W9-APR-353

Also by Thomas J. Leonard

THE PERSONAL FOUNDATION PROGRAM

WORKING WISDOM

THE
28 LAWS OF
ATTRACTION

*Stop Chasing Success and
Let It Chase You*

Thomas J. Leonard

with Byron Laursen

SCRIBNER

NEW YORK LONDON TORONTO SYDNEY

SCRIBNER

A Division of Simon & Schuster, Inc.
1230 Avenue of the Americas
New York, NY 10020

Copyright © 1998 by Thomas Leonard

All rights reserved, including the right to reproduce this book or portions thereof in any form whatsoever. For information, address Scribner Subsidiary Rights Department, 1230 Avenue of the Americas, New York, NY 10020.
SCRIBNER and design are trademarks of Macmillan Library Reference USA, Inc., used under license by Simon & Schuster, the publisher of this work.

First Scribner trade paperback edition December 2007

For information about special discounts for bulk purchases, please contact
Simon & Schuster Special Sales at
1-800-456-6798 or business@simonandschuster.com

DESIGNED BY ERICH HOBBING

Set in Adobe Garamond

Manufactured in the United States of America

1   3   5   7   9   10   8   6   4   2

Library of Congress Control Number: 98-26631

ISBN-13: 978-0-684-85041-2
ISBN-10: 0-684-85041-9
ISBN-13: 978-1-4165-7103-2 (pbk)
ISBN-10: 1-4165-7103-5 (pbk)

Selected parts of this book were derived from CoachVille–owned intellectual property.
Used with permission.

The author and publisher disclaim any and all liability arising directly or indirectly from the use of this book. Further, the publisher is not affiliated in any way with the CoachVille teleclass and/or Web sites sponsored by the author, and disclaims any and all liability associated therewith.

Originally published in hardcover as *The Portable Coach* in 1998.

To Dana Morrison
for getting me on the path

ACKNOWLEDGMENTS

There are over 300 individuals to thank for assistance in the development of the 28 principles described in this book. All were participants in the fall 1997 Attraction Program. See what you helped create? Thank you all.

Special thanks go to Michele Lisenbury. As Executive Director of Attraction University, she has provided the encouragement to keep raising the attraction "bar." And to Dave Buck, a friend and colleague. Dave reminds me that walking all 28 steps (and at the same time) is not only possible, it's awesome. Dave, you're an inspiration.

This book couldn't have come into being without the savvy representation of my agent, David Vigliano. Thanks, too, to Scott Moyers, the editor who saw the potential in this project and helped everyone else at Scribner see it as well. Then there's Marah Stets, who took over editing duties when Scott's career surged to a new level and who brought abundant charm, intelligence, and energy to the process. And some words for the wordsmith: Byron Laursen's talent and dedication were essential to the realization of this book. I'm grateful that someone with a track record of writing best-sellers would see my techniques and programs for personal evolution as not only viable but also valuable.

Finally, I want to acknowledge you, reader, for having the great combination of ambition and self-belief that's necessary for undertaking radically positive shifts in your life. The world needs more people who are classy, constructive, self-embracing, impervious to negative pressures, creative, and who are ready to prove that having solid integrity and high principles is how to build yourself a satisfying life. If this book helps you evolve even a little bit closer to fulfilling your potential, I'll be one extremely happy coach.

Contents

CONTENTS

PREFACE

George Carlin is against positive thinking. It sounds to him like a bad idea, and he's also sure it won't work. (Even if it does, he figures it's probably really hard to do.)

I agree with George. No one should spend their time trying to think positive thoughts. We've all got better things to do.

And yet, by this time, you've probably once or twice taken a long look at your struggles in life, career, or personal relationships and thought, "There's got to be a better way." A better way to have a nice house, a real life, a great relationship, a business of my own, answers to the problems I have now—but without being fried by overwork and stress.

I've got a positive thought for you right now. There definitely *is* a better way.

It's not about feeding your brain lovely bouquets of "good thoughts." It's not about being the meanest shark in the corporate sea. Or any other kind of self-pressuring prescription that sounds halfway-convincing but requires huge effort, or else doesn't work at all.

Before saying what it *is* about, I should probably tell you something of what I'm about: The starting point on my résumé is "certified financial planner." So I began professional life with an emphasis on money skills. But my clients, I soon realized, wanted much more than knowing what stocks to buy. They wanted to acquire much more in life than wealth itself. And I knew I wanted to expand myself to deliver what they needed.

Very recently, the *Philadelphia Inquirer* called me "the patriarch of the personal-coaching movement." Which sounds very graybeard. But I did begin a personal coaching practice in 1982, as an evolution of the work I was already doing for clients. Coaching was a big step, involving money plus career plus personal growth, all pulled together to help my clients become stronger and better and more successful in a well-rounded, lasting way. As far as I can tell—and I have wide access to information sources—I was the first person to start this type of practice.

Within six years, I founded CoachVille to teach others how to thrive in—and contribute to—the field I'd created. It was the first school of its kind. Now there are at least ten in the United States alone, though CoachV remains by far the largest and best known. And it works. CoachV-trained people share great new success stories with me almost every day. Like the man who, in the space of three months, went from welfare recipient to earner of a projected annual income of $60,000. In this book, you will read a number of success stories, and they are all true.

In 1992, my thinking began to evolve a little further. What if a person could consistently attract the good things in life—opportunities, strong finances, rewarding relationships, really useful and desirable material things, self-satisfaction—instead of striving, scuffling, or otherwise struggling for them? What if a person could learn how to become more attractive? (In the sense defined above, not in surface glamour—unless you want that, too.) What if all the squabbles and annoyances in most people's personal and professional lives could be subtracted, to be replaced by big expanses of free and/or productive time?

That questioning drew me to create, and delineate, the material in this book.

The 28 Laws of Attraction is about 28 thought-expanding, surprisingly practical, and highly effective principles, linked to each other like facets on a diamond. These principles will help you shape your life, career, and relationships in the most self-satisfying and profitable way possible. Just look into a single facet, any one that catches your eye. Enjoy it. The deeper you look, the more you'll see parts of all the other facets emerge. You'll intuitively know which one you want to look at next. And you'll evolve toward a more attractive life. More and more, the good things in life will be drawn to you.

These 28 principles are gateways, then, to what you want in both the personal and business aspects of your life. And they are nutrients to help you develop and to sustain your continued growth. Some will mean more to you than others, certainly, because we're all different on the surface. Some will also mean more to you *tomorrow* than they do today, because you will have evolved to subtler and stronger understandings. You can look at them in a straight line, from the front of the book to the back. Or you can choose where to start by intuition or instinct (my favorite way). Every facet connects in some way to a few others—and those others make available further connections, until you've experienced the whole diamond.

Just for a reality check, flip through the book for a while, looking to find a small handful of principles (called steps and numbered 1 through 28) that *already* sound smart and sensible to you, even if they may seem a little challenging. If you can find, say, five that you generally agree with, chances are that all 28 will open up for you by the time you've looked them over closely. If you don't find that many, just close the book now and trust that you'll find your "better way" someplace else, another time. Because this isn't about joining a cult or embracing dogmatic approaches. There's no guru in the building.

Instead, you'll find several practical ways of gaining more access to the brilliance you already have and of making your life become the product of what's best about you.

By coupling what's in this book with your own considerable inner resources, you can make that kind of real-life miracle happen. Reading this book is the closest thing possible to having a series of sessions with a truly great coach. I can give no absolute guarantees, but I feel certain that *The 28 Laws of Attraction* will help you find exactly what you want out of life—or some even better possibility that you haven't even dared to wish for yet.

Sometimes I call these 28 steps the "Principles of Attraction." Sometimes I call them the "Attraction OS," as in "operating system," because they're like advanced software you can upload to enhance the total performance of your mind/body "computer."

No matter what they're called, these principles have worked well, and consistently, with virtually every type of human personality, situation, or problem. They offer a way out of the cycles and loops of self-improvement campaigns. They open a path to achievement that bypasses burnout, soullessness, and hollow striving. They can deliver what everyone with an entrepreneurial bone in their body most craves: making more money with less effort, while having a life that you thoroughly enjoy.

The principles are combined here with self-assessment tests and exercises, just like the ones a CoachV-trained personal coach would administer to a client, to give you an accurate picture of where you are right now and of the higher levels that you can reach.

That's why there's no need for positive thinking: It will be yours as a no-sweat bonus, along with outstanding spiritual feelings and financial/material reality and a life that's lower in stress, higher in satisfaction.

Attraction is the ultimate in being good to yourself. I hope you're ready now to get started!

THE
28 LAWS OF
ATTRACTION

BECOME INCREDIBLY SELFISH

Without You, There Is Nothing and Attraction Isn't Possible

Claim your own at any hazard.
—WALT WHITMAN

From his cradle to his grave a man never does a single thing which has any first and foremost object but one: to secure peace of mind, spiritual comfort, for himself.

—MARK TWAIN

Selfish. It's a little adjective that can carry a big load. In my old *Webster's* dictionary, selfish is defined as "caring unduly or supremely for oneself; regarding one's own comfort, advantage, etc., in disregard, or at the expense of, that of others."

But in my book, it's something else entirely. And it should be in your book, too. For the sake of your personal and professional success, you need to grasp a new way of viewing selfishness. Holding on to, and being ruled by, other people's definitions of selfishness have probably created a barrier that you'll need to break. Because fortune really does favor the brave, and the brave are guided by their own lights. This is just as true about small concerns as it is about larger ones. And you can strip out *Webster's* phrases about disregard of others, and operating at the expense of others. Selfishness, as defined for our purposes, ultimately allows you to be more generous and supportive of others than you have ever been before.

DISTINCTIONS TO DRAW

SELFISH VS. NEEDY—Selfishness is a choice. Neediness means you're driven by unmet needs, without choice.

SELFISHNESS VS. SELFULNESS—*Selfulness* means filling up your soul and your self from the inside. It's a good term to use if you're afraid of *selfishness.*

YOU VS. YOUR ROLES—You are distinct from your roles. Selfulness often requires abandoning or restructuring of roles, so there's room to grow.

NEED VS. WANT—A need is something required to be yourself, fully at your best. A want just provides gratification, usually temporary. Both are terrific. Needs are more important.

WANTS VS. SHOULDS—A want is something you selfishly acquire because it makes you feel good. Wants can be very healthy and motivating. A should is something you believe you must do, or suffer consequences. Shoulds generally slow your development.

GENEROSITY AS A BY-PRODUCT VS. GENEROSITY AS A FOCUS—Selfishness makes you more generous, on a sustaining basis. Lack of selfishness makes generosity too costly to you, your life, and those around you.

JOY VS. PLEASURE—Joy is intellectual excitement, emotional involvement, and physical pleasure combined. Pleasure is mostly physical.

How to know you're making progress with this principle

- You're able to put yourself first.
- You attract others who already know how to be selfish.
- You may find that you need less from others.
- You embrace the notion that "if it's good for me, it's probably going to benefit others."
- You feel more independent, less "pulled" by your roles.
- You find yourself being a lot more generous, because you can afford to be.
- You get a lot more of what you want, more often.

Now, here's how to go about updating your view:

TOP 10 WAYS TO BECOME INCREDIBLY SELFISH

1. SELFISHNESS USED TO HAVE A BAD NAME; NOW IT'S DEVELOPING A GOOD NAME.

When humans were tribal, survival meant common food-gathering, common defense. An overly individualistic member of the tribe, one who dared to be selfish, was a legitimate risk.

This was true for perhaps the first 90 percent of human history. Our ancestors foraged for wild plants, hunted wild animals, migrated with herds or in response to changing seasons. They had to watch each other's backs and depend on the best hunters to feed as many of the less lucky as they could on a day-by-day basis. This is still true of some remote cultures today. And in such cultures, getting singled out is the worst possible fate.

Things began to change a little bit with the development of crop cultivation, and then much more with the rise of cities. As humans became more civilized, some became specialists. They needed, for everyone's ultimate benefit, to be liberated from hunting and farming tasks. In effect, they could afford to become more selfish. Now, not only can we afford selfishness, it's a necessary trait for all those who want to take themselves, and the "tribe" of humanity as a whole, to higher, more evolved levels. Selfishness—along with the specialization and talent-development it makes possible—is a cornerstone of progress, for individuals and for society.

Creativity and excellence *require* selfishness. So does evolution. When you know you're onto something—a potential breakthrough of any kind—you need the purest kind of focus and concentration possible. You need to answer to the callings of your heart and mind *before* you answer to the callings of the tribe. You need to accept that a reasonable and responsible level of selfishness builds long-term benefits for everyone you care about.

2. KNOW WHAT YOU WANT AND SAY SO.

This is great for you, and possibly even more so for all the people around you. Everybody wants *something* from every personal interchange, whether in a school, in a corporate boardroom, or around a Ping-Pong table. Social settings are about interchange. People look constantly, instinctively, for clues about how to deal with you—in your facial expressions, your voice, your posture, even in the way you breathe, not to mention in the words you speak.

When you've clearly communicated who you are and what you want, people can relax. They're drawn to someone who is self-secure, who knows what they want and what they expect to occur. Knowing what you want and saying so is attractive. And it boosts the odds that you will get what you want.

An urgent need-to-know underlies every human contact, from romantic to familial, from play to business. Is the person you're with for real, or just playing some kind of role? How deep is he or she? What will it take to win full effort, full commitment? What kind of ethical code is at work, if any? What hidden agendas are coming up from the bottom, like submarines to the ocean surface?

People want the answers to those questions, and many more, whenever they interact with you. Never leave them foggy, with unresolved ideas about who you are and where you stand. And you deserve plenty of clarity from the people in your life. So ask any questions you want to.

True, being that direct may turn some folks off. But usually those are insecure, vague, indecisive people who—until they finally become more self-secure—are likely to waste big chunks of your time.

One of my clients owns a very profitable business, with a sizeable number of employees. She was constantly frustrated by one of her managers: He had given many years of good service, but had gradually taken an "on-the-job retirement." She had hopes of turning his performance around, but everyone's morale was on the decline as they waited for him to get back on track.

As soon as she grasped that selfishness is good, she let him go. She still felt a little lingering guilt, though, so a few weeks afterward she checked in with him, expecting he'd need some propping up. To her surprise, he said that he'd been going downhill at a fast rate without realizing it, but was feeling great now and very happy about getting on with his life.

When my client wasn't selfish enough, every option looked like lose/lose. As soon as she embraced selfishness, the situation turned out to be win/win.

3. Selfishness is usually the first step to getting your needs met and building a reserve.

Becoming selfish is not really a lifetime ambition. There's no real point of glory in becoming the most selfish person in the world. However, becoming selfish can get you started on a great path—having all that you need and then building a matching reserve. Reserves are a key to becoming irresistibly attractive.

Very, very few people experience having all they need in all areas—time, money, space, opportunities, network, love—so you probably haven't yet observed many good role models in your own life. But having that much is quite possible and definitely desirable. Selfishness and the reserves it will build afford no-strings-attached generosity.

4. When you become truly selfish, you'll have the extra reserves needed to really care about—and be generous with—others.

Being selfish does *not* mean being a jerk. It doesn't mean being pitiless, cold-hearted, unwilling to help lift less fortunate people out of their circumstances. It does mean building yourself a base that will give you the power to be generous—without the burnout syndrome that plagues so many people with good-hearted intentions.

Tremendous numbers of people in this world are struggling and drowning in adversities of many kinds. You can help them by being a lighthouse on a solid foundation; you can help them by jumping into the waves with a buoyancy vest and lifeline to the shore. But you can't help them if you yourself go under.

They say that when one is totally taken care of, his or her "cup runneth over." When this becomes true of you and your life, you'll have extra resources, superreserves that others can freely take advantage of without any risk to you. And you'll have clear, solid boundaries that won't allow anyone to take too much.

5. STOP HANGING AROUND FOLKS WHO ABHOR SELFISHNESS.

People who build their identity on trying to "do good" all of the time, or who try to "evolve" beyond their "ego," are usually drainers. Why? Because it takes a *lot* of ego to pretend you're above having an ego—and a lot of energy to keep up that kind of pretense.

Guess who that energy is going to come from? The people they are "serving"?

Who's serving whom? That's the question to ask.

Those who really do a lot of good also get a lot of joy from what they do. It's good for their hearts and their souls, and they know it. When you can truly afford to do "good works," you're being selfish in the best possible way. Those who are too, too noble—and who let you know it—are on ego trips. If you spend time with them, you'll find yourself paying for their tickets.

6. UNHOOK YOURSELF FROM THE NEGATIVE CONNOTATIONS OF BEING VERY SELFISH.

Selfishness certainly can include egocentricity or insensitivity. But that doesn't make those three words synonymous. They truly are not.

Egocentricity means you think only about yourself or feel that the world revolves around you. *Insensitivity* means you have no heart; you just don't care about others.

But you can be extremely selfish and still be neither egocentric nor insensitive. Really! Most of us have to overcome some of our social conditioning before we can feel good about being selfish. It's worth the effort.

Sally is like many people who give themselves away—sweet, quiet, not wanting to confront anyone, carrying the burden of responsibility for everyone else. If a co-worker got mad, she would apologize whether it was her fault or not.

Through her selflessness, Sally blocked herself off. All of her friendships and relationships had become burdensome, so demanding that she had gradually cut herself off from everyone except people she worked with. She came to a terrific coach named Bobbi Gemma because she was feeling burned out by her job, yet she was getting close to qualifying for a great retirement package after serving twenty-plus years in a large corporation, in various sales-related positions. She needed guidance: "Do I stay on this job, and, if so, how do I make it palatable until I hit retirement?"

Bobbi used diagnostic tests to help Sally understand her own behavioral and communication styles. It was an eye-opener, and from that awareness she became ready and willing to start creating boundaries. Like most people, she had been unaware that you can let people know what behavior you will allow them to display in your presence, no matter the relationship or the extent of the boundary you feel is necessary.

Once Sally began putting some of those pieces in place, unexpected types of people suddenly started showing up in her life—people who brought opportunities for creating relationships of some depth, people able to give her guidance and teach her things. They came because she was sure, internally, of who she was and what she wanted, and because she lightened up on herself enough to regain the terrific sense of humor that had been suppressed for a long time. Becoming incredibly selfish brought back her enjoyment of life and of herself.

Now, because she *is* more fun, she effortlessly attracts more joy and pleasure in her life.

7. SPEND THE NEXT SEVEN DAYS DOING SOMETHING VERY, VERY SELFISH EACH DAY.

So you're having difficulty feeling good about being incredibly selfish? It's time to go on a scavenger hunt!

Make a list of seven things you really want but haven't been able to let yourself have. It really doesn't matter whether they're tangible or intangible.

First, decide that you deserve them. Second, go grab them, one item a day every day, for seven days in a row!

The trick (assuming you won't act counterproductively and mess up your finances) is to quickly obtain what you feel you want or need instead of waiting, thinking a lot about it, weighing the pros and cons until you've talked yourself out of what you desire.

The payoff: You'll develop a warm and positive feeling about how good you can be to yourself. You'll develop the right kind of selfishness, the kind that isn't driven by caprice or by unfulfilled needs but rather by the very practical wish to be good to yourself on a consistent, top-to-bottom, whole-system level.

In most sports, players who stop to think too much about what to do next will soon wish they hadn't. Opportunities blow by those players and vanish. Make this Attraction Principle into a sport. Let the game flow, unhindered, so it becomes beautiful to watch. Allow yourself a new and higher standard of self-regard.

8. SAY NO, JUST BECAUSE YOU FEEL LIKE IT.

Selfishness is a muscle that needs developing. For many people, the easiest place to start is by saying no.

If you have a hard time saying no, get a coach to show you how and to encourage you to say no easily. Saying no trips lots of people up, but it is a learnable skill and pays dividends for a lifetime.

No, in fact, is a beautiful word. And powerful. It's the bedrock for strong boundaries, a topic we'll eventually discuss in greater detail.

Some singing instructors actually advise saying no as a means of locating your best and strongest tones. Try it. Say it, wait two or three beats, then repeat it. Doesn't it feel good? Don't you like how your voice sounds? Practice it some more.

Now imagine how good it will feel when you say no to someone who—whether intentionally or not—is trying to take advantage of you or is wasting your time. Little kids often go through a phase where "no" is their favorite word. That's because it gives them such a definite sense of self. It will do the same for you. And it doesn't cost anything. (It saves you plenty, though.)

Most grown-ups need to rediscover some of what they knew when they were kids.

9. THE REAL VALUE OF BECOMING SELFISH IS TO GIVE YOUR GIFTS ROOM TO DEVELOP.

Gifts and talents are rare, wonderful, and valuable. You undoubtedly have some, whether or not you've focused on them yet in your life. (Going through a cookie-cutter educational system, or experiencing a nonencouraging parenting style, often disconnects people from awareness of their gifts and talents. Among other things, these Principles of Attraction will make your connection stronger than ever before.)

Those gifts deserve and need nourishment; they won't blossom fully without it. Maybe it's still hard for you to be selfish for your own sake. If you've got a special talent or gift—and most of us do—become selfish if only for its sake. Be a good servant of your gifts. Create a setting in which they can flourish, so both you and other people can enjoy, benefit, and profit from them.

Without busting your budget, go ahead and grant yourself whatever amenities you'd grant a winner. Treating yourself well is a powerful strategy.

10. TAKE WHAT YOU FEEL YOU NEED, EVEN IF IT SEEMS THAT OTHERS WON'T GET AS MUCH.

Scarcity can be made to vanish. When you treat yourself to whatever you'd want to give the person you love most, others in your life will adapt, and even be glad. As you become more solid as a person, they'll have a greater sense of (a) the importance of carrying their own weight and (b) being able to count on you if the chips are ever down.

Just as they did for Sally, win/win situations will start popping up for you like flowers after a spring rain.

Carole, a wonderful young woman now breaking into the coaching field, applied selfishness to her private life and proved the point. Her job with a multimillion-dollar shipping firm involves coordinating the schedules and efforts of many different people. Her private life includes the fact that she and her fiancé just recently moved in together.

When that happened, the extra time they spent together took away from the time she had previously spent on fitness. Extra pounds started to show up. So Carole made a selfish decision: To give herself time for jogging in the morning, she started going to bed at nine o'clock. She asked her fiancé to do the same, even if he opted to get up again before going to sleep. How did it turn out? Great for everyone concerned, including Cupid.

Carole's selfishness created a structure in an area that many people have difficulty even talking about. Pretty soon her fiancé started joining her for morning jogs, creating even more shared experience.

Think for a minute. Haven't you known interpersonal problems that could've vanished if everyone involved felt entitled to be definite and totally clear about what they wanted—instead of waiting for hurt to accumulate? That's how selfishness deflects disappointment while it draws success.

Without selfishness, you just can't attract life's best offerings.

EXTREME SELF-CARE

To be selfish in the best possible sense, adopt the concept of extreme self-care.

Living in today's world places many demands on your body, mind, heart, and spirit. The purpose of extreme self-care is to create a positively selfish focus on balance, well-being, and quality of life.

I started thinking this way almost five years ago, but I didn't make a total commitment to the concept until late in 1996—after the rewarding but physically, spiritually, and emotionally intense experience of building up CoachVille to be the world leader in virtual instruction. It was an exciting accomplishment, but it also left me feeling out of balance.

The key word here is *extreme*. Self-care always sounded like a good idea, but I couldn't get interested in it until I could picture how to make a comprehensive and (for me) radical change. During the transition, I was supported by no fewer than ten health-care professionals, including a physician, a coach, a nutritionist, a therapist, and a Rolfer (deep-tissue massage specialist).

Everyone has his or her own way of manifesting extreme self-care, so please adapt these suggestions to meet *your* needs. Some of them may strike you as *too* extreme right now. But, then, your sense of what's possible for you to attain is going to grow tremendously. So don't be concerned, and just give extreme self-care a second look after you've completed this book. By then you may find yourself much more comfortable with the notion of reaching for the best. For now, it's okay if you want to view this section as just a glimpse at where you're headed.

The areas you should focus on are

1. Stress elimination
2. Environment and family
3. Pleasure
4. Well-being
5. Support and experts
6. Ingestion
7. Appearance
8. Sustainability
9. Daily rituals
10. Special-care items

1. STRESS ELIMINATION

Note that we're saying stress *elimination,* not stress *reduction.* If you focus on stress elimination, then, at the very least, you will achieve stress reduction. If you focus only on stress reduction, you may not get enough benefit to make a difference.

- If your job, business, or profession is harming you and you can't seem to make it completely stress-free, either quit, sell it, or change professions.
- Make a list of ten promises you have made to others that are causing you stress, even if it's stress that you can handle. Revoke all ten of these promises and work out alternatives with the promisees.
- Identify the three sources (people, roles, expectations of others) of your current stress. Completely eliminate these three items.
- Get a house cleaner.
- Have your errands run by someone else.
- Arrange to have all bills, paper, and administrative tasks handled electronically or by an assistant who handles everything automatically.
- Completely resolve any legal, tax, or financial clouds or problems.

2. ENVIRONMENT AND FAMILY

We are all products of our environments. But we have the option of designing and adapting our environments to best serve us.

- Revamp your home environment to make it more restful and nurturing. Be fully aware of every aspect of your physical environment and draw energy from it. Fully respond to your environment. If something goes wrong, instantly learn from the experience and grow. If you don't like something, fix it now.
- Back up your computer weekly.
- Your spouse, your children, your partnerships, your friendships, and your pets should all add energy to your life. If they do not, pursue counseling.
- Tolerate absolutely no clutter or messes in or around your house.
- Have everything in your home and office fully and properly organized and filed. (Everything!)

3. PLEASURE

You know what makes you feel great, so please write down your top ten favorite personal, whimsical, intellectual, and entertainment pleasures below.

- _____
- _____
- _____
- _____
- _____
- _____
- _____
- _____
- _____
- _____

Now, for each item listed above, conceive of at least three different ways to put more of each in your life.

4. WELL-BEING

Some of the following steps toward physical and emotional well-being will require using health-care professionals, but there's no better investment you can make. It isn't indulgence; it's a healthy respect for maintenance of a key asset: you. Greater well-being pays off in smoother, more easily sustained performance.

- Give up the future; live in the here and now, and do not chase anything.
- Have a complete physical exam every one to three years.

- Have a complete blood testing workup and discuss the results with a licensed nutritionist.
- Exercise daily for at least thirty minutes, even if you must hire a trainer to keep yourself on track.
- If you react inappropriately to others or to problems, get to the source of the emotional reaction.
- Cultivate excellent posture, move naturally, and keep your body well balanced and integrated through yoga or through the services of a trainer.
- If you find it difficult to eat nutritionally correct meals, arrange for prepared food to be delivered twice weekly.
- Be totally free of adrenalized behavior.
- Arrange to be lovingly touched or held several times per week, each time for as long as you need it. Arrange for frequent massages.
- Know what motivates you.

5. SUPPORT AND EXPERTS

Extreme self-care is made possible by the investment you make in all areas of your life, including the investment you make in the services of experts.

- Work with a personal coach who has a track record of helping others practice extreme self-care and who is a terrific example of the benefits of this program.
- Work with a chiropractor or other bodywork specialist who can remove any energy blocks.
- In addition to regular massage, learn about Rolfing or other deep-tissue bodywork.
- If needed or beneficial, enter therapy with an expert in your area of primary concern.
- Go to a dermatologist and have the skin on every part of your body thoroughly examined.
- Develop a supportive relationship with what you consider to be God, or the Divine Force (or whatever is equivalent for you).
- Be a source of unconditional support and love for a friend or family member and draw on their unconditional support and love in return.
- If you have money concerns or problems, work them out completely, using an expert or team of experts.
- Build a Rolodex of several well-recommended experts that you can call on

for assistance, from attorneys to tree surgeons, from accountants to psychiatrists.

6. INGESTION

Open mouth, insert extreme self-care.

- Drink at least a half gallon of spring water each day.
- Take a timed-release vitamin C (500–1,000 mg) daily, if recommended.
- Take a nutritionist-recommended multivitamin daily.
- Do not smoke. Drink alcohol only very rarely (if at all).
- Do not use caffeine or sugar.
- Eliminate most meat and dairy products (if medically appropriate for you) from your diet.
- Treat your body as the temple that it is.

7. APPEARANCE

Extreme self-care applies to the outer as well as the inner you. As Oscar Wilde said, it is only shallow people who do not judge by appearances.

- Toss every single article of clothing that does not make you look great. Replace them with clothing in colors that flatter your skin tone.
- Have your hair styled and/or colored exactly as you most like it.
- Have your nails professionally manicured.
- If you want or need hair removed, see a licensed electrolysis expert.
- Have (or give yourself) facials at least monthly.
- Wear only great shoes.
- Keep your body in excellent shape, toned and exercised regularly.
- Keep your teeth looking great, and smile broadly at every opportunity.

8. SUSTAINABILITY

Part of extreme self-care is to integrate the changes that you are making. They should become natural behavior for you, not just a temporary effort.

- Restructure your finances (cut expenses, increase income) so that you have absolutely no financial concerns and money does not drive your decisions.
- Work through all of your parental and sibling issues in therapy so you won't be blindly guided by the past.
- Resolve and heal from whatever damage was done to you prior to today.
- Learn to say no easily.
- Know what your strengths are. Install support systems to do for you what you can't, won't, or don't do for yourself.

9. DAILY RITUALS

Extreme self-care is a daily process, not just a one-time program.

- Stretch daily.
- Have a relaxing pre-bedtime ritual (reading, music, touch, etc.) so you fall asleep with a smile on your face.
- Floss well, twice daily.
- Have a waking-up routine that's nourishing and deliberate.
- Make sure that your days are spent doing what you most want to do, not what you should be doing or what others expect of you.
- Underpromise consistently—don't get caught in the trap of overperforming to catch up.
- Each evening have something wonderful to look forward to.
- Have a specially identified time in your schedule just for yourself.
- Stay in touch with yourself and your feelings throughout the day.

10. SPECIAL-CARE ITEMS

On the lines below, please write in the special needs or wants that you have that you haven't seen elsewhere in the program. Use your imagination and, of course, be very specific.

- _____

- _____

STEP 1

- _____
- _____
- _____
- _____
- _____
- _____
- _____
- _____

Unhook Yourself
from the Future

Attraction Works in the Present,
Not in the Future

> If "if" was a fifth, we'd all get drunk.
> —MICHAEL JORDAN

> The supreme value is not the future but the present. Whoever builds a house for future happiness builds a prison for the present.
> —OCTAVIO PAZ

The comedy team of Abbott and Costello was popular for so long that their career bridged vaudeville, movies, and television. Costello was short, round, childlike, lovable. Abbott was tall, lean, hawk-faced, overbearing, with a pencil mustache and a more-or-less permanent frown. Their slightly cracked interplay was a big inspiration for *Seinfeld,* especially the dialogues between Jerry and George.

Abbott and Costello had a famous double-talk routine that went something like this: Both are hungry, but there's only one sandwich. Abbott proposes a bet. He will prove that he isn't actually there. If he's right, he gets the sandwich.

First, Abbott says that he obviously isn't in Chicago. Agreed. Next, that he also isn't in St. Louis. When Costello agrees with that, too, Abbott sinks the hook: "If I'm not in Chicago and I'm not in St. Louis, I must be somewhere else, right?"

DISTINCTIONS TO DRAW

COMMITMENT VS. STRIVING—When you're truly committed, you don't feel the need to strive. It's a lack of sureness that makes you push yourself.

VISION VS. PIPE DREAM—A vision is an inevitable result, based on facts. A pipe dream is hope based mainly on desire.

PRESENT VS. FUTURE—A well-lived present automatically creates a fulfilling future.

"Right."

"If I'm someplace else, I can't be here!" He grabs the sandwich and opens his jaws.

Costello looks flummoxed. Then, suddenly, before Abbott can take his first bite, Costello yanks away the sandwich and takes a big mouthful.

Abbott, of course, protests. Costello, still chewing, runs him quickly through his own chain of logic—from Chicago to St. Louis and back—then finishes triumphantly: "So if you're not here, you must be someplace else, right?"

"Right."

"If you're someplace else, how could I take your sandwich?"

Classic screwball comedy. But our own logic is often just as crazy. For example: When we're worried about mistakes we made in the past, we spend big blocks of our time there, rehashing what already was. "IF I'd only done this . . ." "IF I'd only done that . . ."

When we aren't worrying about the past, we stew and sweat about something we can't possibly know—what's coming next. "If this happens, what'll I do? . . ." "If that happens, I'll have to . . ." Like Abbott, we're constantly someplace else. But the finest place to be, the best possible place to hang out, is right here in the present moment.

It's been said that living in the present moment is the highest form of sanity. I want to add to that: You are most attractive when you're living in the present moment—not living in the future, or striving for it, or trying to repair the past. A smooth, secure, present-time orientation is the sure way to attract a better future. But how *do* you keep focused on today?

That's exactly what you're going to focus on.

How to know you're making progress with this principle

- You couldn't care less about the future, yet you're living responsibly, intelligently, and pleasurably.
- Goals become optional, something to orient around rather than strive for.
- You begin to entertain different goals, interests, and outcomes. Understanding that you can't see the future, you become more human.
- You naturally focus more on enjoying people; you enjoy people more.
- You stop wasting time on people and projects that have potential but no real prospects.

TOP 10 WAYS TO UNHOOK YOURSELF FROM THE FUTURE

1. GIVE UP THE GOALS THAT ARE SEDUCTIVE.

We all have things we want to achieve or acquire. There's absolutely nothing wrong with this. But chasing these types of goals often gets us worked up to the point that we're more passionate about the future than we are about today. That's how trouble starts.

Whether your goal is to get married, to make a million dollars, to change the world, or to become somebody everyone looks up to, you simply can't let it lead you down a seductive path. When the future becomes far more interesting than the present, the destination holds more importance than the journey. So you gradually lose the present, which is where the real gifts are. And the destination, if you ever reach it, is shabbier and much less fun than it looked from a distance.

Why? It's true that some sacrifice to reach long-term goals is necessary. You don't blow your savings every Saturday night just to convince yourself that you're having a good time. But when the habit of squeezing too much pleasure from the present puts you on a self-negating path, you create a rather gray and sunless personal existence. This is not an intelligent way to go.

The antidote? Look to item number 2.

2. PERFECT THE PRESENT.

When your life isn't as you want it to be, the first thing you're likely to do is to set a goal for a better future.

Not bad.

But what if you took the same energy and applied it to perfecting the present right now? You'd probably *attract* a better future instead of trying to acquire it—a very different approach.

Here's the operative idea: A better future will find you, no effort required, because you've made the most of the present you've been given.

Think of yourself as a detective developing leads. They'll come from those things that bring you joy in the present. Those clues show you where to find the future. The great folklorist Joseph Campbell—whose writings on heroism inspired George Lucas to create *Star Wars*—used to say, when students asked him what to do with their lives, "Follow your bliss."

The present is a superb teacher; the future is a seducer.

Steve's story proves the point. He's a very successful entrepreneur, with his own chain of sport shops. He opted for coaching, though, because he felt guilty about not spending enough time with his wife and three small children. Yet, when he was home he thought guiltily about what he needed to be doing for his business.

With Coach Ginger Cockerham assisting, Steve hammered out a new viewpoint, which he expressed as, "My intention is to be fully present with my family while I am here, and to focus completely on my work when I am there."

It worked like magic. Steve now makes better decisions at work, faster and with more confidence. And, more important to him, he's a better husband and father now. He realizes that he used to embrace his guilt—feeling almost righteous about beating himself up over his business-first obsessiveness. He now understands that it was damaging to his mental *and* physical health, in addition to sucking the energy out of the most important things in his life.

Does Steve's story resonate with you? Don't be surprised if it does: It's a story being repeated in lots of lives, by people whose striving costs them the enjoyment of the things they're striving for.

3. STOP WATCHING TELEVISION.

In a recent *Shoe* cartoon, Jeff MacNelly's tweed-jacket-wearing bird, named Shoe, is slumped in his easy chair, passively watching TV. "Okay," he admits in the first panel, "I don't have a life . . ." Still glued to the tube in the second and final panel, he adds " . . . So how come it still takes up all my time?"

It's mind-boggling, but true: The average American spends 40 percent of his or her available free time in front of a TV. Talk about being zoned out! Over a lifetime—or what is mistaken for a lifetime—that much TV viewing takes away ten years.

What could you do with a full decade, lived in the present moment? The possibilities are almost too great to imagine.

TV is a sedative. Its essence is advertising, because advertising pays the bills. All the shows, even the few you might find rewarding, are structured to pay the advertisers back. This is one of the things that make TV hypnotic. The shows unfold to very strong rhythms, always in the service of the ads. Think for a moment. Right after a strongly dramatic moment or after a comedy's best jokes and loudest stretches of canned laughter, they cut to commercial(s).

That's no accident. Ads are slotted into TV's "brightest" moments just the way they're put in prominent and obvious places in magazines—inside the front and back covers and clustered around the table of contents. If that weren't so, they could just run all the commercials in one batch at the end of the day or cluster all the ads in a magazine's final pages. What are the chances of that happening?

Sure, there is *some* good and worthwhile television programming. But most of what's on TV is mind-numbing: a pleasure-provider in the short run, but a thief of the present moment. If your present is unattractive to you, you're more likely to get sucked in. Which explains why people with less education usually watch greater amounts of TV.

Ironically, though, using TV as an escape puts people deeper into a trap. The same as any mind-numbing substance. All those commercial messages cause us to want and "need" more. That can be fun, but it's usually very expensive. Especially if we give up our present quality of life in order to afford that item, tangible or intangible.

In short, TV confuses people about the difference between having a lifestyle and having a life. If you stop watching television, you may have to go through some withdrawal symptoms. The future won't be as seductive.

But in less than a week, you'll notice that your present moments are suddenly more appealing.

4. STOP MOTIVATING YOURSELF.

Giving yourself pep talks, writing endless lists of affirmative thoughts, keeping a stash of motivational tapes in your bedroom or car: These and other "force" measures can be very, very effective. But they're costly to sustain.

The reason they tend to be expensive is because they put blinders on you, like a horse running on a track. I coach people that, instead of slipping themselves into harness, they can actually enjoy all of what they already have. They can be so focused on the present that they realize they don't really need to change a thing. At least until the changes are easy and natural to make.

With that mind-set, a better future will find you, without the expense of motivation. Any necessary changes will flow outward from your higher awareness of the present moment and from everything you've done to tailor the present to your own liking.

5. STOP TRYING TO BECOME A BETTER PERSON.

It's like W. C. Fields said: "If at first you don't succeed, try, try again. Then give up. Don't be a fool."

I've coached too many people who try so hard to be a better person that they lose their humanness. The "better person" you may aspire to be is already present, inside of you, perhaps only partially emerged as of now but ready to come out completely—as soon as conditions feel right.

Your focus on the present moment will create the right conditions.

Ego is a very, very positive part of you. Faults are rich and wonderful teachers. Mistakes are golden. Weaknesses are usually just hidden strengths. Is your goal to have no weaknesses or faults, to make no mistakes, to be free of ego? Playing that game can turn you into a self-deluded zombie or a clenched fist. So stop trying to improve. Get to know 100 percent of YOU, just as you are, with an attitude of loving-kindness.

The future doesn't need you to improve, but it does need you to evolve. Giving up baby steps will result in quantum leaps.

The exact method is something you'll have to work out gradually, after lots of free, open dialogue between your head and your heart. Stay with it. You're evolving.

6. STOP OVERPLANNING.

Ever hear of Righteous Babe Records? Ani DiFranco is an *extremely* independent twenty-seven-year-old singer/songwriter from Buffalo who is blazing a remarkable trail to success. She has sold over 1.5 million CDs and some $4 million in concert tickets, and keeps almost every aspect of her success (T-shirts, CD pressing, posters, etc.) in her hometown, where jobs are sorely needed. Meanwhile, she keeps turning down the major labels and their big, rich contract offerings. I know about Ani DiFranco from a wonderful *New York Times* article that caught my eye just as this book was reaching deadline.

"People have been asking me for years what the hell my plan is and honestly I never had one," she told the reporter. "To me it feels like we're running to catch up with something—this huge horse that's just barreling along."

Not everyone can be that loose. But vast numbers of people are way too tightened up about planning, and it actually hurts them. Especially for certain personality types, it's tempting to think that fully laid-out plans and perfectly identified goals are the right thing to do. In fact, they may simply be a mind exercise to reduce risk and fear.

It's good to identify a vision or sketch out a plan. But there's more: To evolve, you must be willing to hold the plan lightly, and learn—very quickly—as you go.

Rapid assimilation of new ideas, not tenacious loyalty to old plans, is what makes the future arrive magnificently. Far better to become an in-the-moment learner than an expert planner.

Think of how incredibly fast technology has changed our lives and how certain we can be that that trend will continue. Twenty-five years ago seems almost as distant, in terms of opportunities and ways of life, as a century does. Life is now accelerating so quickly that most planning skills become irrelevant before you've had time to master them.

Adaptability is the master skill. Embrace it.

7. STOP HOPING.

Life may improve for you, but not because you're hoping. I once saw a bumper sticker that said it all: "Since I gave up hope, I feel so much better."

If you're living in hope for something to occur or improve, you're simply escaping from the present. We all need to escape from the present from time to time; just don't turn hope (a.k.a. the future) into your personal zip code.

8. GIVE UP FUTURE-BASED POSSIBILITY.

There is a lot that's possible in life. And many of the best things that will happen to you in your lifetime will be things that you never even saw as possible. Will expanding your thinking to consider what's possible actually make these things happen sooner or more often? Maybe. Sometimes. But if you focus on seeing the possibility in the present, rather than what's possible in the future, you'll be a lot better off—and more attractive, too.

9. STOP ASSOCIATING WITH STRIVERS.

People who strive can be fun to be with. For a while, anyway. But because they are so single-minded, hanging out with strivers will drain your energy, usually.

Why? Well, strivers need lots of encouragement and energy from others to keep up their pace. And their views of success tend to be one-dimensional.

Instead of spending time with folks who are always seeking to succeed, find people who are happy with themselves and involved in creative endeavors that express their values. How to find them? Here's the best and easiest way: Involve *yourself* in creative endeavors that express your values.

10. STOP USING IF/THEN FORMULAS.

This gets us back to the Michael Jordan remark that introduced this step. When you start a sentence with *if* or *when,* that usually means you're living in the future. Or, even worse, the past.

Entrepreneurial types, being optimists with grand designs of future possibilities, are especially prone to getting hung up in this if/then fallacy.

The trick is to take out the words *if* and *when* from your vocabulary. "If and when" you hear yourself using them, stop and rethink. What's really on your mind? Get into present time again. Don't set yourself up. Don't start believing that what you want to occur is conditional or hinges on some other person or event. It hinges on you.

For example, you might hear yourself saying, "When I get my degree, then I'll start making some real money." True. But much better to say something like, "I am really, really enjoying my studies." See the difference in orientation?

And if you're not enjoying your studies? Or any other major component of your present activities? Look again at number 6.

OVERRESPOND
TO EVERY EVENT

*By Overresponding Instead of Overreacting,
You Evolve, Which Is Very Attractive*

Is life not a hundred times too short for us to stifle ourselves?
—FRIEDRICH NIETZSCHE

Sometimes something worth doing is worth overdoing.
—DAVID LETTERMAN

Overrespond? To every event? Immediately? Yes. Really. One of the things that make you irresistibly attractive is when you evolve. Of course, you can't evolve unless you change. And you can't change unless you learn to respond to your environment.

Your environment is full of clues: Learn to overrespond, and you'll become more *responsible* to the process of, and opportunities for, creating a more attractive and fulfilling life.

But there's a vital distinction here: overresponding versus overreacting. As we grow up we learn—and this is especially true of men—that we ought to stifle our responses to immediate stimuli in order to be "in control." It's a question of not being pushed around by things. Not flying off the handle, not getting upset. But upset feelings are powerful and are extremely valid as teachers.

What happens when immediate responses are stifled is that people lose track of the full measure of their feelings, along with many things they

---

DISTINCTIONS TO DRAW

OVERRESPOND VS. RESPOND—Wanting a service you cannot find and starting a company to supply it is overresponding. Searching high and low for an existing company is responding.

OVERRESPOND VS. OVERREACT—When you overreact, you nip a problem in the bud. When you overrespond, you get to the root of the problem and find an opportunity there.

LEVERAGE VS. RESOLVE—To leverage is to use a problem as a way to learn something valuable. To resolve is to simply get rid of the problem.

EVOLVE VS. LEARN—When you come out of a situation knowing more, you've learned. When your life has improved significantly, you have evolved.

CELLULAR LEARNING VS. KNOWLEDGE ACQUISITION—Let your body absorb the experience and do the learning, rather than just using your hand to take notes.

EXPERIMENT VS. TEST—A test is rigid; its answer will fall into one of two predetermined boxes. An experiment is more open-ended, an attempt to learn an answer you have yet to define.

---

might have learned from the tendencies revealed by those responses. In order to appear competent and in control, they end up cultivating internal numbness, a widening distance between their minds and their bodies.

Trying to prevent getting stuck in an overly reactive mode, they end up stuck in a response-containment mode, which blocks self-knowledge. And self-knowledge is key to evolving.

What if you could unlearn the operating styles that keep you stuck? What if, by risking a little overreacting, you could become someone who picks up on all possible environmental clues? Wouldn't that give you valuable information? Wouldn't that put you in position to do great things with all your opportunities? It can happen, if you go beyond solving or handling your problems and start using them as a chance to grow.

In this Top 10 List, you'll learn the distinction between overresponding and overreacting. And by mastering that distinction, you'll begin to evolve much more quickly.

How to know you're making progress with this principle

- You surprise yourself by handling a commonly encountered problem in a different, more effective, and lasting way.
- You act on things much sooner.
- By acting sooner, you head off lots of potential problems and/or misunderstandings.
- You truly enjoy overresponding, daily, regardless of the situation.

TOP 10 WAYS TO OVERRESPOND
TO EVERY EVENT, IMMEDIATELY

1. EVERY TIME YOU'RE SURPRISED, MAKE A SIGNIFICANT PERSONAL CHANGE.

When you are surprised, you usually react. And react some more. Then over-react. Then react to the intensity and consequences of your overreactions.

Obviously, this isn't the behavior you really want. In fact, given that your tendency to react and/or overreact to a surprise is rooted in old, obsolete patterns, this is a behavior that keeps you blindly tied to the past. Unless . . .

What if every time something surprising happened in your life—whether good or bad—you made a big change of some kind, even bigger than what that surprise event seemed to call for?

Overresponding has been my personal strategy for several years. It evolved me away from being a certified financial planner, an occupation I didn't enjoy and didn't perform in very well, either.

First, overresponding helped me create a new livelihood as a life planner. That was good, though very goal-oriented and rather lacking in the personal touch that was needed to really help people evolve.

Overresponding to that feeling led me to create a whole new occupational category: personal coaching. I then went on to establish the world's first institute for training personal coaches, a.k.a. CoachV.

Because I hated many of the traditional aspects of selling things—especially the possibility of rejection—overresponding also led to my evolving the 28 Principles of Attraction and to publishers' asking me to put them into a book (this one).

Along the way, overresponding has also made me a millionaire and, what is more important, a guy who's extremely happy with what he does for a living, regardless of income.

But how does overresponding work? Well, you don't have to be mystically minded to notice that we tend to come up against very similar situations and problems over and over again, like turns on a merry-go-round that keep pointing us at the same scenery. It's as if life is conducting a test: "Didja get the message yet? No? Okay, then . . . Here it comes again. Didja get it this time?"

This is something that's hard to prove rationally, but some of the most important things in life are beyond the rational mind anyway.

So, when it comes to overresponding, you need to trust your intuition. That involves investing some trust in yourself, and some willingness to make mistakes as you grow. But as you develop all the muscle groups and skill-sets of your intuition, you will evolve. Sooner or later, your evolution will lift you off the merry-go-round and onto a more rewarding kind of ride.

Making significant changes in your life—instead of just reacting—is how you demonstrate that you've gotten life's message and are ready to stop taking the test. It shows you're operating in the present.

Maybe the change you make will work out brilliantly. If it doesn't work as well as you want it to, you'll soon figure out something better. It's like going from one doctor to another until you get the right diagnosis and a complete cure.

2. LOOK FOR THE FIVE CHOICES YOU HAVE, IN EVERY SINGLE CIRCUMSTANCE.

When faced with a difficult situation, most of us look for two or three options. But there are at least five options in every situation. You may need to think creatively and even consider the kind of things that would normally make you say, "I couldn't do *that*!" But many options are there, every time. Let your thinking stretch to accommodate them.

Because otherwise you're going to keep applying the same solutions and arriving at the same old results. It's been said that doing the same things and expecting different results from them is a good definition of insanity. Maybe, but let's just call it underresponding and agree that it doesn't work.

Why do people underrespond? Not because they really expect a different result. I think it's because they've been conditioned by parents, schools, and employers to have too little trust in themselves and in the value of their intuition. But intuition is a muscle that can be revived in strength. And the more powerful it gets, the more useful it becomes in attracting every kind of success.

Susan enrolled in my first Principles of Attraction teleclass series and wasn't happy with the first few sessions. But instead of stuffing her feelings down, the way a "nice" person might, she sent me an E-mail. That led the two of us into great one-on-one discussions in which she eventually acknowledged that she'd been guilty most of her life of being a "martyr." This time, though, she overresponded. And the extra attention that called forth actually helped her start seeing the Principles of Attraction as a great way to operate. In fact, she eventually coined one of my favorite descriptions of the whole process: "Becoming more attractive," Susan says, "has been an exercise in honoring myself with more vigor."

3. NEVER DECIDE. RATHER, LET YOUR BODY CHOOSE FOR YOU.

As a certified financial planner, I ran true to occupational form. I added up every possible variable so I could make the right decision in every situation. That meant putting everything into numbers, which I'd crunch and crunch until they were almost ready to turn into powder. I'd list all the pros and cons, weigh the odds, consider the short- and long-term consequences, and—eventually—I would make up my mind.

One day I started to realize something very alarming. My decisions were rarely the best ones. They were perfectly rational; they were completely justified by convention. But they were missing something, and that missing element kept them in the middle of the road. Sort of like that joke our northern neighbors tell on themselves:

Q: Why did the Canadian cross the road?

A: To get to the middle.

It finally dawned on me that the middle of the road was never going to be the fast lane. And I was ignoring a lot of information. So, instead of relying exclusively on my mind to make decisions and choices, I started letting my *body* choose for me.

This isn't just "gut" response. Your whole body, from the midsection to the extremities, is naturally wired to take in information and to respond rapidly.

We're so conditioned to "live inside our heads," to value the mind above all, that most of us stop hearing the messages our bodies give us. But body responses are often a whole lot more eloquent, accurate, and straight to the point than mental processes. There are a lot more cells in your body than in your brain. They know more about you, as a totality, than your brain does. And they work in simpler, more direct ways. All you need is enough trust in your feelings, as expressed through your body, to let them guide you.

Trust yourself to your body. It knows, and it communicates what it knows. It's a very smart evolutionary step to start listening to physically felt messages.

4. BECOME EXTREMELY CURIOUS ABOUT YOUR REACTIONS.

The last time you got frightened or angry, did you ask yourself, "Why did I get so scared or ticked off?" Well, you might have asked yourself this. But most of us are so busy reacting and justifying that it's an unfamiliar step and a big change to look beyond that reaction into who we are and why our collection of mental habits makes us react in a certain way.

Rather than trying to stop your reactions, why not let them play out? Then, use them as a way to get to know yourself a lot better. We all react for great reasons. Stop repressing your reactions long enough to find out what they mean. You may have heard the old saying, "Beware the fury of the patient man." That's because the patient man, in most instances, is only keeping his anger bottled up, which is really a lack of an important social skill.

I'm not saying we all have to fly off the handle (though for some people, it would be a step in the right direction). I am saying that anger is just one of many totally legitimate emotions, and if you stop suppressing your emotions, you'll learn valuable lessons and have a richer relationship with your inner self. Work with a coach, analyst, or adviser, if that speeds the process.

At the conclusion of CAI (certified attraction instructor) training, we ask people to say which of the 28 principles had the most impact on them. One man chose overresponding. He said that it "makes a crisis situation less likely to occur (except in a real crisis, and even then cooler heads prevail)."

"Overresponding," he added, "means discovering choices in action that are available, even though they might not be apparent at the moment. Knowing that you can discover several possible choices gets you past feeling threatened and lets you select the one with the most potential to spur your evolution.

"Very soon, response doesn't need as much conscious soul-searching as it did in the beginning. Like a new dance step, it's mechanical at first but then becomes integrated and natural."

5. MAKE OVERRESPONDING A PERSONAL STRATEGY.

If you're alive, creativity interests you. Especially your own creativity. Become creative in how you overrespond. In other words, make it your personal strategy and, as such, *work* it. Whenever something throws you off or in any way impresses you with its singularity or significance, ask yourself: "What's a great way to overrespond?"

It's both a creative exercise and a big part of attracting success. You'll start to develop a healthy admiration for your own creativity, which will lead you to profit from it more. And you'll develop a skill-set that's invaluable at untying the knots in problem situations.

6. STOP SPENDING TIME WITH REACTORS OR NONRESPONDERS.

Some people are an emotional meltdown waiting to happen. Others are numb and could hardly care less. People who strike you as falling into either of these categories are people who are stuck. And they're likely to want you to join them right where they are. They want you to share all the jokes and inside stories they habitually use to validate the idea that we're all really going nowhere.

If you buck their norms by overresponding your way out of life's sticking points, they'll think you've gone batty. Don't join their circle. Overresponding is a progressive way to learn and to advance yourself. If you like its potential, seek out the company of others who, whether by learned strategy or by nature, are on a similar path. Maybe they don't call it by the same name, but if they're instinctively open to fresh approaches and new possibilities, they are the best people to be around. Their company will give you support as you learn the best ways for you to overrespond.

STEP 3

7. TURN EVERY PROBLEM INTO A NONRECURRING EVENT.

Here's a way to flex your new muscle: One, identify a problem in your life; two, take up to ten steps to make sure that it, or anything remotely like it, never happens to you again for the rest of your life.

That's one of the benefits of overresponding—it can fix problems permanently.

It's a terrific skill to be a great problem-solver. People will notice it and bring their problems to you. But consider it your ultimate objective to be a problem-free zone—which is a far more effortless position to remain in. Overresponding can make it possible.

8. EXPERIMENT AS YOU OVERRESPOND.

When you're overresponding to an event, you'll start by doing the obvious things that come to mind. But why not overrespond in very different ways as well? As valuable as overresponding is, the chance discoveries you make about yourself and life will make the biggest difference. These usually result from doing something *radically* different in a situation, not just overresponding well.

For example, say a client fires you or you lose your job. The normal first response is to react with frustration, anger, or sadness. Then you might hit the pavement in search of a new job, possibly with a resolution to work harder or better the next time. And that's a reasonable, healthy thing to do.

But to overrespond, you might

- Take a second look at your entire practice, business, career, or industry.
- Not only correct the "reason" you lost the client or were fired, but also work at becoming someone so obviously *not* afflicted by that particular problem that a similar mishap could never occur again in your life.

When you overrespond, you use whatever happened, good or bad, and you evolve yourself significantly—even beyond the problem itself. You use it as an excuse to make vast improvements in your life, skill-set, lifestyle, standards, or priorities.

9. EVOLVE, DON'T JUST IMPROVE.

What's the difference? When you improve, you do something smarter or better. Not bad! But when you evolve, you fundamentally and permanently change a part of who you are. Improving is good, evolving is better.

Responding and problem solving are examples of improving. Overresponding and becoming a problem-free zone are examples of evolving.

The difference is both in the degree of change you're making and in the type of change. The next time you're in a situation that calls for a change or improvement, ask yourself how you might, instead, evolve. Don't clone. Mutate. Ultimately, you'll come up with a mutation that's better adapted, more likely to thrive. In a personally applied sense, make Darwinism work for you. That way, you'll never be a dinosaur.

10. OVERRESPOND IMMEDIATELY, NOT GRADUALLY.

This is the trickiest part of this principle—overresponding in the moment instead of later. Because, generally speaking, you should adopt the advice in this book at your own rate, as fast or as slow as your instincts tell you. And I'd never coach anyone to be rash or anything less than thoughtful in how they pursue progress. But as you develop this overresponding muscle, it needs room to flex itself.

Perhaps the best analogy, if you'll pardon it, might be to training a dog. If you wait a long time before rewarding good behavior, or punishing bad behavior, the dog probably won't understand the connection between the behavior and its consequences. Your body's reactions are immediate and visceral. If it's too long a time before you respond, you're missing a chance to strengthen the important body-to-mind connection.

Experiment with overresponding radically. Bypass your normal process of decision making. See what you can learn from that. Eventually, you'll start overresponding without having to think about it, navigating your way to new levels of success, and barely even noticing how you've done it. And that is totally exciting to witness.

BUILD A SUPERRESERVE IN EVERY AREA

Having Enough Is Not Nearly Enough for You to Be Irresistibly Attractive

Money is like a sixth sense—and you can't make use of the other five without it.

—SOMERSET MAUGHAM

You never know what is enough, until you know what is more than enough.

—WILLIAM BLAKE

You've already been asked to try some new ideas about selfishness on for size. I hope they feel comfortable, because this is a closely related topic. Let's call it "To Have and Have Not." And let's establish that we're talking about both material and nonmaterial things—love as well as money; time, happiness, and space as much as furniture, houses, and cars; leisure as much as work.

You don't want to be greedy, and you don't want to be needy. You just want to be so well supplied that you will be able to lead a terrific life far enough beyond the reach of scarcity.

Scarcity-based worrying is a leading cause of fear. You can't totally eliminate fear from your life. Nor would you want to; it's a valuable teacher, after all. But you can keep fear from being an overwhelming, personality-distorting presence in your life. The starting point is realizing that having enough to get by is simply not good enough for you.

DISTINCTIONS TO DRAW

RESERVE VS. RESERVES—A reserve is a feeling; reserves are a stockpile. You may need reserves to experience a reserve, but reserves themselves are not enough.

SUPERRESERVE VS. RESERVE—When you have enough time and resources to respond to the opportunities that are always waiting in the wings, you have a superreserve. When you have only enough time and resources to notice and schedule these opportunities, you have a reserve.

BUILDING A RESERVE VS. STOCKPILING—Building a reserve is an integrated process that strengthens your foundation. Stockpiling is an exercise in accumulation, which is a step toward building a reserve.

INVESTOR VS. SPENDER—When you get long-term benefit from what you spend money on, you're an investor. A spender gets immediate gratification that fades.

What can you do about that realization? If it's true that "the rich get richer and the poor get poorer," if it's true that "them that's got are them that gets," how do you put yourself on the side of abundance?

Like so many things in life, it's a combination of attitude and skill. While you begin building those skills, try on this attitude: You deserve a constant, secure supply of everything it takes to have a satisfying life.

Now, act on that attitude until it's a way of life and not just a hope-charged motto. You will begin attracting plenty of those things you want. As a first step, read the following Top 10 List and apply as much of it to your own life as you can.

Remember that your adoption of these ten principles can be gradual, according to your sense of your own readiness. But also realize that the quicker you can adopt them, the quicker you'll feel totally successful.

How to know you're making progress with this principle

- You become a saver instead of a spender. And you'll *enjoy* saving, vs. just doing it because you should.
- You find yourself less affected by life's problems because you'll have more

54

inner confidence and won't have to call on bravado to get things accomplished.

- You steer away from people who don't have a reserve. You see them as risks who are not worth dealing with. This is somewhat cruel, but it's true.
- You feel more generous because you realize you can afford to be.
- You have a large amount of money in the bank with no need for using it.
- You find yourself investing time, money, CPU, and/or space into ideas to test them out, instead of holding back and waiting until you've got them "all figured out."
- You can afford to take more risks because the cost of the risks is almost nil.

TOP 10 WAYS
TO BUILD A SUPERRESERVE

1. PICK A SINGLE AREA IN WHICH *YOU* CAN DEVELOP A HUGE RESERVE WITHIN A WEEK.

Then, once you've done that, double that amount of reserve, just for the exercise of it. Why? Because most of us only develop "more than enough" instead of really developing a reserve.

The area you pick can be anything, from the ridiculous to the sublime. A CoachV student, Marjorie, initiated this principle in a whimsical way, going to the local Sam's Club and buying herself several family-sized packages of toilet paper, which she knew was completely silly. But it was also nice, knowing that this one household fundamental wouldn't have to be thought of again for months. It was a baby step, but it was also a blueprint for future reserve building in other areas.

How often can you open new horizons at so little cost? Pick something either small or large for this step. It should be something that particularly bugs you whenever it has to be dealt with. Load up on a superreserve. You're on your way.

2. IDENTIFY AND REMOVE WHATEVER IS EATING AWAY OR DRAINING A RESERVE THAT YOU ALREADY HAVE.

Building a reserve is a two-part process. The obvious part is composed of addition: acquiring or building things you want. The other part, just as important and potentially disastrous if overlooked, is based on subtraction. When you reduce losses and eliminate unnecessary drains, your cup of prosperity will no longer spring leaks.

How do you accomplish this subtraction part without taking the fun out of life? The answers are totally individualized. But here's a shorthand version: Put your money (and other resources, tangible and intangible) where your values are. In other words, figure out what nonmaterial things *really* matter to you in life. Take some quiet moments and think about it—what are you drawn to (versus what you participate in because you're "supposed to")? Now: How can your key values become more central to the activities and focuses of your life? How can you make your values become your priorities? To paraphrase Shakespeare—How can you make the firstlings of your heart become the firstlings of your hand?

Further on in this book, you'll get some solid coaching on how to clarify your values, which is the first step to fully understanding your priorities.

3. Make a radical change of some sort, just to rattle your own cage.

Most of us are stuck in inertia, particularly in relation to our habits of consumption and saving. If you try to think your way to better habits, you're not likely to get unstuck. As Marianne Williamson, the author of *A Return to Love,* often says, "It's easier to *act* your way to a new way of thinking than it is to *think* your way to a new way of acting."

So, instead of pondering what part of your personality dictates what aspect of your behavior, just shake things up by making a very quick choice. Playfully rewire your pattern in that area. Then stand back and watch that change ripple out to other parts of your life.

What you're after is to create a little momentum. That's important to building a reserve. Later on you can change back to your old ways if you want to. But, just for now, redirect an old, habituated pattern and see what happens next.

4. Become an investor rather than a spender.

The essence of this change is to redirect existing resources. Even without an income boost, you can put yourself on an abundance track. Pick one aspect of how you now spend money or time. Instead of simply spending or meeting expenses in that area, concentrate on building something. This can be as simple as looking for ways to make money from a hobby or as basic as diverting money usually spent at cafes and restaurants into an accumulation of capital that could someday start a business. When you finish paying off a car loan, or any other installment-plan purchase, keep writing the same-sized check every month—to a savings or investment plan. If you work at a job that doesn't offer a pathway to something you might like even better, start looking for options until you find a job that does. They're all around.

Your time is a commodity, your money is a resource; in both cases you deserve a healthy return on your investment.

5. GRAB STUFF EVEN IF IT MAKES YOU FEEL GUILTY.

If you want something for your reserve, take it. Of course, I don't mean that you should steal it or in any other way do an end run on your own ethics. But don't go on a guilt trip just because you take what's readily available. Get yourself in the mode of acquiring things you like, whether it's time, money, ideas, or even people. If you like someone, "take" some of their time and use it for your personal benefit. Ask them about themselves. Don't analyze your friendship to death, but do get a well-rounded sense of why you find them attractive. You'll pick up significant clues that way.

If you have been afraid to charge for your time or your services, figure out a value and begin to charge for them. Real friends will understand and be supportive. They'll respect your right to earn money for what you do well. Users will drop out of your life. Soon you'll be as grateful for their absence, and all the time it frees up for you, as you are for the extra money.

If you learn a good idea from someone, take it. Adapt it to your own talents and circumstances, and run with it.

6. GET YOUR PERSONAL NEEDS MET.

Personal needs that are not met are an insidious drain. They seduce you into wasting resources, without really knowing why or how to stop. No matter how much of a reserve you put together, unmet needs can eventually cause it to leak out.

In the Top 10 List that accompanies Step 13, you will be coached on how to get your personal needs met once and for all, which, believe it or not, really is possible. Until then, focus on this principle: To make your reserve develop faster and last longer, plug all the holes of neediness: You can't capture reserves in a sieve.

7. REDUCE YOUR LIFESTYLE SIGNIFICANTLY.

How much energy does your lifestyle consume? Remember that a lifestyle isn't a life.

Is your lifestyle too big? What amount of time and money do you need to sustain it? Does it bring you flash-in-the-pan thrills or lasting joy?

If "living large" has become a driving force, it's standing between you and the life you want. Simplify. Then you won't have to put out as much to keep it all running. Your body can tell you how much of your lifestyle is really happiness-generating and how much is filigree and trappings. Simplify until you feel your reserves rising steadily, whether they're expressed in time, money, or space.

While you're at it, get rid of the baggage and/or the people who complicate your life. The less you have to lift, the higher you can rise.

8. HAND OVER BIG CHUNKS OF YOUR ADMINISTRATIVE/MANAGEMENT TASKS TO EXPERTS.

Hire an assistant to handle all your unwanted problems or tasks. Someone who, for a reasonable fee, will take over bill paying, sending reminders, client follow-up, typing, ordering, etc.

Because we work together exclusively over the Internet (which is very efficient), I call my administrative jack-of-all-trades my virtual assistant.

Any money I pay my virtual assistant comes right back to me, one way or another. As soon as I hooked up with one, my reserve of time started to grow. This is tremendously important to me. It frees me up to be very generous with my time in other areas of life, including a supremely important one: having more fun.

As much as possible, I've stopped doing errands. Instead of spending hours on end at the supermarket, pushing a cart while canned music and obnoxious ads fill my ears, I usually have my food delivered. I order most things by catalog or over the Internet. I delegate and outsource even those tasks I flat-out *know* I can do easily, and maybe even enjoy doing.

There are costs involved, of course. But time is a commodity. Don't be afraid to invest in things that give you more time to use for the highest possible benefits.

Free your time, and your mind, for whatever is truly special in your life.

9. GET A LOT MORE SPACE.

When you have a feeling of roominess in your life, you have what is called "space." And for all your reserves to have a place to be "stored," you'll need to have a lot more space. You can get it in hundreds of different ways: cleaning the closets, giving up *shoulds* or *coulds* or frustrating projects, taking the path of least resistance, abandoning roles you never chose, or simply taking a lot more vacations.

Get more space. Space leads to reserves.

10. HANDLE THE MONEY, HONEY.

All the reserves in the world in other areas won't give you enough of a reserve until you build up the financial side of your life. You *can* handle the money, either by increasing your income or decreasing your expenses. Or both. Do whatever it takes to begin saving at *least* 10 percent of your current income. Consistently. Because, even though you shouldn't get so obsessed with the future that you tune out the present, there nonetheless *is* a tomorrow.

When you've accumulated a financial superreserve, it will be a tomorrow where you're in control. It takes courage to be this aggressive about savings. The resulting reserve is worth it.

RESERVE INDEX

To further your progress, the following Reserve Index checklist will establish your current level of ten items in each of ten key areas of your life. Please be advised: This is a rigorous test. Your first-time score might seem very low. Don't get discouraged. Time and training will take you higher.

The test will also isolate those areas in which you can make rapid improvement. That will buoy your spirits. Then you can go after the areas that require more time and work.

Doing whatever it takes to achieve a score of 100 on this test will strengthen you. Soon, you will be able to afford—financially, personally, and professionally—to develop and share your unique and special gifts.

Instructions:

1. Circle Y if the statement is completely true. Circle N if the statement is not completely true.
2. Add up the number of Ys in each section.
3. Add up the number of Ys in all sections for the Total Score. You will find the Scoring Key at the end of the test.
4. If a statement doesn't apply to you, please change it so that it does, or replace it with a different one that fits within that category.

1. HOME & COMFORT

Y N 1. My house has extra room/space that I do not need to use very often.

Y N 2. I have twice as much empty available storage as I am currently using.

Y N 3. I always have plenty of clean, pressed clothes; I never "run out."

Y N 4. I have the coziest sheets, comforter, and bedding.

Y N 5. I am physically touched enough to feel satiated.

Y N 6. My home is always clean and orderly.

Y N 7. My home's heating and air-conditioning system always maintains the perfect temperature.

Y N 8. I have more than enough silverware, dishes, glasses, mugs, cooking utensils, and kitchen equipment.

Y N 9. I have a favorite place in my home where I can go to relax, think, and just be.

Y N 10. There is no place in my home that I do not like.

_____ Score   (Number of Ys)

2. CAR/VEHICLE

Y N 1. I have high-quality (10-gauge) jumper cables in the trunk of my car.

Y N 2. I have AAA Plus or similar roadside assistance service.

Y N 3. I have a cellular phone in my car (or I carry one with me when I drive).

Y N 4. I have an extra $100, in ten-dollar bills, hidden in my car—just in case.

Y N 5. I always fill up before the gas gauge falls below a quarter tank.

Y N 6. My car's battery is extremely strong and powerful.

Y N 7. My car's engine is powerful enough to get me out of harm's way immediately.

Y N 8. My car has antilock brakes and air bags.

Y N 9. My car/vehicle is rated "safe" in collision-impact studies.

Y N 10. I have flares, a blanket, extra water, a spare tire, and snow chains in my car.

_____ Score (Number of Ys)

3. FINANCIAL

Y N 1. I have $25,000 in a savings/money market fund, for which I have no immediate need.

Y N 2. I pay my bills early.

Y N 3. I have most of my bills paid automatically by electronic transfer or credit card.

Y N 4. I have arranged with my bank to be able to do wire transfers via the telephone (versus in person or by fax).

Y N 5. I have $500 in cash available at home at all times.

Y N 6. I have no credit card or other installment debt, other than a first mortgage or business loan.

Y N 7. I invest at least 5 percent of my income a year in experiences, books, classes, or environments that will help me earn more.

Y N 8. At least 25 percent of my income each year comes from passive sources.

Y N 9. I work for a company/clients/myself where I am fully compensated for the value I deliver.

Y   N   10. I am clearly on a track to reach financial independence within the next ten to twenty years.

_____ Score   (Number of Ys)

4. SAFETY

Y   N   1. I know what I will do if I am threatened, mugged, or attacked.

Y   N   2. I simply never walk or drive anywhere that makes me nervous in any way.

Y   N   3. I always act immediately to disengage myself from people who will bore, irritate, or consume me.

Y   N   4. I have smoke detectors in every part of the house where they are needed.

Y   N   5. I have a fire extinguisher in the kitchen, car, garage, and bedroom.

Y   N   6. I always use seat belts.

Y   N   7. My home has an alarm system, dead bolts, or other safety equipment.

Y   N   8. I have a remote entry system (called a *fob*) to lock/unlock my car doors from a distance.

Y   N   9. I do not lose sleep over my investments.

Y   N   10. I do not engage in unprotected sex (unless in a monogamous relationship).

_____ Score   (Number of Ys)

5. ENERGY/VITALITY

Y   N   1. I know my cholesterol counts, and they are in the healthful range.

Y   N   2. I get plenty of sleep each night; I am not tired.

Y   N   3. I eat more than enough fresh, healthful foods.

Y   N   4. I drink eight glasses of filtered water each day.

Y   N   5. I exercise at least three times per week.

Y   N   6. I have eliminated the sources of stress in my life.

Y   N   7. I take at least four vacations a year, which completely refresh, energize, and nourish me.

Y N   8. I have something to look forward to each morning.

Y N   9. I have something to look forward to each evening.

Y N 10. I do not use caffeine or drugs.

_____ **Score** **(Number of Ys)**

6. OPPORTUNITY

Y N   1. I am online/have access to the Internet.

Y N   2. I have my own Web page or Web site.

Y N   3. I have much more confidence than I need. I am not held back by fear.

Y N   4. I have at least two to three years' worth of interesting work activities, projects, jobs, lined up.

Y N   5. I always ask for (and get) more than I actually need in any business or work situation, before I need it.

Y N   6. I have developed a highly tuned, consistent, and accurate sense of good judgment; I am rarely surprised.

Y N   7. I have developed a special knowledge, skill-set, or ability that is in high demand; my future appears very secure.

Y N   8. I am part of a company, group, school, or industry that contributes greatly to my ability to succeed.

Y N   9. I have become an investor—I invest my time/money in several things that may take a while to pay off.

Y N 10. I can take the kernel of an idea and "pop" it to become a really successful one.

_____ **Score** **(Number of Ys)**

7. SPACE/TIME

Y N   1. I always arrive ten minutes early to every appointment.

Y N   2. I always promise less than I am certain I can deliver.

Y N   3. I never get talked into doing things.

Y N   4. I end the day quietly.

Y N   5. I always let other cars "in" when I am driving.

Y N   6. I have a virtual or local assistant who immediately handles what I need help with.

Y   N   7. I do not speed when driving.

Y   N   8. I always maintain extra time (one to two hours a day) in my schedule; I never fully book.

Y   N   9. Nothing is distracting, draining, exhausting, or stressing me, period.

Y   N   10. I can easily let opportunities pass me by; I am not Pavlovian (meaning automatically reacting, out of need).

_____ **Score** **(Number of Ys)**

8. CALAMITY PROTECTION

Y   N   1. I have a small 12-volt, automatically charging flashlight plugged into the cigarette lighter in my car.

Y   N   2. I back up my computer's hard drive at least once a week and store the backup away from the computer.

Y   N   3. I additionally back up my computer's hard drive once monthly and store the backup at least ten miles away.

Y   N   4. I have a second ISP (Internet service provider) I can tap into immediately in case the first one is busy/down.

Y   N   5. I have safely listed/stored all of my credit card numbers and 800 numbers to call in case of loss.

Y   N   6. I have a photocopy of my driver's license, passport, social security card, and birth certificate, stored safely offsite or in a safety deposit box.

Y   N   7. I have a will, and my attorney and one other person have the most recent copy of it.

Y   N   8. I have ample medical insurance.

Y   N   9. I have ample car, home, and liability insurance.

Y   N   10. If something happens to me, my family will not suffer financially.

_____ **Score** **(Number of Ys)**

9. SUPPLIES & EQUIPMENT

Y   N   1. I have a six-month supply of toilet paper stored in my home.

Y   N   2. I have enough postage stamps to last for a year.

Y N   3. I have at least one replacement bulb for every light in my home.

Y N   4. I have enough laundry detergent, bleach, and fabric softener to last for a year.

Y N   5. I have thirty days' worth of underwear.

Y N   6. I have two years' worth of vacuum cleaner bags.

Y N   7. I have a 56K, ISDN, cable, or satellite dish modem.

Y N   8. My computer has an extra gigabyte of hard drive storage that is not being used.

Y N   9. I routinely buy the model with more features than I think I'll actually need.

Y N   10. I buy only the quality/grade of tools and equipment that makes me not just more effective, but *a lot* more effective.

_____ Score   (Number of Ys)

10. RELATIONSHIPS

Y N   1. My children show me an incredible amount of love.

Y N   2. My spouse is always showing (versus just telling) me how much he/she cares.

Y N   3. I have a supersharp attorney whom I can immediately turn to for help with any matter.

Y N   4. I treat everyone—spouse, clients, clerks, acquaintances—in the same positive, respectful, and loving manner.

Y N   5. I have no relationships with people who repeatedly disappoint, frustrate, or disrespect me.

Y N   6. I know at least fifty different types of professionals well enough to ask for help.

Y N   7. There is someone I can turn to and ask for help regarding anything without fear.

Y N   8. I know at least five people who are very successful and whom I can ask for advice.

Y N   9. My emotional needs are more than met by my family, friends, and colleagues.

Y N   10. I have a relationship with nature, God, or a force outside myself.

_____ Score   (Number of Ys)

_____ Total Score   (Maximum 100)

And . . . since this is the Reserve Index, it only makes sense that you reach 110 out of 100, right? Here are ten more. Now you'll have a superreserve!

Y N   1. Before I go to bed at night, I prepare for the morning (water in the teakettle, clothes ready, etc.).

Y N   2. I have three extra sets of house and car keys and have placed each set where I can easily get to it if needed.

Y N   3. I keep my car's windshield-washing fluid at least half full at all times.

Y N   4. I buy the larger sizes of supplies and goods because I like having extra, even if I don't need them right away.

Y N   5. I have a tech support contract for my computer, so I can instantly call for assistance.

Y N   6. When working on a project, I always have a backup plan; if something goes wrong, I am "insured."

Y N   7. I work only with people who believe in double-checking.

Y N   8. The moment I sense a potential problem, I address it completely so that it will not actually become one.

Y N   9. The moment something breaks, I take at least thirty minutes to upgrade/strengthen everything related to it.

Y N   10. I am never, never, never a sneak. I am completely forthright and communicate everything, even when it's not ethically "necessary."

_____ **Score**   (**Number of Ys**)

SCORING KEY

110. You can't get any better. Enter your name on the Reserve All-Stars Roster.

100–109. Incredible. Very well done.

90–99. Congratulations. You have a superreserve. Feels great, doesn't it?

80–89. You are well on your way to establishing a superreserve. Keep going.

70–79. You have areas of superreserve but will need to reach 85–95 before you feel the real benefits.

60–69. You have more reserve than the average person, that's for sure. Get ten more points in the next month.

50–59. You are now more than halfway to having a superreserve. Believe me, it gets a lot better.

40–49. This is a challenging area because you're on the verge of getting on the superreserve track.

30–39. You have some reserve, but there is probably something in your life that is preventing a higher score.

20–29. This is where most people first score when taking this test. Identify the next ten points you want most.

10–19. It's important to decide if building a superreserve is important to you. If so, your score will rise fairly quickly.

0–9. Congratulations. You're honest. That's an excellent beginning.

STEP 5

ADD VALUE JUST
FOR THE JOY OF IT

*When You Add Value Because You Enjoy It,
People Are Naturally Attracted to You*

Give what you have. To someone, it may be better than you dare
to think.

—HENRY WADSWORTH LONGFELLOW

We tire of those pleasures we take, but never of those we give.

—JOHN PETIT-SENN

I've said a great deal about claiming your own identity and building your own riches, and I stand firmly behind every word. But it's also vital to remember that life is a team sport, and always will be.

It's easy enough to see this if you work in a structured environment and/or if you're part of a marriage and a family. But it's just as true, and sometimes even more so, when you are entrepreneurial and/or self-employed, or if you're single. Without the steady support of customers and clients, everything can come quickly tumbling down.

How does this principle attract that kind of support and ensure that it will last? How does it strengthen and validate the importance of who you are and what you do—within your family and at your place of work?

The answer: by coaching you to fulfill all expectations and then to do more—at little or no cost to yourself, and with a payoff of joy.

In every key relationship of your life, the success-building thing to do is

---

DISTINCTIONS TO DRAW

ADDING VALUE VS. ADDING MORE—When you give someone more of what they want, you're adding value. When you give someone more of what you want them to have, you're adding more.

ADDING VALUE VS. SELLING—*Adding value* means being inventive and generous in giving potential customers what they want; *selling* is convincing them to buy what you have available.

CUSTOMIZATION VS. PROGRAM—It's more fun to create a perfect fit for a client than to get people to buy your off-the-shelf product.

JOY VS. SATISFACTION—Joy is a feeling that comes from the inside; satisfaction is a sensation that results from an external event.

---

to add value, to go beyond everyone's expectations, but to do it in ways that are relatively inexpensive to you (or even cost you nothing at all).

In business, you need to add value to all of your customers, which will make them feel there's no one better to do business with than you.

To have a very attractive personal life, you simply have to add value to everyone close to you, which will make them glad they are close to you and keep them interested in staying close.

You don't seduce; you don't encourage codependency. You adopt a style of relating that keeps YOU feeling positive. In short, you add value to others for no expectation at all—just for the joy it gives you.

Bees do it right. They do their thing, going from flower to flower, collecting and spreading pollen as they go. Technically speaking, they're just in the honey-making business, working to support themselves and the other members of the hive. But they also create a by-product. They add value to the rest of the world through pollination of the trees and flowers. It costs them nothing, yet the benefits radiate out to practically every living thing on the planet.

If insects smaller than your thumb can do that much, think what you could do!

In this Top 10 List, you'll learn how to add value to others in ways that also bring you joy. In fact, the joy you experience from your value-adding attitude is what will make you more attractive—not the quantity or even the quality of the value you add.

How to know you're making progress with this principle

- You start developing new ideas.
- You get joy and satisfaction from the giving, not from how it's received.
- You get a real kick out of being generous. It strengthens a part of you.
- You find yourself noticing and appreciating people who've been adding value to you, though you hadn't really noticed it earlier. (You may even want to apologize to some of them for having been so clueless.)
- You become more sensitized, feeling the needs and wants of others more deeply, and are prompted to offer or create what will satisfy them.

TOP 10 WAYS TO ADD VALUE, FOR THE SHEER JOY OF IT

1. FIND OUT WHAT THE OTHER PERSON PLACES A HIGH VALUE ON.

Everybody has an opinion as to what adds value to his or her life. Take some time with the people who are important to you and ask them.

What do other people define as value? You may not want to package or deliver what you have to fit their exact description, but the process of being open will add value to you. It will sensitize you to what matters to others.

With this expanded perspective comes wisdom. Eventually, it will emerge: a way to please the people around you that will also nourish you, make you happy, expand your reach.

2. DISCOVER WHAT BRINGS YOU JOY. DO LOTS OF IT.

Very few people know what brings them joy. When they find out, they become more attractive to themselves. What brings you joy? Intellectual pursuits? Giving to others? Solving problems? Designing something?

Usually, people feel joy whenever they're expressing their values. So, whenever you experience joy, you're probably adding a lot of value to others at virtually no cost to yourself. On the other hand, when you don't experience joy as a part of what you do, something will strike the person you're relating to as being out of whack.

David Nelson has it figured out. He's a coach from Kansas City who happens to derive a lot of pleasure from movies. One day he decided to bring that enthusiasm into his practice. This is from an E-mail he sent me recently:

> For years I've been trying to better understand everyone's needs, and help them to get their needs met. I used to carry a little too much of that concern around with me. I also used to think of movies as a luxury, something to indulge in only after the real work was over. All of this changed when I began using movie stories and episodes in much of my training and teaching. People really love it, and they love me for it. After discussions, they start looking at things from their hearts, not just their eyes.
>
> Now I go see movies more frequently, and enjoy it even more than before. The guilt is gone, and my presence with clients, friends, and family is enhanced, more joyful. I'm writing articles now which I hope someday will grow into a book—about the images and scenes I've used, and what thoughts and feelings come up for people in the discussions. All of this new momentum came about because I found a way to add value that was really pleasurable for me.

3. FIND WAYS TO BROADCAST WHAT YOU HAVE OR KNOW WITHOUT A COST TO YOURSELF.

Thanks to the Internet and electronic distribution of information, you can add lots of value to others at little or no cost. For example, you can set up a weekly E-newsletter, teach a teleclass, train others, write a book, create audiotapes, set up a Web site (which actually costs very little).

These are all ways to increase the distribution of what you know, which will have you adding value all along the way.

4. STOP TRYING TO SELL, CONVINCE, ENROLL, OR HYPE YOURSELF—OR WHAT YOU OFFER.

You immediately become more attractive as soon as you stop pushing yourself, or what you offer, onto people. Adding value usually occurs least expensively to both parties when one party takes it from "your doorstep" instead of you having to knock on their door. This occurs because they've preselected the experience and are pretty much bound to be happy—as long as it meets their core expectations. Easing off the "push it, hype it" mentality is a pretty big change in style, especially since hype has become such a constant in our lives. But very few people who push their offerings hard actually experience joy.

Stop pushing. Find a better way to make your business work or to reach your goals. You may have some rough spots in transition as you review and try out different nonpushy strategies, perhaps even a temporary decrease in income. But most people find that the extra joy in their lives is a great consolation and that income eventually rises above all previous levels.

Todd proved it to himself, with the help of an enthusiastic coach. Todd is an insurance salesman in Dallas. He was frustrated and feeling unsatisfied after fifteen years on the job: Even though he led the large agency where he worked in the number of new policies sold, his income was rising only slightly, while he was working harder and servicing more clients. Then he shifted focus from selling more to adding more value. That inspired a decision to spend his time mainly with clients whose businesses could grow faster with the benefit of his help. His decision doubled the amount of time he spent working with clients. Because the focus was on their wants and needs, and because great results quickly started to materialize, Todd started feeling new enthusiasm for his career. Now he serves fewer clients but in a more meaningful way. Instead of waking up anxious about getting out and making sales, he's concerned only about building relationships by adding value to others at low cost. In one year, his income shot up 38 percent. Now he speaks at meetings, letting other agents in on his "competitive secret."

5. Help others create tremendous value from what you provide.

Just as you can fill your mouth so full of food that it's hard to chew and swallow, you can overwhelm your customers and potential customers with too much value.

It's much better, and much more manageable, to simply help people get maximum value from what's already there.

How do you show your customers and potential customers how to make the most of what you've provided? Give them instructions, coach them, stay connected to them as they use your product or service until their skills and their appreciation have fully blossomed. That will make them the best spokespersons in the world and will also make it much easier for you to follow Principle number 4 above.

Your customers may even uncover new uses for your product or service, which will be pure gold for you.

Remember, you can create more value without giving more product.

6. DON'T GET YOUR PERSONAL NEEDS MET BY ATTEMPTING TO ADD VALUE TO OTHERS.

"Adding value" is an attractive mantra, but it becomes less attractive when it's simply a way to get your needs met, as when you recognize that you're "playing the angles" with somebody, holding a hidden agenda in your back pocket. Like that old soul song says: "Smiling faces sometimes don't tell the truth."

No matter how clever the manipulation, people feel the difference. The added value feels more like a hook or a setup, not a gift. They may bite, but the bad taste will remain, and they won't be back again.

What's tricky is that manipulativeness can be pretty subtle, even unconscious, especially if you're feeling extremely needy about the desired outcome. But it can be sensed, and it puts people on the lookout so that they're automatically less receptive to the good points of your service, your product, or you yourself.

Add value because it brings you joy, not to fill a personal need.

7. MATCH WHAT YOU HAVE TO THE PEOPLE WHO WANT AND NEED IT: CUSTOMIZE.

One of the easiest ways to increase the value you deliver without a lot of extra work is simply to repackage or customize pieces of what you offer to fit the exact (and I do mean *exact*) needs of your best customers.

Buyers are getting very picky and exacting; each of the forty shades of beige/ecru/bone matters a great deal to the person buying those shoes. The same is true for almost every product or service today. Plus, if you're at all creative, you'll find that it's fun to customize. It increases your sense of being a master of your trade, and it increases the amount of happiness you'll see beaming back from your customers.

8. GET IN SYNC WITH A LARGE TREND AND MOVE FORWARD TO THE HEAD OF IT.

Because the bulk of what is called "value added" in our information age is intangible (information and skills, not brick and mortar), the more value you can add to other people's intangibles, the better. Keeping up with trends that will affect the value of information and other intangibles is the perfect lookout position!

Right now, two meta (transcending, overarching) trends are the Internet and "meaning," the ongoing search for relevancy and fulfillment in life. The Internet is, obviously, a wheel that's still in spin. Fortunes are being made; fun is being had; personal, business, and social patterns are being revamped. "Meaning" is a wide-open category: Some people are jettisoning traditional religions; others are becoming more "fundamentalist," or looking to other cultures and other eras for spiritual foundations. Some are experiencing the sense that they can forge a connection to the Divine through New Age–style inner journeys. Still others are rejecting such searches but embracing the here and now more passionately than ever, finding their meaning through full-tilt aliveness. On a lower, but still important, plane, some people are trying to rekindle their ethnic identities or to borrow religion, music, dance, or anything else that's joyful from other cultures. Therapies of all kinds, from the AMA-approved to the most way-out, are flourishing. Yoga classes aren't just filled with aging hot-tub hippies any longer; they now attract a rich cross-section of young and old, careerist and seeker, male and female, the athletic and the fitness-deficient. Spiritual hunger, and its fulfillment, is simply one of the keynotes of our times.

Attune yourself to metatrends like these and to their implications. Let yourself explore and find a natural, totally and authentically "you" way of relating to them. You'll discover inexpensive ways of adding a lot of value to everyone important to you and your life.

Applying your insights will upgrade what you currently offer without you having to upgrade tangible features or specific performance.

9. PUT PEOPLE TOGETHER IN NETWORKS
THAT MEAN A LOT TO THEM.

You can add a significant amount of value by doing what may come naturally to you—putting people in touch with each other. Whether you have a big Rolodex or are now developing one, the more people you put together, the more value everyone receives. If you can sponsor, host, or create special-interest networks, that's even better.

Esther Dyson, who I think is one of the smartest people going, went from being a journalist to becoming a Wall Street analyst following high-tech stocks to helping produce a computer-industry newsletter. Eventually she took it over, just in time to write about a charming little startup located in Bellevue, Washington—Microsoft. In 1983 she took over PC Forum, an annual computer conference, that had previously been just one afternoon session within a bigger industry conference. It became a place to talk about the problems of a growing industry. People like Bill Gates and Mitch Kapor waded into deep arguments, while other folks convened in corners to strike deals, learn what was new, make job connections, find new partners and capital sources. PC Forum just keeps thriving, and so does Esther Dyson as an expert on the potentials of personal computing and the Internet. I'll be citing examples of her thinking in other parts of this book. Her example proves how, more than ever, people need to belong to groups and networks for emotional reasons just as much as they need to for professional resources. You can fill those needs. It will strengthen your connections to all the people and things that are important to you.

10. BECOME A COACH AND/OR MASTER THE FULL SET
OF COACHING SKILLS.

A coach is someone who shows you how to do or master something, whether it be reaching an important goal or making a difficult change. A coach stays with you and helps you select the goal, engage with it, progress through it, achieve it, and integrate the accomplishment into your life—just as this book aims to do but on a one-to-one, custom-tailored basis.

With a coaching background, you can show people how, not just tell them. Everyone needs this level of care and personal attention.

AFFECT OTHERS PROFOUNDLY

The More You Touch Others, the More Attractive You'll Become

Do not wait for leaders; do it alone, person to person.
—MOTHER TERESA

Isolation is the sum total of wretchedness to man.
—THOMAS CARLYLE

Without communication, life becomes cold and daunting. But when communication flows, people feel one of the best things there is to feel—touched. Even if that communication comes in the form of a deep, sad story about mortality and loss, we're still reminded of our aliveness. The message itself can be less important than the openness and honesty behind it. And a profound connection can happen in any human interchange.

People who are skillful and practiced at helping people feel alive and connected are more attractive, more sought after, better remembered. We all affect others anyway, more than we generally realize. That's why this step can be related closely to Step 5. When you affect people, when something you say or do touches them, you've added value to their lives. And they're certain to store that positive association somewhere in their hearts and/or their minds. So why not aim to tap into your abilities and affect them profoundly?

Here are ten proven ways to touch people where they live. All of them

---

DISTINCTIONS TO DRAW

PROFOUND VS. HELPFUL—Helpful gives someone what they seek; profound gives them something bigger than they knew was possible.

INSPIRE VS. MOTIVATE—To be inspired is to be pulled toward something; to be motivated is to be pushed by yourself or others.

AWARENESS VS. KNOWLEDGE—Knowledge can be transmitted; awareness can only be catalyzed.

PEOPLE VS. INFORMATION—Focus on the person, and information will be created; focus on information and the person will either accept it or reject it.

FEELINGS VS. DATA—When you focus on other people's feelings, they can absorb more of the data you want to deliver.

WHO VS. WHAT—Because information is becoming essentially free and accessible to everyone, who you are and who you know is more valuable than what you know.

---

will make you a lot more attractive to others—and to yourself. They're just as applicable to business and career as they are to being among friends.

How to know you're making progress with this principle

- Life starts to appear very, very simple. You wonder why it seemed so complex before.
- People respond to what you say with a jerk of the head or a start of some kind, just because you've said what's true for you.
- You realize that you *need* profundity in order to evolve quickly. You seek it out. It becomes a currency for you, not just information.
- You discover the gifts you have that do affect others and develop this part of yourself.
- It becomes easier to work with other people because you can reach them efficiently.

TOP 10 WAYS TO
AFFECT OTHERS PROFOUNDLY

1. LISTEN FOR AND POINT OUT THE SPECIAL GIFTS, TRAITS, OR TALENTS OF THE OTHER PERSON.

Most people just listen for what they *need* from the other person. They wait out a string of words until they hear a period landing at the end of a sentence. Then they deliver the phrases they've been holding at the ready, which they hope will trigger a result and allow the "communication" to stop.

Listen instead for what's special or unique about a person—and take a moment to point it out. You'll affect them positively with very, very little effort on your part.

What if you did this during every conversation you had for the rest of your life? It would mean trusting that your needs were eventually going to be met, possibly on a bigger scale than you'd originally hoped for. Taking neediness out of the loop always opens up grander possibilities.

2. LISTEN AND RESPOND IN KIND TO THE UNDERLYING EMOTION OF THE OTHER PERSON.

Facts and information are valuable but are rarely profound.

What *is* profound? People, emotion, and concepts. Next time you're listening to your child, client, or friend, feel what they are feeling and respond in kind to that instead of just to what they are saying.

Ronald Oltmanns, a coach who recently completed attraction training, wrote this account of his experiences:

> Instead of soliciting business and hunting for clients, I've started asking people questions like, "Where would you like to be in the next quarter of this year?" and "How do you want to be remembered when you're gone?"
>
> Questions like these inspire people to think deeply, and I really listen to what they say. I've gotten a reputation for facilitating people's success by being their mirror (that's what my clients are calling it). Since I'm not soliciting, people don't feel so guarded and I really feel like a partner

with them. I'm building longer-term relationships, and I'm learning patience. My client base is mushrooming. Word seems to get out.

Believe this truth: You *cannot* give away more than you get back.

Feelings are the fastest way to a person's heart. Besides being a good-feeling, human thing to do, and totally worthwhile in its own right, addressing someone else's feelings makes great business sense.

3. DELIVER NUGGETS/MESSAGES THAT CAN BE REMEMBERED AND RETRANSMITTED.

Memes are basically the idea equivalent of genes. They are expressions of concepts and ideas passed along from person to person. Memes are capable of changing and adapting as they are transmitted and applied to real-life situations. And they're likely to perpetuate themselves if they succeed in the environment.

Following the laws of evolution, the best memes live on, sometimes even flourishing, while others pass into extinction.

The idea to hold on to about memes is this: When you can package information, concepts, or truth into nugget-sized packages, (a) they land easily on the person you're talking to and (b) that person can also pass them on to others easily.

The biggest thing in life right now is the competition between memes and genes: between being ruled by centuries-old programming in our DNA and improving on the cards we were dealt by evolving on a socio-cultural level. (By the way, memes have a cool edge on the competition: They can mutate and retransmit millions of times faster than genes can.) So, become memetically attractive. When you're in a reflective mood, express what you feel and believe in words. Take some time to play with your phrases until they feel polished, compressed to few words yet filled with provocative thought.

You will always have simple, worthwhile, intriguing things to say. It's as simple as that.

4. Accept and endorse your worst weaknesses so that others feel safe around you.

A lot of attraction works without you having to "work it." It happens by itself, behind the scenes. And one of the ways to profoundly affect others is to be so self-secure that they, too, can feel secure.

We're all gripped by eye-popping fears and compelling desires, but when you've reached that place in life where you aren't affected by any of this—because you've fully accepted your humanness, faults, *and* talents— then others can have the same experience of themselves. It's magical. And profoundly attractive.

In Step 17 we'll focus directly on this concept. Other steps will support this process as well. For now, just realize that what you experience as your faults may be clues, gateways, signposts, to your deepest strengths.

Part of your life's journey is going to be finding out about those things, unlocking doors, taking a different attitude about "scary monsters," and finding key, powerful elements of your humanity, which you ultimately will tap, for huge benefits.

When you radiate a confidence in being basically okay, your faults and setbacks notwithstanding, others pick up a cue and become more comfortable with themselves. They may not know what they're experiencing, but they'll be attracted to the feeling.

5. Open up new worlds for people, in their thinking, feelings, or priorities.

In other words, pull the rug out from under others whenever you can— but quickly give them a new chair to plop into on their way down. How? You can draw a missing distinction, question an antiquated assumption, challenge a strongly held belief, plant a seed of a different crop, be strongly inquisitive, or give them words to express what they are barely able to sense and cannot yet say. If you play fair—never being abusive, always being respectful of boundaries—you'll make deep, positive impressions.

Okay, so that's a lot to learn if the above communication skills are new to you. But boy are they fun! And as long as you practice them with a spirit of kindness, not as a squad-room inquisition, they cost absolutely nothing.

6. SHOW OTHERS HOW TO BETTER EXPERIENCE
WHAT THEY ALREADY HAVE.

We've already given some focus to unhooking yourself from the future so you can be fully present in today. But that principle (from Step 2) is the parent of this one—showing others how to get more benefit from what they already have, whether it's a problem or an attribute.

Most folks are so future-oriented that they miss out on the opportunities staring right at them in the present. Be their eyes and ears for a minute. Help them see the value of what's already all around them.

I'm not suggesting you should deliver one of those speeches that start with "Cheer up—lots of people have it tougher than you!" I'm talking about gently, mindfully helping people see that the present moment, and their present circumstances, are full of powerful connections to happiness, to improvement, and to fulfillment. If you can teach that to others, you'll really develop a great understanding of it for yourself.

Esther Dyson tells the story of Vittorio Cassoni, an Italian executive for AT&T. When she asked him what his managerial job entailed, he said, "I absorb uncertainty." The rapid changes in our lives and workplaces mean that we're constantly saying good-bye to familiar routines. As a result, people need to experience stability. If you can honestly communicate that quality, you'll be a key individual.

7. REMIND PEOPLE WHO THEY ARE INSTEAD OF JUST
COMPLIMENTING THEM ON WHAT THEY'VE DONE.

Praise and acknowledgment are nice, but that's a bit like telling your dog that his tail wags really well. The tail-wagging is fun, but keep your focus on nurturing the happiness that makes his tail wag.

In terms of two-legged animals, you want to be more aware of the *person* than you are of the accomplishments, or the problems, with which they're connected.

It's the fundamental distinction between who they *are* and what they *do*.

Your attention will help the person get more in touch with who they are. So, naturally, they'll produce better results. Let them feel recognized and appreciated on a deeper level, related more to potential than to performance. They'll relax, drop some of their am-I-good-enough? tensions, and start living up to those potentials.

If you focus primarily on the "whats" instead, you'll soon be expecting the tail to wag the dog!

8. GIVE PEOPLE SOMETHING MEANINGFUL TO DO.

Sad to say, but it's also accurate—most people are pretty bored. They're waiting for something interesting and meaningful to do. Many aspects of modern life, including its fast pace and the too-common reliance on television and other prepackaged entertainment for stress relief, have people going around in a sort of excited stupor (if such a paradox is possible).

If you're up to something intriguing, and if you're willing to, include eager people in your game or project. Most people will get meaning from that and will appreciate it very much. It's as if you're inviting them to play. They'll enjoy the game itself as well as the new people they'll meet along the way. You'll get valuable help, often for free, while they get personal growth. With nurturing, it could lead them to a rewarding change of career.

If you're working on a promising project, OPEN IT UP and profoundly affect a lot of other people. It's a perfect path to attraction.

If you don't yet see yourself as the project-launching type, be on the lookout for people who have that talent or any special enthusiasm to express. Go into their project well informed, with a mutually agreed-on sense of what rewards to expect and what not to expect. And join up only with "playmates" who are totally ethical and aboveboard. Then plunge right in. Learn from the people who have a gift for initiating things. You can only go upward.

9. GIVE PEOPLE THE TOOLS THEY NEED TO IMPROVE AND EVOLVE.

I'm very high on computers. I see them as machines to multiply the reach of our intelligence, our personalities, whatever is essential to our being human. In my eyes, the growing popularity of computers is a flashpoint in a progression toward a much greater civilization. The great Winston Churchill said it best: "I am an optimist. It does not seem too much use being anything else."

E-mail, Web sites, and other relatively new features in our culture are among the tools that help me build my optimism.

My evolving toward computers began in 1987. A manager at the firm where I worked said he had an extra copy of Lotus 1-2-3. Did I want it?

I barely knew that I *should* want it, but I faked a resounding "Sure!"

It only took about ten seconds, but that single event changed my life forever! The manager offered me a tool that, for some reason, he felt would help me. And it opened up a new world for me to explore. As you're definitely aware by now, computers and the Internet are enormously important to me. I wasn't born knowing about them—I learned more and more as I was drawn forward by a sense that these amazing tools can make lots of great things happen. And fantastic things really have happened in my life through that exploration. The lion's share of my prosperity is directly linked to what computers and the Internet have made possible.

I no longer use Lotus 1-2-3 or any other spreadsheet program. But the exploration is still in progress. All because somebody took a few seconds to be thoughtful and generous.

What tools do you currently have available to you that would profoundly affect others? Share all of them!

10. DON'T TRY TO AFFECT OTHERS PROFOUNDLY.

Okay, I had to toss this one in here. Not just to be a wiseguy but maybe to show some slightly tricky wisdom.

It's great to affect others profoundly. But if that objective is too much "out in front," it's going to get you in trouble. Because even though everyone, deep down, wants to be profoundly affected, no one wants to be manipulated, condescended to, or patronized.

If you try *too* hard to affect people, you might spark some potent negative feelings instead. "Get away from me!" they'll shriek. You get the picture.

However, what you can do is to care for others and share your knowledge with those who want it. That way, "profoundly affecting others" won't become your cause, banner, or reason for living. That would be pretty unattractive all around.

Besides, we often profoundly affect people without really knowing it. And that may be the best way of all.

I was rather concerned about a student who seldom talked during any of the twelve sessions of a recent Principles of Attraction teleclass. But later on, when he called to inquire about another class, he said, "I haven't told you this, but I want you to know how much you've affected me. The principles opened up so many possibilities, it's like the class began for me at the moment it ended."

My modus operandi for profoundly affecting others is this: Make them feel good about themselves, immediately, but also leave them with something that has a life of its own—something that will support them personally or professionally—like sourdough starter added to bread dough.

It's deliberate, but you don't keep score. Basically, it's an act of faith: You do it and move on. The rewards are terrific.

100 WAYS TO IMPROVE YOUR COMMUNICATION STYLE

Here's an activity where the rewards are also terrific, but you *do* keep score. You'll learn wonderful things about yourself and pick up a lot of guidance on how to have the greatest possible effect on other people.

BAR CHART

Color in the boxes below, left to right, to create a bar chart that reflects your current score for each section.

Update this chart as you make progress in this program.

Keep going until you reach a full 30 points in each category!

The 10 Areas of Communication	10	12	14	16	18	20	22	24	26	28	30
1. How well do you come across?	□	□	□	□	□	□	□	□	□	□	□
2. How well do you listen?	□	□	□	□	□	□	□	□	□	□	□
3. How well are you understood?	□	□	□	□	□	□	□	□	□	□	□
4. What do you talk about?	□	□	□	□	□	□	□	□	□	□	□
5. How well do you converse?	□	□	□	□	□	□	□	□	□	□	□
6. How believable are you?	□	□	□	□	□	□	□	□	□	□	□
7. How positive are you?	□	□	□	□	□	□	□	□	□	□	□

	10	12	14	16	18	20	22	24	26	28	30
8. How do you affect others?	☐	☐	☐	☐	☐	☐	☐	☐	☐	☐	☐
9. How effectively do you communicate?	☐	☐	☐	☐	☐	☐	☐	☐	☐	☐	☐
10. How aware are you?	☐	☐	☐	☐	☐	☐	☐	☐	☐	☐	☐

Current Overall Score is: _____

Maximum is 300 points

Percentage Score is: _____

Maximum is 100%

INSTRUCTIONS AND SCORING

This self-test contains ten pairs of statements for each of the ten categories listed above. In the middle of each statement pair are the numerals 1, 2, and 3.

Please read all 100 statement pairs and circle the appropriate numeral for each.

Circle 1 if the statement on the left is fairly true or often true.
Circle 2 if the statements on both the left and right are both somewhat true.
Circle 3 if the statement on the right is almost always true.

SCORING TIPS

A. If you're undecided about a statement, be a hard grader and circle 2 or 1. Circle 3 only if you (and others) feel that you've really mastered that element of your communication style. Even fairly good communicators will usually score a 1 or a 2.

B. A score of 3 really means that you are a model of this statement. You've probably been complimented many times for it. All parts of the statement on the right must be true, not just selected parts.

C. If you find that only one aspect of the statement on the left is true but other parts are not, give yourself a 1.

D. If you find yourself being overly generous, please deduct 10 percentage points from the overall total. Likewise, if you have been overly hard on yourself, add 5 percentage points to your overall score. The best thing is to be fair and honest, yet rigorous, in your self-assessment.

E. This profile is for you to take for yourself, but you may want to give it to friends or colleagues and have *them* profile *you*. In the training business, this is called "doing a 360." Even if you are completely honest in answering the statements, most of us have blind spots and can't always see ourselves as others do. Give others a chance to help you.

AFTER TAKING THE PROFILE

If after taking this test you find that you would like to improve your score, ask your coach for assistance. If you don't have a coach, please visit the free Coach Referral Service at *http://www.thomasleonard.com*.

In January 1998, CoachVille began awarding the Certified Communication Coach designation to coaches who have been specially trained in the elements and nuances of this profile.

1. HOW WELL DO YOU COME ACROSS?

1.	Loud, coarse, booming, domineering, intense	1 2 3	Refined, subtle, graceful, polished, quiet	
2.	Manic, charged up, hyper, too eager, too "on"	1 2 3	Naturally paced, calm, composed, present	

3.	Slow, plodding, flat, monotone, draggy	1 2 3	Naturally paced, enthusiastic, vibrant
4.	Complaining, whiny, screechy, grating	1 2 3	Pleased, thankful, grateful, happy
5.	Sugary, puffery-oriented, too "nice," fake	1 2 3	Expressive, not syrupy, genuine, accurate, honest
6.	I speak at the person	1 2 3	I share with the person
7.	Heavy, significant, overly concerned	1 2 3	Light, not weighted down, yet respectful, caring
8.	Complicated, convoluted, or technical	1 2 3	Simple, easy to grasp and understand
9.	Suspicious, distrusting, negative, cold	1 2 3	Friendly, open, positive, expectant, warm

10.	Rigid, measured, dogmatic, linear	1 2 3	Flexible, fluid, casual, three-dimensional

Section Score _____ (Maximum 30)

2. HOW WELL DO YOU LISTEN?

11.	I listen too attentively, too intensely	1 2 3	I feel what is being said, without needing all the data
12.	I hear mostly the facts or information	1 2 3	I hear what is behind the words
13.	I wait for overwhelming evidence before trusting myself	1 2 3	I trust my intuition fairly quickly
14.	I acquire and consume information; I am always seeking	1 2 3	What I hear is absorbed and integrated fully
15.	I listen passively, blindly, dumbly	1 2 3	I know what to listen for; I recognize clues
16.	While listening, I am busy preparing a response	1 2 3	I listen fully to the person speaking
17.	I react negatively to what's being said	1 2 3	I accept what's being said; I don't resist or react

18.	I interrupt; attempt to correct, advise, or fix	1 2 3	I prompt or encourage the person to say more
19.	I can hear and handle only one thing at a time	1 2 3	I can listen to and handle multiple lines of conversation
20.	I hear only part of what's being communicated; I filter input	1 2 3	I hear everything that's being communicated

Section Score _____ **(Maximum 30)**

3. HOW WELL ARE YOU UNDERSTOOD?

21.	I launch in with new information or ideas recklessly	1 2 3	I first contextualize new information or ideas
22.	I lecture at others; I push information	1 2 3	I educate others; I notice how well the listener is absorbing
23.	I ramble, confuse, overexplain	1 2 3	I am succinct, clear, easily understood
24.	I use clichés, jargon, technical language	1 2 3	I make points in simple, compelling messages
25.	I seek to convince or to sell	1 2 3	I seek to respond to the needs and interests of the listener

26. I speak in a rote manner, using the same format and content for everyone	1 2 3	I personalize and customize the message for each listener
27. I use general or vague terms; I oversimplify	1 2 3	I use exact, highly descriptive words
28. I say what the other person wants or needs to hear	1 2 3	I say what needs to be said; I don't hold back
29. If misunderstood, I repeat the same thing, probably louder	1 2 3	If misunderstood, I say it very differently, using examples
30. I have limited vocabulary or understanding of words	1 2 3	I have extensive, full vocabulary and command of language

Section Score _____ **(Maximum 30)**

4. WHAT DO YOU TALK ABOUT?

31. Life's symptoms, circumstances, problems	1 2 3	The source of a problem or its possible solutions
32. The negative side of things; what's wrong	1 2 3	The positive side of things; what I am happy about
33. The past or the future	1 2 3	The present

34.	What I should, could, or ought to be doing	1 2 3	What I really want to do or am excited about
35.	What interests me; my agenda exclusively	1 2 3	What interests both parties in the conversation
36.	Mostly just facts, information, historical data	1 2 3	Concepts, ideas, possible trends
37.	Others	1 2 3	Myself
38.	What I know	1 2 3	What I am learning
39.	What the other person should do or not do	1 2 3	What the other person most wants to do
40.	Things I am trying to get the other person to believe	1 2 3	The other person's situation, goals, or problem

Section Score _____ (Maximum 30)

5. HOW WELL DO YOU CONVERSE?

41.	I push my mood or style onto the other person	1 2 3	I match the tone, mood, and pace of the other person
42.	I speak *or* listen; I can't do both at the same time	1 2 3	I can speak *and* listen at the same time
43.	I am easily distracted, inattentive	1 2	I am very attentive without being intrusive

44.	I am interesting	1 2 3	I am interested
45.	I respond mostly to the information being shared	1 2 3	I respond mostly to the person asking
46.	I am lost until the information is fully understood	1 2 3	I easily get the gist of what is meant
47.	I lock on and don't stop until my point is fully made	1 2 3	I dance back and forth easily; I am quick on the draw, nimble
48.	I give pat answers; I employ clichés, sayings, quotes	1 2 3	I respond with personalized, fully related comments
49.	I respond with non sequiturs; I am disjointed, off the subject	1 2 3	I track, follow, respond to what has just been said
50.	I pepper the speaker with questions	1 2 3	I clarify what was said or meant

Section Score _____ **(Maximum 30)**

6. HOW BELIEVABLE ARE YOU?

51.	I am pretentious, name-dropping; I attempt to impress	1 2 3	I am simple, humble, real
52.	I am too eager to please, two-faced; I flip-flop	1 2 3	I am happy to help and please, but not at the expense of honesty

53.	Sneaky; I say only part of the truth or facts	1 2 3	Forthright and forthcoming; I easily state all the facts
54.	Dishonest or partially honest; I justify	1 2 3	Completely honest always; I can afford the consequences
55.	I overpromise, overstate	1 2 3	I underpromise, understate
56.	I sell, promote, enroll, hook, hype	1 2 3	I tell, inform, respond to the other person's interests
57.	I perform for the listener or try too hard	1 2 3	I relate as an equal; collaborative
58.	Hungry, desperate, needy, pleading	1 2 3	Legitimate, experienced, secure, assured, confident
59.	Insincere, disingenuous, fake	1 2 3	Sincere, caring, salt-of-the-earth
60.	I sound too "on" or too up; adrenalized	1 2 3	I am present, relaxed, "with" the other person

Section Score _____ **(Maximum 30)**

7. HOW POSITIVE ARE YOU?

61.	I am critical, insensitive, or harsh, even if accurate	1 2 3	I am constructive, yet direct and honest
62.	I ignore, one-up, downplay, or diminish the other person	1 2 3	I endorse, celebrate the other person's accomplishments
63.	I exclude people or groups; bigoted, intolerant	1 2 3	Inclusive, tolerant; I learn from diversity
64.	I am disrespectful to the other person; I use barbs or digs	1 2 3	I am highly respectful, even when the person is mistaken or wrong
65.	I judge, ignore, label, disregard others	1 2 3	I treat every person as a positive, well-intentioned individual
66.	I hold a grudge and show it; I gossip, backstab, thwart	1 2 3	I am generous, forgiving, compassionate; I seek to mend or heal
67.	I tear people down, point out flaws, undermine	1 2 3	I build a person up, consistently
68.	Righteous; I push my own views relentlessly	1 2 3	Curious; I seek to understand and evolve

69.	I talk more than listen	1 2 3	I listen more than talk
70.	Win (exclusively self-interest) oriented	1 2 3	Win/win oriented

Section Score _____ (Maximum 30)

8. HOW DO YOU AFFECT OTHERS?

71.	I annoy or irritate others with style, content, personality	1 2 3	I impress others without trying to
72.	I leave others doubtful of my skill level or expertise	1 2 3	People find me credible and knowledgeable
73.	I leave people feeling hurt, bruised, or in pain	1 2 3	I am always unconditionally constructive, even when joking
74.	I leave people feeling unheard	1 2 3	People feel like I am really interested in them
75.	I leave people feeling like they witnessed a performance	1 2 3	People feel I am fully present in the moment
76.	I leave people thinking, "hasn't got a clue"	1 2 3	People feel I am wise and knowing, yet humble
77.	I leave people shaken or shocked by a torrent of emotion	1 2 3	People feel touched and inspired by my presence

78.	I leave people with their eyes glazed; information overload	1 2 3	People feel I helped them learn something easily
79.	I leave people wondering why they bothered to listen	1 2 3	People want me to keep talking
80.	I leave people crossing me off their Rolodex immediately	1 2 3	People invite me to spend more time with them

Section Score _____ (Maximum 30)

9. HOW EFFECTIVELY DO YOU COMMUNICATE?

81.	I am results-driven, at the expense of individuals	1 2 3	I easily invest in others and harvest results there
82.	I speak from theory, book learning	1 2 3	I speak from hands-on or observed experience
83.	I ask obliquely or hint at what is wanted or needed	1 2 3	I ask or tell directly and straightforwardly
84.	I merely inform	1 2 3	I naturally inspire
85.	Silent, passive, weak, or wimpy; I don't fully communicate	1 2 3	Naturally confident; I request and say what's on my mind
86.	I need immediate gratification, results, response, outcomes	1 2 3	I can easily afford to plant seeds and nourish the process or the person

87.	Problem- or circumstance-oriented	1 2 3	Solution-oriented
88.	I focus on symptoms or irrelevant aspects of the situation	1 2 3	I quickly identify and articulate the source of the problem
89.	I say only what I am certain of	1 2 3	I experiment while speaking; I create on-the-fly
90.	Conspiratorial, tribal	1 2 3	Collaborative; partner- or team-oriented

Section Score _____ **(Maximum 30)**

10. HOW AWARE ARE YOU?

91.	I assume I am a good or great communicator	1 2 3	I have a 360-degree view of myself and how I communicate
92.	I keep talking even though the other person has gotten the point	1 2 3	I instantly know when the other person has gotten the point
93.	I am unaware of how I am being perceived or reacted to	1 2 3	I am aware of the reactions I am causing in others
94.	I am narrowly focused on what I know	1 2 3	I have a greater sense of life, things, priorities
95.	I react to or am surprised by events and trends, locally and globally	1 2 3	I understand exactly why things are happening as they are

96.	Ignorant, uninformed	1 2 3	Educated and informed; up on current trends and events
97.	Goal-oriented	1 2 3	Vision-oriented
98.	I consume space and energy; I intrude on physical space	1 2 3	I add to the space or energy in a conversation; I am respectful
99.	I am guided by my own thoughts or knowledge	1 2 3	I am guided in what to say by my body, intuition, reactions to the other person
100.	I speak in "I" terms almost exclusively; I experience life from a single, self-oriented vantage point	1 2 3	I speak in "you" terms most of the time; I experience life from multiple vantage points

Section Score _____ **(Maximum 30)**

Grand Total Score _____ **(Maximum 300)**

Divide by 3 to arrive at your percent score

_____ %

SCORING KEY

Here's what your score says about the current status of your communication skills:

Score	Comments
90–100%	You are an extremely good communicator. If you aren't currently working in a field that benefits from your obvious communication talents, switch. Please consider becoming a certified communication coach; you'll have a lot to offer your clients.

Score	Comments
80–89%	You are very close to becoming an extremely good communicator. Within several months, you may well reach 100% on this profile. If this interests you, it will likely be a worthwhile investment, given that very few people score this high.
70–79%	Congratulations. You are a very good communicator, but you probably know this already, based on what others have told you. If you wish to develop and master the communication skills that would result in your scoring 100% on this profile, a coach can probably help you reach that level of expertise within nine months.
50–69%	You are a decent enough communicator. Your score may have been pulled down by low scores in several of the ten categories. Work on those problem areas, and you'll likely see your score increase dramatically.
30–49%	You are an average communicator. Seriously consider focusing on this area of your life for at least a year; you'll find that other, seemingly unrelated areas of your life will also improve. Communication can be the gateway or leverage point for overall quality-of-life improvement.
10–29%	Don't be disheartened. The author of this test scored in this range at an earlier stage of his life, before receiving training and coaching. You really *can* improve, if becoming a good communicator is something that you desire.
0–9%	Career in politics?

MARKET YOUR TALENTS SHAMELESSLY

If You're Embarrassed About What You Do Well, You Won't Be Very Attractive

'Tis God gives skill, but not without men's hands: He could not make Antonio Stradivari's violins without Antonio.

—ANTONIO STRADIVARI

If you put a small value on yourself, rest assured that the world will not raise your price.

—ANONYMOUS

Market shamelessly? How can this be at all related to attraction?

Good question!

Some people naturally assume that attraction is a passive process. It is very much an *active* process—based on planting seeds, adding value, telling (versus selling), responding, and, yes, even marketing. The big difference is, attraction sets up a system that begins drawing people and opportunities to you.

As I've confessed, I'm very intrigued by computers and the online world. Communication takes on a different shape there. People have so much freedom to tune in or out as their impulses dictate. The more our business culture gets Web-savvy, the more opportunities there will be for people who can market themselves successfully. The information itself will always be paramount. But it will become only slightly less important

DISTINCTIONS TO DRAW

MARKET YOUR TALENTS VS. MARKET YOURSELF—It's better to know exactly what parts of you people want to buy, rather than assuming you are the entity they are buying. The buyer's decision won't be personal, so you'll never suffer rejection.

CONFIDENCE VS. ARROGANCE—Confidence is knowing exactly what you do well and don't do well; arrogance is a way to cover up what you don't do well.

INVITE VS. OFFER—When you're offering, you're trying to serve a perceived need; when you invite, you're simply sharing whatever extra value you have to give.

INFORM VS. BOAST—Boasting is trying to make yourself sound special. Informing is educating the other person as to what you can do.

ARTICULATION OF SKILLS AND BENEFITS VS. KNOWING SKILLS AND BENEFITS—When you can articulate well what you do, you'll become even better at it.

MODEL (OF WHAT YOU'RE MARKETING) VS. EXPERT—If you're an expert, you know the subject extremely well. If you're a model, people can learn what you know just by observing your life. You show instead of just tell.

CAPILLARY SYSTEM VS. PROMOTION MACHINE—Promotion pushes business to you; a capillary draws it.

than having the skills to package and present it intriguingly. Success on the Net will come to people who are irresistibly attractive.

In this Top 10 List, you'll learn how to feel incredibly attractive as you market yourself. It's going to make a tremendous difference—selling something you really believe in, without limit.

How to know you're making progress with this principle

- You stop selling yourself, yet people ask to buy.
- You find yourself incredibly curious as to why an ideal buyer says he or she isn't interested. You care more about knowing why than you do about pushing them harder.

- You become fearless. Rejection ceases to feel personal.
- You become someone who's interested in others, instead of someone who is just interesting.
- You learn exactly what it is you offer that matters most.
- You develop confidence in other areas of your life.

TOP 10 WAYS TO MARKET
YOUR TALENTS SHAMELESSLY

1. KNOW EXACTLY WHAT YOU PROVIDE/DELIVER TO OTHERS.

Do you know what you offer to others? If you're a physician, for example, is it relief from suffering? Well-being? Referrals? Diagnostic services? Stern lectures about smoking? Medicines? Preventative care? All of the above, perhaps.

What you need is a way to share with your patients the full scope of what you offer, so that *you* are the doctor who comes to mind at the exact time they start to realize they need something you can provide.

Here's a demanding but very rewarding exercise: Try to express the essence of what you offer in two or three words.

This usually takes some concentration, so think of your first attempt as a lump of carbon and keep compressing it until you create a diamond. Your phrasing should be broad and universal, yet clever enough to stand apart.

Paradoxically, compressing your expression of who you are and what you do is something that will enlarge your thinking—and your market, too.

For example, I've long felt that when local school districts realize they're in the entertainment business, people will learn a whole lot faster. Of course, schools will entertain in ways that also transmit culture and create an appetite for learning skills.

Meanwhile, some entertainers are in the happiness business. Others might be in the thought-stimulating business.

When you perfect the exact description of what you offer, you'll never hesitate to share it with anyone at any time. And you'll smile while you're sharing it, because you believe in it so much. The phrasing makes it even more real for you and the client. What you have to offer becomes a meme.

2. Make it impossible for potential buyers not to buy or leave with something.

What if you decided to provide some service or product to everyone who expresses interest in what you offer? Take CoachV, for example. Some people are ready immediately to plunk down $2,995 for two years of training to be a coach. Others find that commitment too tall. So . . . how about a three-month course on attraction for $295?

Still too much? There's a LaserPhrasing tape set for $59.

Still not ready? No problem! Let's get you signed up for a free teleclass. You can learn the basics of coaching for four weeks at no charge at all.

Too busy, you say? Then, how about a free subscription to the *Daily-Coach*? You'll learn a bit about coaching every day, for as long as you want, at no charge.

I'm sure you see the point. When people are attracted enough to come near you, make sure it's easy for them to say yes to *some*thing you feel good about providing them. They may not buy your premier product or service. That's okay! In many cases, they will upgrade later, when they are ready—with absolutely no effort on your part. We all want the premier-product clients, and lots of them! But if you have something to offer just about everyone who expresses interest, you'll have a more secure base, one that will lift you as it experiences your value and grows to want more of what you offer.

Have something to offer everyone who may come calling on you for help, at various levels of intensity and at several price points, even down to zero. And, of course, add lots of value to all those who buy.

3. Feel incredibly proud of what you do and what you offer.

I used to be a certified financial planner, which was ironic because I really didn't do very well at it financially. Why? The truth was, I didn't believe in what I was doing.

I realized that, no matter what title it went by, I was primarily a product salesman/stockbroker. Nothing is wrong with that, but I wasn't personally excited about it, certainly not proud enough of it to tell the world. I tried to fake the enthusiasm for it and I barely got by. It helped me evolve into coaching, however, which I became *very* proud of.

What was so different with coaching was that I enjoyed doing it and I saw that my clients benefited, measurably and consistently, by my direct efforts—at almost no risk to them.

Coaching was an outgrowth of being a financial planner, yet it created an entirely new realm.

If you don't totally love what you do, are not proud of exactly how you do it, or don't feel good enough to tell the world about it, it's going to be difficult to be very attractive. You may need to change jobs, occupations, or employers. Like me, you'll probably find that your changes will evolve out of what you're doing now, but with a significant "mutation." Or else you'll need to master your craft until you do experience pride, joy, and absolutely no shame about letting everyone know what you're about.

4. BECOME A MODEL OF WHAT YOU'RE SELLING.

Karen Wright is much newer to coaching, but her experiences remind me of my first few years in practice. And they're living proof of this particular point within Step 7.

First, she started weaving into her life some of the principles that felt very relevant to her. "Tolerate Nothing" (Step 15) was especially powerful, as it is for a great many people. As the benefits started showing up in her life, she felt more in the present, more fulfilled. The quality of clients, as well as friends, began to rise. She became engaged to someone she describes as "the man of my dreams." And all the changes must have showed, because gradually she attracted new clients who told her, "I want what you have." Karen recently wrote to me: "At least six clients in the last six months have said they hired me strictly on the basis of being attracted to who I am and what I have in my life."

What if you were a marketing expert but your brochure was a dud? That wouldn't be very attractive. What if you were a coach and your life wasn't up to snuff? Who's going to hire you without a hard sell?

This point is obvious, but it still bears stating: The more you've personally benefited from what it is that you offer to others, the better a "living brochure" you will become! Printing is not required. Be honest, be yourself, but be conscious that prospective customers will want to read the brochure. So . . . how's it looking? Throughout this book you'll be finding methods and suggestions to help you radiate your best qualities.

5. PERFECT OR CUSTOMIZE WHAT YOU'RE SELLING SO THAT IT FITS YOU PERFECTLY.

In number 2 above, I talk about tailoring what you offer so that it can fit more than just a single set of clients. This principle is related but a little bit different.

I'm suggesting here that you perfect or customize what you do so that it's a better, more complete expression of your talents—in other words, a better fit for you.

This is a trend you can see happening a lot in most professions: the physician who learns chiropractic and becomes a much more complete healer; the psychologist who becomes a coach and can better diagnose clients' needs and accelerate clients' progress.

In addition to the synthesis of professions, you can also customize a product or service around a special talent you have. And we all have them. As you proceed through this book, especially the various self-tests, you'll probably emerge with a more complete and exact sense of your own special talents and gifts.

6. KNOW WHAT YOU WANT PEOPLE TO DO, TELL THEM TO DO IT, AND SHOW THEM HOW.

There are so many choices out there, it's overwhelming for most. People need, appreciate, and benefit greatly from direction. And none of us had Goal Selection 101 in high school.(If you did, I want to know about it!)

Whether during the selling process, when using the product, or when experiencing the service, people need direction. Without it, they won't draw the full, intended value, which is a key cause of what's called "buyer's remorse."

Don't be afraid to tell people what to do! It's a huge way to add value. The few who don't want any help will quickly let you know so. If you feel the buyer should buy your product or service, and you feel good about selling it to them, don't take no for an answer. But do show them how to maximize its usefulness and every nuance of its benefits. Chances are that they'll be lastingly grateful.

7. SHOW CUSTOMERS HOW TO SELL FOR YOU.

This builds nicely on Principle 6 above.

I almost never ask my clients or customers to refer their friends or associates to me. But they do. A lot. Why? Because I show them how to sell for me, without being blunt about it. And so can you.

I often tell very quick stories about what some of my clients have gone through and how I advised them. I don't talk about the client, nor do I talk about the client's situation, because that would be against my ethics of confidentiality. Rather, I describe the feelings and spaces my clients had to move through. Remember, facts are important but feelings are even more so.

This kind of storytelling strikes a deep chord with almost any listener, and credibility is established. Plus, the person I'm sharing this with (usually a client) now knows who else they can refer to me!

Ethics are key. You don't share stories to be devious or seductive; you share them as a way to educate a client about themselves, their needs, and the fact that others have evolved through similar situations and gotten to a better place. But the sharing does have a nice bonus!

By the way: As you warm up to marketing yourself shamelessly, you'll understand that the selling process is part of everything you do. You don't have to set aside a special segment of the day. It's built in, which makes your marketing much easier.

8. MAKE CERTAIN THE CLIENT KNOWS ALL OF THE VALUE THEY ARE RECEIVING.

My clients, as well informed as they are about what we're doing together and the value they are receiving, still probably understand only about 30 percent of the value that they are getting. (But, hey, I'm working on it!)

I want clients to really feel, see, and understand the complete 100 percent of how what we're doing together is benefiting them today, next month, next year, and next lifetime. Not because I need the kudos, but because they will then take our work much more seriously.

One of the ways to lock in the value is to say something like, "The reason X is so important right now, John, is that . . ." Or, "What you did right here, Jane, was called a . . ."

See how this works? It not only builds appreciation, it also invites people into fuller participation in the satisfaction of their own needs. It's telling, not selling, and it naturally creates more sales and referrals.

9. ALWAYS HAVE A COMEBACK FOR THOSE WHO DOUBT OR CRITICIZE YOU.

You may not need to have a collection of comebacks, but I do. They are like arrows in my quiver, giving me the extra confidence to market shamelessly. If someone thinks that coaching is a sham, I say, "Hmmm, why do you think, then, that all those Olympic gold medalists credit their coaches for their wins?" Or, "Why do you think top-echelon coaches in professional sports now make almost as much money as the athletes?"

When confronted with the opinion that coaching is a luxury, suited only for trend-crazed Californians (or their Manhattan counterparts), I say, "Yes, coaching is worthless for those who don't want much out of life."

If someone complains that my fees are too high, I say, respectfully, with an innocent and inquisitive look, "Don't you have any goal worth that much?"

I almost never have to actually use these. But they are available, and they have been helpful once or twice.

No matter what you're marketing, there will be times when you have to deal with doubters. Some of them may be nastily sarcastic and cynical. That's their right. Don't be defensive, but have some countering words within reach.

By the way, some people have a hard time with trust. Sarcasm and cynicism are a sign that they don't trust even their own judgment. That's probably because they've made colossal mistakes in the past. And are likely to do so again. So they have to equip their opinions with barbs.

That's why you never force-market what you have to offer. Stay away from the hard sell. Not only is it very unattractive, with a lousy ratio of efforts to results, it will often blow up in your face. Much better to deal with attraction and the more even-tempered, open-minded people it brings to you.

10. DEVELOP A CAPILLARY SYSTEM TO SELL, SCREEN, AND FILTER FOR YOU.

I think if I had my way, my Capillary System would handle every part of the sales/buying process so all I would have to do is my coaching, at $400 an hour.

My Capillary System is composed of the various things I've put in place to help people learn about me, what I offer, and the benefits they will receive. The idea is that new clients can "work" their way to me the way fluids are drawn up a tube. They have some curiosity. They have easy access to information. They decide whether to learn more, to sign up, or to find what they want without involving me.

Thanks to my Capillary System, I spend zero time selling my services. But I do spend the equivalent of 10 percent of my billable time feeding my pipeline: I have about 25,000 daily subscribers to various newsletters; I teach several free teleclasses each month on subjects I find interesting or wish to develop further (so it's really research and development time, not selling); and I regularly add information to several dozen Web sites.

The point is, I refuse to sell. Not interested. But I am interested in providing value for all who want it. So the Capillary System gives me a way to nourish and attract others. By the time they reach me by E-mail or by calling me, they're ready to hire me or to buy something.

This may sound cold to someone who hasn't gotten acquainted with the power and potential of the online world. But it's just a system of dispersing information. People receive it at their own convenience. They're free to decide whether they're attracted or not.

Isn't this a better way to build a business than becoming an expert at cold calls or networking?

One of the great benefits of having a strong Capillary System is that I add so much value to so many people that I don't feel at all hesitant about charging what I think it's worth. I know from experience that the client will ultimately get at least ten times the financial value from our time together. Because by the time they've come through the Capillary System, they've identified and built their own readiness. They are primed to make huge strides.

My 10 percent investment in a Capillary System not only brings me lots of clients, it saves me from having to take them through "baby steps." I can usually get straight to what I do best, and that makes me more attractive to myself.

BECOME IRRESISTIBLY ATTRACTIVE TO YOURSELF

How Can You Attract Others If You Don't Feel Irresistibly Attracted to Yourself?

YES! WE'RE OPEN!
For what it's worth.
(sign in the window of The Low Self-Esteem Cafe)
—from a cartoon by JOHN CALLAHAN

True happiness is of a retired nature, and an enemy to pomp and noise; it arises, in the first place, from the enjoyment of one's self.
—JOSEPH ADDISON

Get rid of what makes you most unattractive to yourself.

Superconductivity is an exciting corner of science that many researchers are now eagerly working on. When they've solved its riddles, superconductivity will allow electrical current to travel—even at great distances—with just a very tiny amount of its power lost to energy-robbing resistance. The result will be huge savings for everyone who uses electricity.

Superconductivity makes a great metaphor. Less resistance equals greater efficiency, a more direct relationship between the amount of energy applied and the magnitude of the results.

A kind of personal superconductivity will happen in your life as you get rid of any patterns or habits that keep you from feeling totally attractive to yourself.

DISTINCTIONS TO DRAW

ATTRACTIVE VS. ENAMORED—Feeling attractive to yourself is a healthy, self-affirming feeling. Being enamored is a step toward being narcissistic, which is very unhealthy and self-defeating.

PROUD VS. PRIDE—Being proud of yourself (as a parent feels about a child) is empowering. Having pride means you're so convinced of being right that you can't learn from others, which is power-depleting.

ATTRACTION VS. GRATIFICATION—Loving who you are should be enough. Needing to give yourself "rewards" is something very different from finding yourself attractive.

ATTRACTION VS. NARCISSISM—Attraction is what happens when you naturally feel great about yourself; narcissism is what results when you *have* to feel great about yourself, and seek external validation.

Obviously, the owner of the imaginary Low Self-Esteem Cafe has a few items getting in the way of being attractive to him- or herself. But we all do (until this particular step is completed).

It can be troubling to look at those items, mostly because they seem to have a lot of power over us. Yet they may not be as almighty as they seem, and eliminating them is a vital step in creating the life you want. Unattractive elements, from whatever source, need to be edited out.

We just need to realize that these things are only items on a list. Courage is required to face them. Some will yield more easily than others. But at every step you will experience payoffs, which will accumulate faster and faster, giving you power to eliminate even more items.

As you subtract them, you will also eliminate the possibility of self-sabotage. You will spend less and less effort while attaining more and more rewards. And that will present you with a pleasant choice: either attaining even more or relaxing more.

Either way, you win freedom!

With today's focus, you're on your way to becoming superconductive. Following is a Top 10 List to help you. Please read it carefully and ask yourself some tough questions, knowing that doing so will surely make your life easier and more attractive.

First, ask yourself, "What am I doing in my life that's unattractive to ME?" You may want to write out a list. Do it fearlessly. Pin the bugaboos down on a page. Exposing them to daylight is like pouring disinfectant on bacteria.

Second, think for a while about this: What might you be doing in life to compensate for doing those things you find unattractive? Many people recognize, while pondering this point, that they've been sort of unconsciously supporting some significant energy-robbing and money-draining activities—which they could get rid of, at great savings.

Third, ask yourself what you're doing—or what changes you're making—that may look unattractive to others but that are *very* special or attractive to you. After all, you're now in a process that involves breaking out of old boxes, loosening former restrictions, creating room to grow. You have a right to design your own standards.

Fourth, ponder a few moments: Are there things that you find unattractive yet you don't think you'll ever be able to change?

How to know you're making progress with this principle

- You start doing things that make no sense but give you a sense of joy or pride.
- You feel more deeply about yourself and others. You experience others more than you have before.
- You do not have to motivate or pep-talk yourself.
- You make decisions faster because you know what does—and doesn't—make you attractive to yourself.

TOP 10 WAYS TO STOP BEING UNATTRACTIVE TO YOURSELF

More questions: Would you spend money on a paint job for a dented-up car? Would you spread a fresh coat of paint on a house with split, wood-rot-infested siding?

Not likely. It wouldn't make sense.

It's always good to undertake improvements. But they have lasting value only when you've dealt with what's underneath the surface.

So . . .

1. Stop doing what you know is bad for you and start nourishing yourself.

There are two important points here.

First, and most obvious, is that extreme self-care will help you be attractive—both to yourself and everyone you meet. It's nothing more than acknowledging yourself as valuable and then following through with the self-care that someone valuable deserves. Other people will notice and, consciously or unconsciously, they'll honor you for it.

Second, and more subtle, is that *bad* is both a relative concept and an evolving one. There are probably things you once did, and were okay about, that have since become bad for you.

As you progress on the upward pathway you've begun, your mind and your body are going to become more sensitized. Think of a pond. After a sudden downpour, the water will be a bit muddy. Then it will settle out and once again you'll be able to look through from the surface to the bottom.

In just the same way, your personal perceptions are going to gradually become less muddied, more clear. You'll naturally notice a stronger wish, and a greater willingness, to let go of unappetizing foods, unhealthy substances, destructive or even just growth-inhibiting relationships of all kinds. And so you'll be less willing to put up with any nonnourishing things, including personal habits, that were part of your routine before.

Some people appear to be "getting away" with wrong actions or bad habits. That's an illusion. Sometimes it might take a long while before the damage shows. But when it does, it's significant damage. And the remainder of a lifetime may not be enough to deal with the ill effects. Lung cancer from smoking is only one example.

On the other hand, even if you can't see immediate results from clear-headed actions and good habits, the truth is that they're accruing like money in the bank.

As you absorb these principles, your integrity will become stronger. For you, the rules will be different. This illusion of "getting away" with things will become more obviously foolish and self-defeating.

Learn that, and make the necessary behavioral changes. The tip is to upgrade your self-care to reflect where you are NOW.

2. STOP TRYING TO MEET ANYONE ELSE'S EXPECTATIONS AND START MEETING YOUR OWN.

Unhooking from others' needs or expectations is an essential part of your growth process. It's a good thing to be responsive to other people, even to be highly responsive. But the fun stops when you cross the line and begin responding to *their* expectations of you. There's a big, big difference. For many people, this is an aspect of personality that's hard to see because it's gotten tied up, inappropriately, with survival needs. So be patient with yourself.

And, while you're at it, start unhooking other people from *your* expectations of them. After all, it's a two-way street. If you want to grow, you must also let others grow.

Believe me, the more evolved you become, the more good you and other people can do for each other—without suffocating each other's creativity through role expectations.

3. STOP BEING GOOD AND START BEING RADICAL.

Maybe what I really mean is "start being bad," instead of just "start being radical." Growth involves breaking chains—of history, of proper roles, of acceptable behaviors, even of cultural norms. And you may have to be experimental at first. You may have to swing the old pendulum *way* over, just to break the "good guy/good girl" grip that most of us have held so tightly. *Nice,* after all, rhymes with *mice.*

I recently saw a sign on the picture window of a car dealership. It said "Home of the nice guys." I'm sure they meant "C'mon in, we're *so* easy to deal with." But it made me think for a minute—being a "nice guy" or a "nice gal" all the time, that's a lot of pressure. That's a lot of stunted growth. And just maybe a lot of passive manipulation on the part of the person being "nice." What's so wonderful about being a "good guy"? Is it your true nature, or your hiding place? What good is being nice doing you? Isn't there a better way?

Worrying too much about being "good" is a vestige of those days when one misstep in life could ruin your status in the pack, possibly ruin your future, or even threaten your very survival. Women in particular get lots of socialization designed to ensure that they'll forever after be "nice," meaning compliant. But things have changed. Today, "doing the right thing" may very well be the wrong thing for you.

I'm not suggesting that you be irresponsible or do anything illegal. But do lighten up. Take a week off. Eat a pizza tonight if you want one, regardless of what you're trying to do with your diet. Let go of doing something that you're being pressured to do.

Be *bad,* if it feels good, and open a pathway to a new way of seeing yourself. Valuable, but lighthearted, and able to courageously follow personal instincts. In short, show everyone—yourself included—that you don't want to live inside a box.

4. STOP COMPARING YOURSELF TO OTHERS
AND START IDENTIFYING YOUR OWN MEASURES.

It's normal and even healthy to compare who you are and how you're doing against how others are doing. Reference points are fine. But using these reference points as a way to build self-esteem is not smart. Why? Because it makes you dependent. Also, it's human nature to compare yourself one day to people whom you feel are steps above you, and on another day to people who you feel are steps below you, depending on your ego needs of the moment. And that's a pointless exercise.

Far better, spend some time and some thought on coming up with your own measures of who you are and how you're doing. Those are the only measuring sticks of lasting importance in your life.

5. STOP SETTING YOURSELF UP
AND START MAKING LIFE EASY ON YOU.

Do you ever set yourself up for stress or failure? Many people do. Maybe they think that they need the stress in order to create adrenaline, so it can carry them to greater accomplishments. Or maybe they think that peace is just the first stage of terminal boredom. Actually, peace can be the first stage of getting out of a rut, as the following story will show.

George came to his coach as an entrepreneur in his late forties who'd been through many different business efforts—primarily with start-ups that were oriented toward sales. None of them seemed to be working very well. A lot of anger was apparent. He was flippant about himself and his feelings, but he obviously wasn't comfortable in his own skin. He asked for help in staying focused and in deciding what he should do "when I grow up."

Even while jumping from one project to another, George was managing to support a family, though always by the skin of his teeth. But he was looking at his life and thinking, "I can't do this for the rest of my life. I need to make some profound changes."

This quandary is very common for entrepreneurial people.

George's coach focused him on narrowing down the number of his projects. At the same time, she let him know he was okay just as he was. He really only needed to change tactics. He initially resisted the message: Like many entrepreneurs, George had always felt like an outsider. "Maybe I just need to get a regular job," he suggested.

"But you won't be happy doing that," his coach countered. "You'll stay a few months, it will get on your nerves, you'll move on." When he felt the truth of that in his gut, he also started to feel the truth of what she was saying about him as a person, too.

George agreed to work on only three things at one time. Within four months that had opened up his schedule enough so that he could consider dealing with his internal workings, begin to recognize who he was, and start taking care of himself. And he saw that not only had he been harsh with himself in the past, but he'd been strong-arming potential clients as well. Now he can laugh at himself, accept his tendencies, and still be okay. And that allows him to lighten up on himself and on other people so that all of his interactions go better.

Changing a stress-producing business tactic opened the way for personal evolution and got George out of the Angry Guy Club.

My coaching tip is this: Look at your current life and ask yourself, "Where can I see that I've set myself up for stress or failure?"

There are probably a couple of people in your life, or projects, activities, goals, or "shoulds" that come to mind as you ponder this question. All right. Pick one of these and look very closely. Take it down several more levels until you're looking at the reason that motivated you in the first place to set yourself up.

Now, get to know that part of yourself really well. Because to become really attractive, you'll need to make peace with it and come to respect it as a very powerful force in your life. Don't wrestle with it. Don't begin attacking the problems that it causes. Simply respect its power. Acknowledge it. Own your awareness. That's a very powerful step on your part; it's going to pay dividends.

6. STOP SETTING OTHER PEOPLE UP
AND START UNDERPROMISING.

If you are someone who overpromises, don't just underpromise. Stop promising anything at all! You need to break this cycle. If you're someone who seduces people, recognize it. If you're someone who makes people dependent on you, fix that.

Michele Lisenbury handles a huge array of responsibilities for a multimillion-dollar trucking firm in the Pacific Northwest. At weekly organizational meetings, whenever someone needed any kind of help she found herself saying, "I'll take care of it!" That felt powerful. It positioned Michele as a can-do individual, which she definitely is. But with all the deadlines and conflicting demands from different people and departments, she also was perpetually stressed out.

After studying attraction, Michele took a different approach. She started saying no whenever she could. When people asked her how long something would take, she'd silently make an estimate and then double it. Pretty soon she found herself being twice as creative—picking the times when she was most inspired, jumping from project to project as it fit her mood, and doing things far better than ever before. Faster, too. Because she no longer overpromises, people now take the time to outline their needs really, really carefully. And because she no longer builds up their expectations, they're thrilled with the value and quality she delivers. Michele learned something big: It's much easier and more fulfilling to deliver something you've never promised.

As a footnote, her work-related tensions diminished so much she had energy left over to open up a sideline business: coaching. And she's doing great!

When you release yourself from the pattern of overpromising, you gain more freedom and create a huge reserve of unburdened time. That's a promise. Not an overpromise.

7. STOP WAITING AND START TRUSTING YOUR INKLINGS.

If you blindly followed your intuitions and inklings, would your life be a lot better than it is today? Even with all the mistakes you would have made because you misread a feeling or intuitive thought?

I think that for most people the answer is yes. Because no matter how rational or dispassionate you may strive to be, you can never be 100 percent accurate anyway. And even if you could, your life would become stale, boring, and unfulfilled.

It's better to become more attuned to feelings, intuitions, and inklings. And here's another reason to build superreserves: You can afford the consequences of whatever rookie mistakes you may make in the process of learning to trust and honor your inner voice.

Here's a nice example. After a long hiatus spent vacationing and playing with sideline projects, Joan wanted to get very active again in her seminar business. But a lot of momentum had been sacrificed to her time off. So, against the conventional advice many associates offered, she decided she would book a hall, run advertisements, and invite anyone who was interested to attend a free seminar.

"I'm the one who gets to decide," she told me. "I'm going to give away something I normally charge a lot for and keep on doing it as many times as I want to." And with a glinting smile she added, "It's going to feel great, walking into that room and having everybody owe me."

Sometimes you make yourself feel great, really attractive to yourself, by doing something everyone else thinks is crazy. So what? How you feel about yourself is the fundamental issue here.

In Joan's case, her tactics, and the good feelings they amplified, catalyzed so much response that her seminar business began netting her a quarter million per year.

I hope you've begun to see that there's a wonderful interlocking value to the Principles of Attraction. For example, learning to trust and respond to your intuitions will make you a much faster learner. In a Top 10 List coming up very soon, you'll focus on how much smoother, more efficient, and opportunity-maximizing your life becomes when you can respond immediately to things.

The pathway is to act on your inklings. Live THERE instead of just in "reality." Because by the time the present has become provably real, it's already the past. And the present moment is always the best possible place for you.

8. STOP CHASING AND START APPRECIATING.

Probably the most common unattractive and self-defeating thing that I see people do is chasing after dreams, hopes, goals, "coulds," people, love, feelings, fantasies, opportunities, etc.

It can be fun, but it's generally fruitless.

I'm certainly not saying, "Don't dream." I'm not saying you shouldn't ever chase your dreams. But please let up on the chase for a moment. Take a new look at any dreams (goals, people, etc.) you're currently chasing.

How would you benefit if you let them go? What else might that energy and dedication bring you? It's often very smart to follow the path of least resistance. Remember superconductivity? Well, you can increase energy flow in two basic ways—reduce your own internal resistance, or reduce the resistance level of what you seek.

It's better to spend your energies attaining all of a nearby goal than absolutely none of a distant goal, right? Because you'll be building strength instead of exhausting it. At the same time, you just might be bringing that distant goal nearer to you.

9. STOP TRYING TO BECOME SOMEBODY AND JUST BE YOURSELF.

You've probably recognized a recurrent theme by now, the notion that striving is fairly unattractive. One of the ways we strive is trying to project ourselves as somebody more than, or other than, we really are. Aspirations are healthy; striving can get ugly.

You can be yourself and still wish to develop yourself. That's fine. In fact, it's terrific!

But don't try to become somebody else. That's a hookup with the past—somebody else's past, as a matter of fact. That's why it lacks freshness.

Give up trying to become somebody else. And you'll truly begin growing up. You will begin to discover more fully just who you are. It's a sure bet that you're going to end up delighted and positively amazed.

10. STOP HAVING PROBLEMS AND START SOLVING THEM.

You can become either an expert problem solver or a problem-free zone. The latter is less "rewarding" and dramatic, but it is far more attractive and extremely energy-efficient. Overrespond to a problem instead of just fixing it.

One of my earliest clients was a magazine editor. Stewart shared a large office with a chronically quarrelsome editor-in-chief. Just about everyone in the organization had experienced her unwarranted blowups, Stewart included, though he seemed to have a knack for defusing her volatility.

Privately, he often wondered why she didn't get fired. One day, after another unpleasant incident, the truth dawned on him: He was letting himself be the organization's "shock absorber." Because he so often corralled and/or deflected her moods, management didn't have to deal with the problem.

Stewart decided that shock absorber wasn't the highest and best use of his talents. In fact, for management to use him in that way subtracted from his pride. So he moved into a smaller office across the hall from the editor-in-chief, kept up his work, maintained cordiality, but completely stopped "fixing" problems.

Within four months, management stopped living in denial. She was gone, he was promoted. The first issue he created won an industry award.

It's terrific to fix a problem. But if you're a problem-fixing "specialist," a long line of them will show up at your door. And your creativity will be stifled. Value yourself for the skills you most want to employ, and the path of least resistance will lead you forward.

GET A FULFILLING LIFE, NOT JUST AN IMPRESSIVE LIFESTYLE

A Great Life Is Attractive; a Lifestyle Is Usually Seductive

Attachment is the great fabricator of illusions; reality can be attained only by someone who is detached.

—SIMONE WEIL

All you have is your soul.

—TRACY CHAPMAN

Let's make a distinction: attraction versus seduction. At any given moment when you are faced with a choice, which one are you experiencing? The difference is crucial.

Attraction ultimately leads you to feeling bigger, more complete, more integrated and connected. Seduction ultimately makes you regretful, poorer, made up of conflicting pieces. One is about substance, the other is about surface. One is joy and elation, followed by fulfillment; the other is rush and thrill, followed by emptiness. Pick up on what your body says. It will tell you straight out.

As the subtitle for this step says: A great life is attractive; a lifestyle is usually seductive. Do you buy a ranch set among rolling hills because you're tired of cities, love horses, and stepping onto your porch at night to see infinite numbers of stars does your soul an infinite amount of good? Or do you buy it because you wish you had more of an identity and one fateful,

---

DISTINCTIONS TO DRAW

LIFE VS. LIFESTYLE—A life is based on YOU. A lifestyle is based on externals.

FULFILLMENT VS. GRATIFICATION—To be fulfilled is to radiate your positive feeling consistently. To be gratified is to consume experiences, resources, or people.

NATURAL VS. NORMAL—Natural is what's best for YOU. Normal is what's average for others.

EMOTIONAL COST VS. FINANCIAL COST—Most costs are measured in terms of money or time, but emotional costs are much higher. If you're working long hours to keep up with your lifestyle, you are losing a part of yourself along the way.

SUSTAINABLE VS. MANAGEABLE—A fulfilling life sustains YOU; you don't have to manage IT.

---

impressionable day you looked into a catalog advertising fringed Beverly Hills Buckaroo–style jackets? Scenario one might yield several years of contented living. Scenario two offers no real chance of it. Did you pay $10,000 over list price to buy a Porsche Boxster because you've been a sports car enthusiast since forever and this one looks to you like a modern-day classic, or because you can't remember the last time you turned the head of a good-looking stranger? Is it because of a wonderful, self-sustaining feeling that you choose a certain vacation spot, neighborhood, spouse, or restaurant? Or are you guided in such choices by what you think others will think someone like you ought to choose?

Seduction by lifestyle is huge right now, across the whole social spectrum. It's the old confusion between consumption and fulfillment. The following Top 10 List will guide you toward consistently attractive choices.

How to know you're making progress with this principle

- You start to enjoy your "trappings" for the real qualities they have and how they feel rather than for what they tell others about you.
- You simplify aspects of your life because they no longer are that appealing to you, not because you feel an overt need to simplify.

- You find yourself watching and learning about people with simpler lives to see how they live. You'll be curious.
- You find yourself less willing to pay the emotional costs often associated with traditional success. Your body just won't let you pay that price any longer.
- You start saving a lot of money!
- The people who come into your life are there to know you, not your lifestyle.
- You feel proud of you, not just of what you have.

TOP 10 WAYS TO GET A LIFE, NOT JUST A LIFESTYLE

1. UNDERSTAND THE DIFFERENCE BETWEEN LIVING A LIFE AND HAVING A LIFESTYLE.

An ad for a financial services firm says: "Are you working for a living or are you working for a life?"

I'll change it a bit: "Are you working for a lifestyle or are you *living* your life?"

In a sense, life and lifestyle are synonymous. As in: You choose how you want to live. That becomes your lifestyle. It makes you happy. And you can afford it.

At the same time, the two can be mutually exclusive. As in: You choose how you want to be seen—whether by yourself or by others. You make expensive decisions based on whether or not you're achieving the desired effect. You aren't necessarily happy, given that it's a strain to support the expenses. But maybe the happiness will accrue later on.

Life and lifestyle are like love and lust. Ideally, they can go perfectly hand in hand—to your great delight. But if you aren't clear about which one is which, it's easy to get confused. Lust can be a great servant of love or a thief, depending on your instinctual judgment. The same is true of lifestyle and life.

The key question to ask yourself is, "How much of my *life* is being consumed by my *lifestyle*?" In other words, there's absolutely nothing wrong with having a lifestyle. But please make sure that you have it, and it doesn't have you!

There are vast numbers of people, of every possible economic condition, paying way too much for what they get out of life, chasing a lifestyle when they could be living a life. This has applied to quite a few people I've coached. Maybe it applies to you, and maybe not. Everybody is different.

One thing is for sure—it's hard for most people to admit to themselves that they've been seduced.

If you can't decide, discuss it with a coach. Once the complications are pared away, it's a simple equation: Less lifestyle (trappings/geegaws/merry-go-round pursuits) results in more life (freedom/space/self-satisfaction). And it *really* becomes simple when you orient yourself around your values (Step 23) and get your personal needs met, once and for all (Step 13).

2. START LEARNING ABOUT DIFFERENT WAYS OF LIVING.

Sometimes I'm shocked by how few options people feel that they have, or how rarely they'll consider that they might live differently. Look around and notice who has a life (or even a lifestyle!) you find intriguing. Have lunch with those people. Ask them lots of questions about how they live, what's important to them, how they have changed their life or lifestyle significantly, and what other changes they may still want to make.

Sometimes, making a change in life or lifestyle might make you feel as though you are being disloyal to your peer group. It may seem you are negating what's highly important to them, whether it's regularly having drinks to unwind, shopping at certain stores, sticking with just one kind of music, loving miniature golf—whatever.

Real friends grant you plenty of license to experiment, discover, and even renew yourself. Those who become jealous are energy-drainers anyway. So grant yourself room to flex. Explore. Report your findings back to yourself.

Just learning new things is liberating. New choices are always optional.

3. IDENTIFY WHAT ABOUT YOUR LIFE ISN'T REALLY YOU AT ALL.

We're all products of our culture and our environment; of peer pressure and group norms; of advertising and the desire to get ahead; and so forth. That's why so few of us really examine who we are. It can feel easier to live a prescribed role or drive the right car.

It's safe to say that most people haven't really chosen their lives; they've only chosen their lifestyles. Or perhaps a lifestyle has chosen them.

Break the cycle by working with a coach who can help you identify what about yourself and about life is most fundamentally important to you. Some of the checklists coming up in this book will help you confront these personal choices. Then you can drop the parts that are just excess baggage.

Think of the relief you feel in your shoulders after you put down heavy bags you've carried out of an airport. Now, think of feeling that kind of relief on a cosmic level.

4. Identify what is natural for you, even if it's not normal for others.

Of all the countries in our world, Americans are thought to have the most individualistic culture. We tend to do what we want and to heck with what others think.

The trend of "doing your own thing" continues, and it's accelerating. In the sixties, doing your own thing was in its pioneering phases. Sometimes it meant doing the opposite of convention, sometimes it meant doing something of your own design. With practice, we've gotten better and better at this skill-set. The rebirth of entrepreneurialism in America is one piece of evidence. Today, we have wonderful new tools and technology to support the trend. And the very abundance of new tools and technology compels us, as a society, to value those who discover the best ways to use them.

Creativity and freedom are held in high regard; normalcy is often scoffed at. You now do have the societal and cultural freedom (even more than you may realize) to discover and orient yourself around what is natural for you, because normal isn't natural for many.

Now, just give yourself that freedom.

5. Lifestyles are expensive to support and they prevent you from evolving.

In that great old thriller *Key Largo,* Johnny Rocco, the murderous gangster played by Edward G. Robinson, was asked what he hoped to get out of his bullying, criminal activities. His answer? "MORE!"

Constant advertising, along with whatever trace of Johnny Rocco we all embody, seduces us into wanting more. And that isn't so wrong, actually. But choosing lifestyle over life is about *having* more instead of *becoming* more—and being glorified for the role you're playing, not for who you are.

A few years ago I worked with a client who had plenty of MORE: a new Lexus, an eye-popping house (with mortgage to match), beautiful children. He was a lawyer and had a strong personality but not a strong underlying sense of himself. He and his wife were busy acquiring tons of the best of everything. They thought that was building a reserve. Reserve is an emotional space, though, not just a financial space. He wasn't really getting fulfillment out of his lifestyle. But by spending money, he covered up things he didn't want to face, and he was too busy to make any fundamental changes anyway.

And then changes demanded to be made. "I need to raise my income by fifty percent," he said in our first conference. "I'm getting a divorce, and I've got kids, and I'm cash-flow poor."

"Well, you can do that. But you can also simplify your lifestyle."

"No. I really can't do that," he said. And he reeled off numerous reasons, such as keeping the kids in a private school and other nonnegotiable "must-haves."

In a few months, we got his income to double and then triple its former level. But, guess what? That just made the problem worse. As he worked harder, he also figured he deserved more. Including a girlfriend who was very expensive.

Propensity to spend is the term used by financial planners. No matter how much you make, you will spend that and just a little bit more. People like this are going to be magnets for more problems if they don't solve the source of the lifestyle problem first.

To get a life means there is room to enjoy. You can have a really big life and a big lifestyle, but only if the lifestyle isn't costing you excessively in time, emotion, space, risk, pressure, adrenaline. Most people don't have enough of a life to enjoy their lifestyle. And that's how MORE becomes less.

If you're living paycheck to paycheck, supporting a lifestyle rather than saving money, your lifestyle is too expensive. You're trapped in it. You must keep working in the job you already have instead of initiating something you'll like better.

I'm not knocking lifestyle. I'm just pointing out something that's true: As long as you feel the pull to fund a lifestyle, and you can't afford to stop working, your rate of development and evolution will be much slower than it could be.

Rapid personal development occurs when you have the time, space, and reserves to afford to experiment with new ways of thinking, working, and living. If you're living wonderfully yet close to the edge, you can't really afford to progress in some very important ways. And you probably won't be attractive. A lifestyle is generally seductive; a person is attractive. Do you want to be seen as a person or as someone who represents a lifestyle? Take your pick.

Note: If you have a reserve, enjoy your lifestyle completely! If not, it's time to simplify.

6. IDENTIFY WHO GIVES YOU LIFE AND WHO ARE MERELY PLAYERS IN YOUR LIFESTYLE.

One's lifestyle has a theatrical element to it—people are constantly entering and exiting, like actors in a film. Everyone from valet parkers to tailors. Housekeepers to architects. And scenes shift, too: Starbucks to Lutèce, hotel to home. In and out of your life, just long enough to advance the plot.

For those who are too caught up in their lifestyles, other people take on the quality of being extras, bit players in the movie that is their life. It's important to make a distinction—who is an asset and who is just an adjunct—because shallow relationships tend to be high maintenance, either in money, time, or both.

Again, I'm not knocking wonderfully rich lifestyles at all! I'm just suggesting that you identify who in your life adds joy and energy versus who merely supports, entertains, or assists you.

7. DOWNSIZE, RIGHTSIZE, OR EVEN TOSS OUT YOUR CURRENT LIFESTYLE, JUST FOR THE SHOCK OF IT.

Most of my clients refuse to downsize their lifestyles until they experience a crisis—usually involving money, a divorce, or health problems.

I've given up pestering them. But I am also not surprised when I see them struggling to become more attractive. They can't figure out why it's not working as easily as advertised.

The primary reason? They are unwilling to give up some of the trappings they have. And yet, to many of them, "downsizing their lifestyles" means a vacation in the Caribbean instead of Australia. Business class instead of first class. An Infiniti instead of a Lexus.

Again, I'm not knocking luxury. In fact, I live luxuriously. But my lifestyle is optional. It's a source of fun, not my identity. I'd immediately downscale it at any sign of financial concern.

I don't suggest you renounce all material pleasures, shave your head, and take up a begging bowl. It isn't necessary to become an ascetic. But what if your lifestyle chokes away your ability to be yourself?

Lifestyle should support life, never the other way around.

8. SPEND AN HOUR AND WRITE DOWN WHAT AN IDEAL LIFE FOR YOU WOULD LOOK LIKE.

Have you ever done that before? Write down the people, objects, work, feelings, and home that would make up your ideal life? Why not put on some tea or coffee right now, sit in a comfy place, and start writing it out? Not for the sake of living in the future but to try a possible future on for size.

You can use the online system if you'd like help getting started. It's available at *http://www.thomasleonard.com/ideal/default.html.* It's nothing fancy, just something that presents you with good questions and choices!

9. GET TO KNOW WHAT YOUR VALUES ARE.

Let's define your values as those things in life you find yourself naturally drawn to—so much so that you have a desire to express them. In this sense, beauty, peace, creativity, discovery, and harmony are examples of values.

To live your life in tune with your values brings more real fulfillment than any lifestyle possible.

But don't get this notion of being in tune with your values mixed up with being holier-than-thou. That's one of the most intensely *un*attractive attitudes going. Don't make a big deal about proclaiming your values— just make a solid commitment to expressing them as much as possible in what you do and how you live. That is *extraordinarily* attractive.

Most people long for it but don't trust that they can find the way. At least, not without giving up too much of their lifestyles.

In Step 23 you'll be coached in how to precisely identify the values that have the most power in your heart.

10. STOP STRIVING, ACQUIRING, PUSHING YOURSELF.

What if you "gave up" right now—checked right out of the rat race? How would your life be better? How would it be different? What's the worst thing that could happen? What would you lose that's not replaceable? How would you change as a person? How would you spend your time? Is there a path you might start down, very different from the one you're on now? What goals would you let go? How would you motivate yourself? Would you even need to?

These are questions worth asking. The answers are different for everyone, of course. I'm not saying to cut all your moorings loose. I'm suggesting that if you invest some time playing with the above questions, you'll envision things you've probably never thought of before. Fears may arise but so will wonderful possibilities. Your sense of possibility is a muscle that thrives on exercise. The bigger it gets, the more present-moment opportunities you'll be able to see.

PROMISE LITTLE, DELIVER EVERYTHING

When You Consistently Deliver More Than Was Expected, New Customers Are Drawn to You

"Do-so" is more important than "say-so."
—PETE SEEGER

You can't build a reputation on what you're GOING to do.
—HENRY FORD

"Deliver *more* than was expected? But I'm already stressed out!"

Why do we promise so much? Is it because we want to be valued?

Here's an irony: When you master the practice of promising less (yet delivering more), you'll fulfill much more of your own potential and greatly increase how people value you.

How can this be? Well, if you don't crowd yourself with promises, you're free to reach a lot deeper into your resources for performance.

This principle may not *sound* practical, but it really is. Especially because of the transformations in our economy, driven by downsizing on the one hand and the possibilities of the Internet on the other. More and more people are now transforming themselves into freelancers and entrepreneurs. So it's more important than ever to build and maintain a great reputation. Information gets around fast these days; to be known as exceptional can really light a rocket under your career.

The idea is to build a reserve of expectation between what you *promise*

DISTINCTIONS TO DRAW

UNDERPROMISE VS. OVERPROMISE—Overpromising is seduction; it makes you become either a workaholic or a liar. Underpromising (and overdelivering) is extremely attractive because you *keep* impressing the client.

EXCEED EXPECTATIONS VS. SATISFY—Being satisfied has become the norm. The next level, which is now required if you want to be attractive, is to exceed expectations.

DELIVER VS. OFFER—When you deliver something to a potential or current customer without first offering it, they will be stunned—and very attracted!

---

and what you ultimately *deliver.* The wider the gap, the more "vacuum" you'll create, and therefore the more you'll surprise and profoundly affect folks when they take delivery.

The more pleasantly surprised people are, the more excitedly they will sing your praises.

Note: I'll be using the words *client* and *customer,* but this list truly applies to all your relationships, whether they're based on money, love, or any other affinity.

How to know you're making progress with this principle

- You discover there are ways to deliver twice what you promised without having to spend twice the time. You innovate!
- You start to seek out vendors and providers who think as you do. Their level of service makes overdelivering even easier for you.
- Several clients and/or customers are impressed and tell you so. Because it's fun to share this kind of good news—and it makes one feel quite savvy—they also tell potential clients/customers. Your reputation soars, and your business grows.
- You place a lot less pressure on yourself to perform.
- You have a lot more time and space to customize and perfect what you're delivering.

TOP 10 WAYS TO DELIVER
MORE THAN YOU PROMISE

1. UNDERPROMISE AND OVERDELIVER.

The key here is to promise far less than you know you can deliver. Promise even less than the client or recipient is asking you to. Reduce their expectations whenever possible—you will gain a lot more maneuvering room.

If you recall Michele, the woman who worked with a multimillion-dollar trucking firm, overpromising created a lot of stress in her work life. Underpromising took it out and at the same time helped her produce better (and more gratefully acknowledged) results.

Another reason to underpromise: It gives you the freedom to deliver something different (not just more) from what perhaps either you or the client was expecting. It gives you the room to create and invent, which may serve the client better than whatever they had considered possible at the outset.

Remember, clients don't usually know what they really want, just that they have a need that must be filled. Don't let yourself get too tightly boxed in at the beginning. But DO give them what they paid you for. And then some.

2. DISCOVER WHY YOU NEED TO MAKE PROMISES AT ALL.

Now, that's an interesting thing to think about. Are you the type of person who's always in the promise/deliver mode? Why do you think that is? Aren't there other options?

Some people feel that if they can't or don't make promises, they won't have the motivation or structure to deliver consistently. So, promises become deadlines, and keeping your word becomes necessary. This is something we'll talk about in Step 11: being *pushed* forward versus being *pulled* forward.

I'm all for you keeping your word. In fact, I take it so seriously that I'm really careful about when I'm willing to give *my* word. Most of us give our word too readily and then find ourselves ensnared by the effort it takes to keep it.

I used to hang out with folks who deeply needed me to keep my word, which meant there was a dependency of some sort. I'm a rather free spirit, so this type of promise/deliver system caused me grief until I stopped promising anything at all—which quickly brought an end to performance anxiety.

It may not seem possible for you to stop promising entirely, but I think that everyone can progress by enjoying the space and freedom that comes from promising less.

Think about it anyway: Why ARE you making promises? Is there another, better way? Maybe one that fundamentally makes you more attractive to yourself?

Promise *yourself* to address those questions honestly, okay?

I can tell you about a coach who is now glad that he did. "I filled my life with busyness," he says, "to show people how important I was by how *busy* I was. But by underpromising and overdelivering, I suddenly created big gaps of time. One day I heard myself saying, to my own astonishment, 'I have plenty of time!' It was an epiphany. Now, when a client calls and wants extra guidance, but qualifies the request by asking if I have the time, I love to say the words 'I have a reserve of time.'

"I can practically hear them smile over the phone. It makes me so much more attractive."

3. DELIVER FOR THE PLEASURE OF IT, NOT BECAUSE YOU SAID YOU WOULD.

Some people feel so relieved when they deliver something that most of their pleasure comes from the delivery rather than from the joy of having created what they delivered. Other folks can enjoy both the doing and the delivery.

The point to ponder here is this: What's motivating you after you make the initial promise, and also what "mode" are you in throughout the project?

A woman who has developed into an exceptional coach told me the following story:

> When I first began my practice, I was so often anxious to please that I promised too much to my clients and then had to scramble to carry out those promises. As a result, I was often frustrated and resentful that I never had time to get everything done. As soon as I realized that I was focusing on the promise I'd made instead of the gift I had to give my clients, things shifted. So I committed to making absolutely no promises at all for three months. I continued to add value, faxing spe-

cific tools to help them find a solution, introducing them to people who could help with their problem, and so on. They had no expectation and were grateful.

It was magic for me to give something and know it would be a surprise. Now I do promise things sometimes. But my emphasis is on delivering value and on the joy I feel seeing the surprise and pleasure they get.

One thing her story shows is that the anxiety that leads us to make big promises, while extremely effective and motivating, is fundamentally a net loss for the provider and the recipient both.

The remaining items on this list should help you understand why.

4. DELIVERING EVERYTHING IS EVOLUTIONARY.

The principle reads, in part: "Deliver everything." What does *everything* refer to? Well, it refers to the fact that you can create a bigger solution or product instead of just delivering what the client asked for.

When you focus on delivering everything, you create more. That will evolve both your skill-set and your client's as well. Instead of waiting until you can "break into the big time," you practice the skill and attitude of being big-time creative. So both you and your client move forward instead of just getting your needs met. As the progress builds up, it will make you and the client more and more of a team, drawing each other forward. And it will help you attract finer clients.

Again, whatever the client asked for is just the starting point! In other words, orient what you're working on for the client so that it brings them—as well as you—to the next level. Don't be a machine spitting out predictable and unvarying products. Let the project and the client affect you greatly. Use what you're doing to really evolve.

5. DELIVER WHAT THE CUSTOMER EXPECTED, BUT ALSO DELIVER SOMETHING DIFFERENT.

This is a slight variation on number 4. The idea is to add a twist or an additional component to what the client expected: not just more, like eleven apples instead of ten, but tossing an orange in with the eleventh apple. The orange is something to surprise them with, but you haven't given them any fewer apples.

Perhaps the client will be fascinated by the orange, decide they need more oranges, and that can lead to your next piece of work.

6. DELIVER ALL THAT OCCURS.

This, again, is subtly different from adding something different or delivering more quantity or quality than was expected.

As you're working to create and deliver the product or service, you might stumble upon something surprising to you, either about the client, the product or service, or the situation the client is in.

What you've learned may be totally unrelated to what you're being paid to deliver, but it usually makes sense to keep the client fully informed. These chance discoveries can lead to additional work. They often end up being worth more to the client than the project they paid you to deliver. Call it "Chaos Theory" or something else, but it works.

Be careful not to push what you discover, though. Just casually advise the client. It's their call, and it may take them a while to warm up to what you've shown them before they can decide what—if anything—to do about it. Tell, don't sell.

7. BY NOT MAKING PROMISES, YOU WON'T BE LIMITED IN YOUR CREATIVITY.

I'm a freedom/no pressure junkie. Even though I know that I produce really great results under pressure of deadline or performance, I finally came to realize that the personal and opportunity cost of working that way is far higher than the rewards and results generated.

Results produced under stress have less chance of being creative. They're more likely to be run-of-the-mill, with patched-over rough spots or even mistakes, than to represent what a terrific job you can do. Think of how a basketball team that's just two or three points behind when the game gets down to the wire often will end up losing by eight or ten. Under stress we tend to make chancier decisions that hand our competitors more opportunities.

It's always better to be playing to win than to be playing to come from behind. It's easier to score a win if you haven't overpromised.

8. NATURE DOES NOT PROMISE; NATURE JUST DOES.

This isn't easy to explain, other than to say that genes just do their thing. And, as a result, we have nature, and ourselves.

Delivery, then, is a by-product, not the objective. Interesting, yes? Perhaps the ultimate creativity occurs when you just do what comes to you to do. At a certain point, promising may become unnecessary.

9. JUST DO WHAT YOU CAN DO; DON'T SAY WHAT YOU *CAN'T* DO.

When I lived in Utah I used to see a TV ad for the Mormon Church that featured that thought, and it made a lot of sense. The image in the advertisement was of a neighbor simply mowing the lawn for an elderly couple, without even asking if it was needed.

Rather than offering to help, rather than telling folks what you can do for them, rather than getting people interested enough to say yes, just MOW THEIR LAWN.

It's possible, and sometimes very creative, to just do what you want to for others, without even offering to do it first.

True, you'll miss the mark sometimes. But most people do enjoy surprises, and it's fair to say that there's no delay or performance anxiety because there was no promise, just delivery.

10. HAVE SUCH A RESERVE THAT YOU NATURALLY DELIVER EVERYTHING, WITHOUT HAVING TO COUNT OR LIMIT YOURSELF.

This puts you in a rarefied league, but it's a place where you can really have fun!

This is the idea: Have not only enough reserve to do the other nine things described above, but also have enough to do them with such grace and style that your grace and style become as integral to what you're delivering as the product or service itself.

When you reach that level, very few people can resist wanting to do business with you.

STEP 11

CREATE A VACUUM
THAT PULLS YOU FORWARD

Being Pulled Forward Is Attractive;
Pushing Yourself Forward Isn't

Life is to be lived. If you have to support yourself, you had bloody well better find a way that is going to be interesting.

—KATHARINE HEPBURN

The thing always happens that you really believe in; and the belief in a thing makes it happen.

—FRANK LLOYD WRIGHT

As you know by now, the central idea of the Principles of Attraction is to *attract* people, opportunities, and all other worthwhile things to you instead of chasing after them in some way. So, if you're not pushing or grasping, how do you go about moving all this in your direction?

In terms of physics, you'll need to become either a magnet or else a vacuum of sorts. Both are great concepts, and depending on how a situation inspires you, you can alternate between them.

The magnet comes to mind first, since the nature of magnets is to attract. But for now we'll home in on the less obvious choice: how to use the pulling power of a vacuum—to either pull yourself forward or pull things to you.

DISTINCTIONS TO DRAW

PULL GOALS VS. PUSH GOALS—Joy, happiness, fulfillment, and community are goals that pull you forward, creating a more effortless style of achieving. Money, success, winning, meeting quotas and deadlines, are goals that push you forward, which is more expensive emotionally.

INSPIRATION VS. MOTIVATION—Inspiration is when you are motivated by a person or idea; motivation is when you are inspired by an object.

SUPERCONDUCTIVE VS. ENERGETIC—Superconductivity is the absence of resistance; being energetic is what one does to overcome resistance.

VISION VS. GOAL—A vision is a beacon that is *quite* clear to you once you see it; a goal is what you set when you can't see the vision.

How to know you're making progress with this principle

- You're surprised to find yourself pushing less yet accomplishing more.
- You find yourself noticing the quiet (versus the noise) as you produce results. It may be unsettling at first.
- You find yourself unwilling to push as you used to, whether it's pushing yourself or others.
- You learn how to select the path of least resistance without compromising yourself or your values.

TOP 10 WAYS TO CREATE A VACUUM THAT PULLS YOU FORWARD

1. REALIZE IT'S BETTER TO BE PULLED FORWARD THAN IT IS TO PUSH YOURSELF FORWARD.

Most cars today are front-wheel drive: pulled forward via the front wheels instead of pushed by the rear wheels. It's a lot more efficient, and it eliminates the bulky drivetrain hump running through the middle of your car.

But aside from the trend in automobiles, the notion of being pulled forward is usually a lot more efficient than being pushed. Think of the planets and gravity, maglev (magnetic levitation) trains, magnets, pursuing a vision versus pursuing short-term goals, being motivated by incentive versus being motivated by threat, and so on.

Sure you *can* push yourself forward, and it does work well for many people. But it can be exhausting. In some cases, it's a recipe for burnout.

Most of the time, you'll find that being pulled forward is easier on you than being pushed forward. There is a natural pull somewhere in your life—something that opens up your energies and makes you feel great. Identify it and simply hang on for the ride, instead of trying to propel yourself forward. One of the newer coaches to complete training told me, "I've struggled most of my adult life to 'be in the present moment,' and 'stay present' with situations. I read books, undertook therapy, concentrated on trying and then trying harder. Then, a couple of months ago, I realized I could simply quit trying.

"I've become a lot more productive, and I may even be working harder. But I don't 'try.' It's a wonderful transformation!"

Note: Some folks call this pulling phenomenon "flow," and it is partly that, but it also goes a step further—as you'll discover via the remaining points below.

2. BECOMING MORE SUPERCONDUCTIVE CREATES A VACUUM.

As you know, there are two key aspects in the process of becoming more attractive. One is to spend as much time as you can becoming lighter and less resistant. The other is putting energy into adding value, overresponding, and investing in things.

Creating a stronger vacuum comes from becoming less resistant, more superconductive. Getting your needs met; building a reserve so you can afford to take chances and try new things; surrendering to truth as it occurs to you; letting go of rigid beliefs, assumptions, and dogma; taking the path of least resistance; eliminating tolerations; fixing your integrity—these are all ways to streamline. Some you've already read about, others you'll meet up with soon. What they have in common is that they make you be more conductive, naturally. Thus you are more easily drawn forward by the natural pull in your life.

3. A VISION IS BETTER THAN A GOAL AS A WAY TO BE PULLED FORWARD.

When you identify a goal, it becomes a beacon to strive for, a source of motivation, something to orient yourself around. Goals get you focused on propelling yourself toward them. There's nothing really wrong with this, but it's usually expensive for several reasons.

One, you are focusing on the future, which limits your connection to the people and opportunities around you in the present.

Two, you are measuring your progress against an external reference. This takes you outside yourself and makes your own fulfillment subject to the measures of others.

Three, goals are usually based on unfulfilled wants or needs, which themselves often give you ideas for silly goals. That's why so many folks have a hard time identifying goals that are consistently meaningful.

When you have a vision, however, you are released to focus 99 percent on the present. You don't have to create the future—it's already clear to you. You just proceed from here to there.

By my definition, vision is simply an extrapolation of what's already occurring in the present. It's nothing more than looking calmly at what is— the big and little trends that are reshaping our world, as well as at things that seem likely to endure no matter what—to find clues as to what will be. Therefore, it is present-based, not future-based. It's not something to acquire or achieve, because it's probably going to happen anyway, given enough time. With or without you, most likely. But if you can see in that vision something that meshes with the natural pull in your life, then you will become a part of it.

So, what good is a vision if it's going to happen anyway? It simply provides a non-ego-based, non-performance-based focus. It provides you with context and meaning as you focus 99 percent on responding to the present.

4. PUT YOURSELF INTO CREATIVITY-STIRRING SITUATIONS.

You can push yourself to start or complete a project. Or you can put yourself in an environment that will either pull you forward or pull it out of you.

Whenever I get stuck—and it does happen from time to time—I usually host a conference call on the subject. Within an hour, I'm unstuck.

And all the people on the call have in some way furthered their own understanding. So everybody wins—which, of course, is very attractive.

I create situations that solve the problems *for* me, instead of making myself push through problems.

I know, it's the easy way out, but THAT'S THE POINT! If it's effective yet ultra-low-cost emotionally or financially, it's probably attractive.

Other examples of this point would be joining a training program, taking on a project, writing a book, joining a company that you know would bring you to the next level, signing up for a marathon, etc. USE situations to your advantage; whenever you find yourself struggling with something, find a situation, a group, or an environment to put yourself into. The easy way out usually works extremely well.

5. PUT YOURSELF AMONG FRIENDS AND COLLEAGUES WHO BRING OUT YOUR BEST.

You can use willpower and self-reliance to always perform well, or you can surround yourself with people who always perform at *their* best. This is similar to number 4 above, but it's different in that people are the "who" whereas situations are the "what."

People provide the support you need emotionally. I rely on my personal network to both motivate and acknowledge me. And they always come through.

The trick is to select *only* those folks who do this naturally and in a positive fashion. I don't mean you should surround yourself with people who tell you only what you want to hear. I mean that it's natural to be drawn to people who are both positive and creative.

If a friend or colleague seems to bring out your worst or to slow down your progression, find out why and make the necessary changes.

6. SAY THINGS THAT OCCUR TO YOU, EVEN IF THEY ARE NOT YET TRUE.

Back in 1989, while being interviewed by the *San Francisco Chronicle,* I casually and unthinkingly remarked to the reporter, "I feel that goals are overrated and unnecessary."

The reporter made mincemeat out of my remark. Because at the time I said it, I actually felt that goals were pretty darn important. As a matter of fact, he was talking to me about a course I was then teaching called "Life by Design," in which goals were an essential part of the process.

It was painful being hung out to dry in a major metropolitan newspaper, and I don't necessarily recommend it to you. And yet, that slip of the lip put an important question in my mind. Ultimately, that question helped me to evolve.

Six years later, I started feeling that goals weren't all they were cracked up to be, and that attraction was more interesting and effective.

Chance remarks, Freudian slips, errors, and other unplanned utterances may well be true, but your mind may need some time to catch up with them. I can't *prove* that my chance remark led directly to the development of the Attraction OS, and this book, but I know in my bones that there's a connection.

In other words, my "mistake" left me inquiring, "Hmmm, if goals *aren't* in fact the best way to accomplish stuff, what *is* a better way?" The gap created a vacuum, which naturally pulled my thinking forward, without my putting any energy into it.

The tip is that when you say something that seems to be the opposite of what you meant or what you know to be true, take yourself seriously. Don't dismiss inconsistencies and "unconscious" slips. Let yourself ponder them.

There's a highly useful vacuum in there somewhere!

7. DELIBERATELY CREATE A CONFLICT OUT OF WHICH CAN COME A SYNTHESIS.

Deliberately cause a problem or conflict, just for the opportunity to create a synthesis?

Well, almost. Maybe what I should say is to let point and counterpoint have a go at each other—just to get the positions unstuck and open up new possibilities.

Remember, the objective is to create a vacuum that will pull you forward. An odd but viable way to create a vacuum is to create a problem for yourself. Examples: Make a promise that will be hard to pull off. Change your mind about something and deal with the consequences. Call someone up who violated your boundaries and let them have it. Give out an ultimatum to someone who is frustrating you. Start behaving the opposite of how you have been behaving. Surrender to a whim.

The idea here is to swing the pendulum, even if you go too far or it goes in the wrong direction. It may seem counterintuitive, perhaps in opposition to everything that's been said about attraction and effortlessness, but life is rich in paradox. Remember how my then-inexplicable remark set the stage for a bigger way of looking at things.

8. MUTATE, AT WILL.

As the DNA in your body (and in all of nature) divides, splits, and recombines millions of times, mistakes occur. Sometimes it doesn't perfectly match up on recombining. This creates what's called a mutation.

Mutation and natural selection, of course, are the basis of the theory of evolution.

The same is true with thoughts and ideas (which are called "memes," instead of genes). So, one might say that truth itself—in the sense of shared thoughts and beliefs—is always evolving.

Of course, everything else is rapidly evolving, too: law, business theory, philosophy, science, marketing—everything.

When something mutates, there's a chance that it may create an improvement in the species. A mutation—whether of yourself, an idea, or a meme—might bring you a competitive advantage. As a sentient being, you have the option of trying and keeping, or discarding, an infinite amount of personal transformations.

Experimentation, and the freedom to experiment, are the basis of research and development departments. R&D is what leads to more products or product variations—more mutations, if you will. So, then, one of the ways to become more attractive is to experiment more with yourself, with others, or with ideas, words, products, life, companies, situations, feelings. Take it as a given: The odds favor that at least one of your experiments will create real progress for you, thus making you more attractive, either to yourself or to the marketplace.

To have the freedom to experiment frequently, you'll need some sort of reserve. Reserve affords you the time and energy to take risks and can reimburse you for your mistakes. Experimentation leads to attraction.

9. Unhook yourself from who you were; this will let you be pulled forward.

Many of my clients are quick to describe their skills, talents, and successes, because they do have many of these! So far, nothing's wrong. But the tendency is also to define yourself by your skills, talents, and accomplishments—or at least to be reassured by them. This leads you astray in two areas: complacency and ego. Complacency in that you don't feel the need to experiment and advance as much. Ego in that you begin to identify yourself by what you're good at.

Neither complacency nor ego is bad. However, take them lightly even while you enjoy them. Otherwise, they begin to act more as an anchor than a foundation.

For example, I used to think that I was a really good communicator and especially masterful at articulating ideas, thoughts, and distinctions. So much so, that I let myself perform like a seal to anyone who would stop by. I'd get praise for how good I was and I started not only to believe it but to have it be reassuring to me.

It was a trap, because I stopped learning and advancing in this skill area. I was like the kind of athlete that sports coaches call a "floater." That's someone who's gifted enough to succeed without working much on their skills yet likely to come up short when really challenged.

I now regard myself as an acceptable communicator and coach, but I feel I am only at the 30 percent level, not at the 90 percent level I formerly felt I'd achieved. And I wasn't bitten by the humble bug, either. I simply unhooked myself from a slightly complacent and egotistical self-definition. Since then, I've been progressing very nicely!

Paradoxically, though, "making progress" can become a real trap as well. But let's save that for another Top 10 List. The point here is this: Stop thinking that you're really good at something, or at least stop saying that you are. Even if you really are. And even if lots of people say that you are. In fact, the moment they begin to praise you is usually when you need to do some more work!

There's always plenty of room for self-confidence *and* improvement. Think of star athletes who go back to the gym on their own and take time to add new dimensions to their existing skills. Think of Magic Johnson, already one of the best basketball players of all time, adding that "baby, baby hook shot" to his arsenal, then using it to knock out the Boston Celtics at the buzzer.

10. TELL THE NEWLY DISCOVERED TRUTH ABOUT SOMETHING, EVEN IF YOU CAN'T SEE A WAY TO IMPLEMENT OR HONOR THIS TRUTH.

The most significant and immediately applicable way of creating a vacuum is to remove something that's blocking the path of truth. Flow is important to truth and to progress, and lies of any kind—deliberate or unintentional—can clog the pipeline.

Every day, something new is occurring to you. Your awareness is increasing, you are coming to better understand yourself and your needs, and you are getting smarter about life. But sometimes something big will dawn on you that seems to be very, very true, yet you can't figure out how to change your life enough to honor what you just discovered or noticed that's true. So, you either disregard it or panic and become paralyzed, or you dilute the truth because it makes it hard for you to justify your current life.

Ah, but there *is* a better way. And that's just to TELL THE TRUTH about a situation, your life, yourself, another person, even if you *cannot* change yourself or the situation in the foreseeable future. Communicate the truth to someone, instead of just merely thinking it. When it leaves your lips, you *have* done something about it. You've put it into play. If it's strong enough, it'll get communicated more and more, until so many minds focus on it that they create a breakthrough. Then, it becomes something you *can* do something about.

A truth spoken creates a vacuum for you. It's *that* easy.

ELIMINATE DELAY

Time Is Expensive;
Using Too Much Is Very Unattractive

Nothing is so fatiguing as the hanging on of an uncompleted task.
—HENRY JAMES

Lost time is not found again.
—BOB DYLAN

Here's a topic where the Attraction OS is very obviously in sync with today's trends in everyday life and business. Can you remember when there was no such thing as Federal Express? Twenty-five years ago it was a baby-sized company—a few planes and not many customers. But FedEx soon thrived, and in doing so it proved a point: Overnight delivery is worth a premium. It helps people get things done a lot quicker, which is another way of saying *more competitively.* Because time really is worth money.

Pretty soon a host of bigger companies, even the U.S. Postal Service itself, jumped into the trend FedEx had started, bringing to bear huge commitments of their considerable resources. And yet FedEx has remained dominant. It's even become a verb: People will say, "I'll FedEx this package to you," even if they're actually using another courier.

I'm a big believer in the notion that consumers, given choices, will naturally eradicate every single source of waste or inefficiency in business: everything from the high cost of telephone service (as in Internet phones) to segments of entire professions, such as car salesmen and even Realtors.

DISTINCTIONS TO DRAW

IMMEDIATE VS. SOON—When you respond to a phone call within ten minutes, that's immediate. When you respond by the end of the day, that's soon.

SPACE VS. TIME—When you create more space for yourself, time stops feeling like a scarce commodity.

If it's a middleman/woman, they're GONE—unless they are adding a lot of value to their clients throughout the day, instead of "wasting time" hustling prospects.

One of the cool things about the Attraction OS is that attracting business, results, people, things, *to* you is just about the most efficient process of all, especially when compared to hustling, searching, selling, acquiring, seeking.

Delay, the focus of this principle, is simply one of the many unnecessary expenses that consumers are now rejecting. Delay is something that you can really do something about on a practical basis, and right away.

Following are ten ways to get started—immediately.

How to know you're making progress with this principle

- You start to see where you're delaying and reduce or eliminate it as much as possible.
- You find yourself unwilling to tolerate the delays of others. You seek out vendors and associates who respond immediately.
- You take pride in responding immediately.
- You set up a system so that everyone who comes in contact with you (personally or professionally) experiences virtually no delay.
- Serendipity becomes so much a natural part of your life, you expect it to happen regularly.
- You do not depend on a to-do list.
- Customers are delighted by your immediate response and buy more from you.
- You stop missing opportunities, especially those of brief duration.
- You attract other "quick" people who realize the incredibly high costs of delay.

TOP 10 WAYS TO ELIMINATE
THE HIGH COST OF DELAY

1. REFUSE TO WAIT FOR THINGS; BECOME DEMANDING.

I deal only with companies or individuals who respond immediately to what I want, have a Web site and online ordering, offer overnight delivery, and respond promptly to E-mail.

I'm not obsessive or hyper about it. I just know that delay of any kind is wasteful or, at the very least, expensive. Delay slows down my creative process, so I'm not willing to tolerate it.

I don't get upset if something doesn't arrive when it should. I simply work with someone else next time.

To put it another way, quick response adds value—which makes you more attractive. And, believe me, there are *plenty* of folks who value immediate response as much as I do. So choose which group you wish to join—the Immediate Response Club or the Delay Club. It matters.

2. BECOME THE TYPE OF PERSON WHO RESPONDS
TO OTHERS' REQUESTS IMMEDIATELY.

We all get too busy to be completely on top of all things all the time, so this may be something you'll progress toward instead of instantly adopt. But when you respond immediately to inquiries or questions from customers or prospective customers, their trust expands greatly, without your having to do anything else.

People fear delay. They are reassured by immediate responses. That dynamic alone will make you a lot more attractive to yourself and to others, because delay sometimes signals a shortage of integrity. Not always, but often enough to make people wary about whether you'll really come through.

There's a trend many coaches are now picking up on, and that's eliminating the practice of scheduled weekly sessions in favor of being available throughout the business day so they can respond to a client's needs whenever an emergent situation makes the client realize exactly what he or she wants to work on. In other words, there's no delay between the experiencing of a need and the delivery of service.

There's an emotional change necessary. You have to bond with your clients enough to have a real relationship. You may need to set up your life to have almost no inventory of consuming projects; keep your bandwidth (the amount you're able to receive) wide enough to handle all that comes at you. The payoff is that you and your client will find yourselves getting more done in less time.

So, while eliminating delay is a great thing in and of itself, it's often just the beginning of what's possible.

3. MAINTAIN NO INVENTORY OF TO-DO'S.

Wouldn't this be terrific? I'm going in this direction but, like most of us, still have lots of room to improve. Still, the point warrants making: While there's nothing wrong with to-do's, there is still an inherent delay, isn't there?

To-do lists are about the past and the future, *not* about the present, right? So, if attraction and opportunities occur primarily in the present, to-do lists could very well get in their way.

Sharon Eakes, a warm and highly skilled coach from Pittsburgh, told me recently:

> I used to pride myself on being a great "time manager." I made huge lists and prioritized the items every day, and always started on the most difficult and *did*, in fact, get a lot done. But I was crabby. I operated in an "efficient" way toward the future but without zest.
>
> I still have a vision now, just a different way of getting there. Now I have more fun. I kind of respond to what comes up, which means that I change focus a lot in the course of the day. I enjoy the process. Amazingly, the hard stuff still gets done—but in due time and at less cost to me. I am happier with myself, and the feedback I get is that people find that very attractive.

Interesting thought, yes? As I've admitted, I'm still working on the solution myself. But I know it's all about installing systems and practices that can handle projects and needs as they come in. It's a challenge but well worth addressing.

4. LEARN QUICKLY: INTEGRATE CHANGES IMMEDIATELY AND RESPOND ACCORDINGLY.

As I've remarked earlier, and probably will again, computers and the Internet are among the most important changes of our era. And as I've also noted, Esther Dyson is an acknowledged expert on where these changes are likely to lead us. In her recent book, *Release 2.0,* she affirms that the most important talent in the online world is creativity—either artistic or intellectual. In the future, the companies that stay ahead will do so by generating an abundant stream of new technology and ideas.

"The second key attribute," she writes, "is a performance personality." In other words, people who respond quickly (versus people who think slowly) will thrive.

How quickly do you both assimilate new ideas and implement whatever changes are called for as a result of what you learned?

For most people there is a lag. In some cases it runs into a day or so; in others it's a lifetime.

New information, truths, or new ways of doing things have to filter into our heads and through our systems. If they are delayed on the way, they'll probably get either diluted or completely lost before we can benefit from them.

"Turning on a dime" is one way to describe the preferred mode, and the place to start is to understand how long your "delay/integration process" takes. Then seek to shorten it by 90 percent.

True, you'll make some mistakes by responding too quickly to false signals. But it's better to master the signals in your body and in life than to play it safe and miss out on the real opportunities that life presents. In other words, use your intelligence to the maximum, but DON'T stop to think. In sports terminology, you should play to win, instead of playing not to lose. Think on the fly, and respond equally fast, so the game won't pass you by.

You know you're a rapid learner if you substantially change your thinking or behavior even *before* you truly understand what you're learning. That represents a very advanced level of skill.

5. REDUCE YOUR "PERSONAL PROCESSING TIME"
BY ELIMINATING FEAR-BASED DELAYS.

The John D. and Catherine T. MacArthur Foundation gives tremendous sums of money, called "Genius Grants," to people whose work shows great potential, so they can advance the evolution of knowledge in their field without fear of going broke.

Having reserves is a lot like giving yourself a Genius Grant.

First, you deserve that kind of backing (even though you're providing it yourself).

Second, having a reserve is the best way to reduce fear.

This is a key point. Reserves work because they reduce the consequences—perceived or actual—of threat or risk. And it's risk and threat that cause fear. And fear that causes constricted decision making. And constricted decision making that causes delays. And round and round you go.

Rather than consciously trying to learn or process much more quickly (although that's nice if you can do it!), you can simply focus on building reserves. Very soon you'll find yourself learning and evolving faster, because fear no longer slows you down.

6. SENSITIZE YOURSELF SO YOU CAN RESPOND
EVEN BEFORE A DELAY IS POSSIBLE.

As you reduce tolerations (a topic that gets full treatment very soon), you become less numb and increasingly more sensitive. Tolerations have a numbing effect. As you build a reserve, you can afford to feel MORE than you're currently feeling. You'll be like a radio that's suddenly able to receive more signals.

Being sensitive is not about being a fragile little hothouse flower; it's about being open and UNAFRAID to notice what's alive in the present moment.

Step 18 will focus on the how-to of becoming more sensitive. For now, I'll just introduce the ultimate objective: being able to feel, sense, hear, and see future events before others can.

A lot is said about being proactive and anticipating changes. That's good. But sensitizing yourself—so you can respond even before a delay is possible—is much more advanced.

In other words, if you really understood how costly delays are to you,

you'd quickly make changes to eliminate them. And respond *thisquick* to events. It's more than just avoiding delays; it's about being a scout—sensing what's around the next bend, even before the competition knows there's a bend coming, and making immediate changes to take advantage of what's ahead.

7. DEVELOP A FILTERING SYSTEM TO SCREEN WHAT COMES AT YOU.

One of the best ways to eliminate delay is to keep your intake system from getting clogged. You don't respond to every piece of mail you receive. Some of it is junk. Should you respond to everything that comes to you? Could you realistically do this?

Probably not.

But you can filter what comes at you so that you *do* have time to respond immediately to whatever really matters.

One way I filter out stuff is by maintaining just a few key and mutually supportive friendships and relationships. Managing and supporting several relationships consumes bandwidth. For me, having a few friendships and relationships of terrific quality proves that less equals more.

Another way to filter is to let an assistant, whether local or virtual, handle your incoming E-mail and even regular mail. Just instruct your assistant on what matters to you, yet give him or her freedom to include whatever else *might* interest you.

Another way to filter is to know what your vision is. (This is another upcoming focus, in Step 27.) When you're clear on this and on your personal values, your clarity will automatically filter out unwanted stuff. You'll be attracting the appropriate information, along with people who have a similar vision.

Joy is an excellent filter as well. If something is not going to bring you joy, it shouldn't get into your life.

Now, you may be wondering if the above filters are too narrow, meaning that they might make you miss out on something really cool or isolate you from radical ideas. Well, there *is* a danger of becoming too insulated. What I do is subscribe to *WIRED* magazine; that alone keeps the pipeline for radical ideas pretty full, so I don't get stale or limited by the thinking of my closest associates.

There are lots of other provocative forums out there. Spend some leisure time soon at a bookstore with an extensive magazine rack. Select a few that look like they'd be fun and maybe eye-opening, too. Sample. Take one or two home and stretch out.

8. AUTOMATE YOUR RESPONSES
SO YOU DON'T HAVE TO BE THERE.

We've covered this a bit in number 7 when I mentioned having a virtual assistant.

Just for a minute, step into the shoes of all the people who contact you via phone, E-mail, fax, or the U.S. mail. Think how you might develop a system to immediately confirm that you received their request and to let them know when you'll get back to them.

Again, you're eliminating delay. Even if you can't handle their request right away, people are reassured that you *know* of their need and intend to *do* something about it.

On the E-mail front, autoresponders are the way to go. I changed my E-mail address of *thomas@coachu.com* to be an autoresponder, so it directs people to places they can get most of what they want. You can also set up a fax-on-demand system or voice-info on demand so callers can get most of what they need without your having to call them back.

The solutions will likely be different for you than for me, but the idea is to eliminate the delay between the time a person contacts you, for any reason, by whatever means, and the time they receive at least a confirmation—if not the solution itself. It means taking yourself out of the response loop, which is yet another way of filtering what comes at you.

One of the interesting ways I used to handle inquiries regarding the Coach Training Program at CoachVille was to steer callers and E-mailers to the Web site, the fax-back, and the autoresponders. Then I went a step further and set up the system to let them know when the next Coaching Q&A free tele-class was scheduled and how to register automatically.

That way, I could spend my time more efficiently, talking only with those who had enough interest to show up. It saved *hours,* yet gave folks personal attention from me, as the founder. It worked great.

9. ALWAYS BE INCREASING YOUR BANDWIDTH AND CPU WAY BEFORE YOU NEED TO.

If you're successful, or plan to be, it only makes sense that the demands on your time will increase. Think of a computer. One that's okay for an elementary school student to do homework assignments on will probably be too limited in speed and memory to handle a small business's inventory, shipping, customer base, projections, etc. In other words, its CPU (central processing unit) will be underpowered relative to what's needed. And if that small business really grew, the computer would soon be a bottleneck—until it was replaced by perhaps several computers linked in a network or by a giant mainframe.

Given that success is bound to happen, the only responsible thing to do is to consciously scale up your support system and personal capacities in order to handle the oncoming demands. Most people are in the mode of scrambling to keep up. Instead, always operate at a 50 percent reserve factor. Scrambling to keep up with opportunities puts you behind the curve. Being ready for opportunities takes you to the next level, where you will once again scale up your support system and personal capacities.

Be responsible—develop a personal system that generates quick responses.

10. WHEN YOU FIND YOURSELF DELAYING, FIND OUT WHY.

Learning slowly, deferring decisions, or playing wait and see can sometimes be the very best approach! Occasionally, the best decision is going to be no decision at all. This is sometimes known as "good timing."

However, if you find yourself always putting things off, or delaying in any manner, ask yourself why. There's ALWAYS a reason, and it's always worth knowing—even if you choose to do nothing about it, which may or may not be good timing, depending on outcome.

GET YOUR PERSONAL NEEDS MET, ONCE AND FOR ALL

If You Have Unmet Needs, You'll Attract Others in the Same Position

Our greatest pretenses are built up not to hide the evil and the ugly in us, but our emptiness. The hardest thing to hide is something that is not there.

—ERIC HOFFER

Facts do not cease to be because they have been ignored.
—ALDOUS HUXLEY

To go Mr. Huxley, the author of *Brave New World,* one better: "*Needs* do not cease to be because they have been ignored." In that little maxim, one of life's great mysteries is solved. The mystery is why, in spite of special talents and great desire, do so many people stay stuck in self-limiting patterns?

If you recall, the lawyer whose story I related in Step 9 managed to triple his income and still have, in the words of a country song I heard one time, "too much month at the end of the money." How is that possible?

Here's the answer: unmet personal needs. They loop us back again and again, because we can't help communicating to others the pressures caused by those unmet needs. We do this through our eyes and through our actions as much as through our words. And we experience, even if unconsciously, a sort of dysfunctional connection with those who carry around the same, or very similar, unmet needs.

DISTINCTIONS TO DRAW

NEEDS VS. WANTS—Until your needs are met, you really can't make the most of what God gave you. People who don't have their needs met have an awful lot of wants.

NEEDS VS. VALUES—Needs are what you must have to be you; values ARE you.

NEEDS VS. PSYCHOLOGICAL PROBLEMS—Needs can be satisfied only after psychological problems have been healed.

NEEDS SATISFACTION VS. NEEDS GRATIFICATION—When your need gets met without your having to repeatedly focus on it, it's being properly satisfied. If you keep "feeding" the need, it's being gratified.

PERSONAL NEEDS VS. SURVIVAL/PHYSICAL NEEDS—Personal needs are those emotional, physical, mental, spiritual, and environmental things you need to be your best. Physical needs are about surviving physically, as an animal.

We find a level of comfort in all that agreement, but unfortunately we don't find very many clues about how to evolve.

The clues are evident, though, when you learn how to spot them.

This may sound beyond human reach, but you *can* evolve upward and outward from your patterns of personal needs. You really can get them met, once and for all, and never get spun back to square one again.

There are two categories of needs: survival needs and personal needs.

Survival needs include water, food, shelter, and (to a degree) love. Personal needs are what you need to be your best and to progress in life. They can include inspiration, information, support, solutions, focus, people, touch, skills, avocation/vocation outlets, context, character, and so forth.

Survival needs, when met, keep you alive. Personal needs, when met, let you truly be yourself—in the best way possible.

Either kind of need, when unmet, can stir up reactions ranging from restless discontent to abject fear.

Most people do not have their personal needs met, for several reasons. First, they don't know what their needs actually *are*. They have a general idea, but it's not really clear or exact enough to act on.

Second, even when they are in touch with what their needs are, they aren't comfortable or confident that they can *really* get them met.

Third, when they do get them met, it's only temporarily, not permanently.

This Top 10 List includes tips on how to identify your personal needs and how to get them satisfied once and for all. When you've reviewed all ten list items, use the NeedLess Checklist, developed by CoachV, to help you illuminate your own situation by trying on a comprehensive list of 200 Personal Needs for size.

Before starting, we need to clarify two key points:

First, needs are distinct from values. Needs are what you need to be your best. Values are those interests or behaviors you most enjoy or are most attracted to. At first, it might be hard to see the distinction. But eventually you'll be able to accurately label whether something in your life represents a need or a value.

Second, needs are not optional (even though we often treat them that way).

If you're starving, food isn't an option—it's a need. The same is true if you have an unmet personal/emotional need. To really be yourself, you MUST get this need satisfied. It's not optional. The basic problem people have with this particular Attraction Principle is that they see needs as "important" to identify and get taken care of. They're way beyond important.

Satisfying your needs is ESSENTIAL to your evolution.

How to know you're making progress with this principle

- You start going out of your way to get a need satisfied, just as you now go out of your way to get a top-quality product instead of a generic brand.
- You are excited about getting needs met, instead of chagrined, embarrassed, or hesitant. In other words, you're proactive instead of reactive.
- You find yourself becoming more creative and energetic.
- You find yourself factoring in your needs to whatever work, client, project, or relationship you now have. You ask yourself, "Will this get in the way of getting my needs met? Will this person drain me or nourish me?"
- You open up special parts of yourself that have been hidden by unmet needs.
- You feel more confident because you know how to get what you need from others.

TOP 10 WAYS TO GET YOUR PERSONAL NEEDS MET ONCE AND FOR ALL

1. UNDERSTAND THAT YOU DO HAVE NEEDS AND THAT GETTING THEM MET IS ESSENTIAL TO YOUR BEING IRRESISTIBLY ATTRACTIVE.

Humans have many needs. We're aware of only some of them. Others lie in our "blind spots."

Aware or not, we are still motivated and driven by these needs, sometimes positively but sometimes negatively. Even when we *have* identified a key need, getting it met properly still requires some time and investment.

Knowing what your needs are is a terrific start, then, but really just the beginning. And yet, needs satisfaction will reward you for a lifetime. So make your beginning, then move to the next steps and phases with confidence. You're setting yourself up for a freer, fuller life. You'll have more room and love for other people, without competing. You'll feel and project dramatically more self-confidence, without arrogance. You will be full-time attractive to yourself.

2. IDENTIFY AT LEAST ONE PIVOTAL PERSONAL NEED.

What do you need most, do you think? Is it to be heard? Touched? Respected? Loved? Cared about? Is it freedom? A healthful environment? Security? Money? Beauty? Success?

Choose one that seems likely and ask yourself this: "What if I had an unlimited amount of it? Would it make my life incredibly perfect and allow me to be my best almost all of the time?"

Your pivotal personal need (PPN) can be something big or small, but it needs to be really specific, not general. Identify it, so you can act on it. This is your starting point.

3. IDENTIFY AT LEAST ONE OTHER PERSONAL NEED EXACTLY.

I usually suggest that someone identify his or her pivotal personal need and at least one other personal need. So, in addition to what you identified in number 2 above, what else is really important for you to have in your life?

It can be big or small. Try to pick one that is barely on your radar, meaning that it's a "quiet" or "emerging" one—one that you've either not let yourself admit to or not taken *that* seriously.

4. DISCOVER THE SOURCE OF YOUR PIVOTAL PERSONAL NEED.

Now we're back to the pivotal personal need again. Why do you think you have *this* pivotal personal need? Was it something you never had as a child? Is it part of your genetic makeup? Something you discovered about yourself in conjunction with an important event or juncture in your life? Something that someone told you about yourself and it clicked and made sense?

Do you think you absorbed this need from your parents' way of thinking? Is it culturally or ethnically based?

The point here is that needs exist for a good reason. If you can uncover that reason, you'll probably be able to more readily accept it as a need and *respect* it.

It's vital that you respect and honor your needs. People generally want to deny their needs. Sometimes they overcompensate for them, or dress them up to look prettier, or try to eradicate them with an Uzi. But the best thing to do with a discovered need, especially a pivotal personal need, is to *honor,* respect, and eventually understand it better.

Don't be in too much of a hurry to satisfy or eliminate it. You'll miss a gateway to understanding and leveraging other important areas of your life.

5. DOCUMENT HOW THAT UNMET PIVOTAL PERSONAL NEED (PPN) HAS HELPED YOU GET WHERE YOU ARE TODAY.

Needs are good things—they often force us to create strengths or muscles in other areas of our life in order to compensate for the big black holes that pivotal personal needs often are. We're better off for having unmet PPNs. Well, not really. But they have propelled us forward, at least for now. Entertainers and athletes provide more examples than you can shake a stick at: kids concentrating on their talents to lift them to a better life away from tough neighborhoods, dysfunctional parents, or other spirit-deadening circumstances growing into adults who've made it but who are still missing some important aspects of adulthood. Go to any newsstand in the country, pick up a celebrity- or sports-oriented magazine, and you'll find several stories following those contours.

It could almost make you think that life is going to trip you up, one way or another, no matter how successful you get. And that's true—as long as you're walking around with unmet needs.

What's great is knowing that as soon as you get your PPNs satisfied, you'll find much smarter, more effective, less emotionally costly ways to get motivated and create progress in business and in life.

But don't criticize or denigrate the good your unmet needs have done for you thus far in your life! Make a list of five very specific ways in which your life is *better* because of an unmet PPN.

6. IDENTIFY WHAT YOU'D NEED IN ORDER TO HAVE THAT PPN SATISFIED PERMANENTLY.

Is this even possible? Yes. That's part of the theory (and promise) of this Attraction Principle. You really *can* identify and get needs satisfied, permanently. It takes some work, but it's worth it.

So, what would you need to happen, or happen regularly, for your PPN to feel satisfied forever? Big question. You may need to inquire into it for a while. If you'll accept the possibility that one *can* satisfy needs permanently, you'll open up enough to realize how to go about it.

There are two basic ways of getting personal needs met. One is healing via therapy or other psychological or spiritual means. Let's face it, many needs are simply scars left over from something bad that happened—or something good that didn't happen—during your childhood years. If it has to do with childhood, work with a therapist or other healing expert. However, many needs are not childhood-based. They are probably gene- or meme-based and need to get satisfied in a way other than permanent healing. This leads us to number 7.

7. BEGIN SETTING UP AN AUTOMATED NEEDS SATISFACTION SYSTEM (ANSS).

I used to have a driving need to feel appreciated. I'd bend over backward to do things for people in the hope that, maybe 10 percent of the time, someone would notice and thank me enough. A dribble for filling up a big black hole, but a dribble is better than nothing, right? Only when I recognized this as a need (versus a desire) and took it seriously did I realize that I'd have to install some sort of system to water the need until it didn't need any more water.

So I told all of my clients and friends about this newly understood need and asked them to help me get it watered. Not to overpraise or butter me up, but just to let me know whenever my coaching, or my friendship, really turned out to be important to them. There's an old saying, "Nothing improves my hearing like praise." But some of us need to hear *lots* of praise before we start letting ourselves believe that we really deserve it. I once was just like that.

It took about six months of watering, but the need no longer drives me. (And it used to drive about 90 percent of my actions, which was very expensive!)

The people around me became the ANSS. I told them what I needed from them, and I had enough willing partners in this project to take care of the need permanently. You can do the same.

In addition to what you're learning here, Step 16 should be a tremendous help in your needs satisfaction process.

8. MAKE SIGNIFICANT CHANGES IN OTHER AREAS; SATISFY THE PPN AS A BY-PRODUCT.

There are a couple of ways to get PPNs satisfied. You can focus directly on the PPN, as I did in number 7 above, and/or you can focus on other parts of your life and strengthen them. The key is to come to understand the PPN. Once you reach that point, you can focus either directly on it or on other aspects of your life, and the PPN will start to get satisfied.

In the example given from my own life above, I could have also worked with a psychotherapist, or another coach, to become better at seeing my own value and hearing the generous amount of praise already coming my way. Or I could simply have written down all the praise I heard and kept it in a file, to look at whenever I felt the PPN. I chose to rely on friends and clients, which turned out great, but I could have explored other options, too.

9. KEEP WORKING AND FINE-TUNING THE ANSS.

In number 7, I explained my ANSS. The key is to SHARE your need with others—that starts the satisfaction process. You'll also discover who has quality time for you and who doesn't.

One of the confusing things about personal needs is that we very often attract people who *cannot* meet our needs, especially our PPNs. Weird and unfortunate, but true. You may be surprised, if not hurt, by how few people have the capacity for or interest in helping you. Remember, they probably like you as you are. Some people need *you* to be needy in order for them to get *their* needs met.

The point here is to keep tweaking your ANSS until it works well and automatically. Think of an automated watering system for your lawn. It doesn't require you to keep flipping the switch. *That's* automatic!

10. IDENTIFY OTHER NEEDS THAT HAVE DISSIPATED AS A RESULT OF GETTING THE PPN SATISFIED.

Part of the value of this Attraction Principle is simply to pay more attention to needs and their satisfaction. So, notice how your life (and awareness of other personal needs) is changing and improving as a result of your working on your PPN.

This may seem to be an obvious point, but it's worth pursuing. The point of getting your needs met is *not* just to get them met permanently but also to come to understand yourself better in the process. By noticing how your life is improving in all areas as a result of your focus on needs, you'll become more sensitized (another one of the principles) to everything and everyone. That is another important part of being irresistibly attractive.

BECOMING NEEDLESS

Read this list of 200 needs. Circle approximately 10 that resonate for you. You are looking for a *need*—not a want, a should, a fantasy, or a wish. A need is something that you *must* have in order for you to be your best. The first step is to TELL THE TRUTH ABOUT WHAT YOU ACTUALLY NEED.

This may be the first time you have ever admitted this to yourself. Some of these you will know intimately; others may require some soul-searching. Please be willing to try on words you might normally skip over. These may be hidden needs. If so, you may have one or more of the following reactions:

- No, no, no; I don't want *that* to be a need.
- If that is true, I'd have to change my life a lot!
- I flush, blush, or shake when reading the word.

Got the idea? Good. Now circle the ten words that you believe to be personal needs. Ask yourself: "If I had this, would I be able to reach my goals and vision without struggling?" (Work equals good; struggling equals not so good.)

BE ACCEPTED	BE ACKNOWLEDGED	BE RIGHT
Approved	Worthy	Correct
Included	Praised	Not mistaken
Respected	Honored	Honest
Permitted	Flattered	Morally right
Popular	Complimented	Deferred to
Sanctioned	Prized	Confirmed
Cool	Appreciated	Advocated
Allowed	Valued	Encouraged
Tolerated	Thanked	Understood

TO ACCOMPLISH	BE LOVED	BE CARED FOR
Achieve	Liked	Get attention
Fulfill	Cherished	Helped
Realize	Esteemed	Cared about
Reach	Held fondly	Saved
Profit	Desired	Attended to
Attain	Preferred	Treasured
Yield	Relished	Treated with tenderness
Consummate	Adored	Given gifts
Win	Touched	Embraced

CERTAINTY

Clarity

Accuracy

Assurance

Obviousness

Guarantees

Promises

Commitments

Exactness

Precision

TO CONTROL

Dominate

Command

Restrain

Manage

Correct others

Be obeyed

Not be ignored

Keep status quo

Restrict

BE FREE

Unrestricted

Privileged

Immune

Independent

Autonomous

Sovereign

Not obligated

Self-reliant

Liberated

BE COMFORTABLE

Luxury

Opulence

Excess

Prosperity

Indulgence

Abundance

Not work

Taken care of

Served

BE NEEDED

Improve others

Be a critical link

Be useful

Be craved

Please others

Affect others

Give

Be important

Be material

HONESTY

Forthrightness

Uprightness

Truthfulness

Sincerity

Loyalty

Frankness

Nonscheming

Directness

Candor

TO COMMUNICATE

Be heard

Tell stories

Make a point

Share

Talk

Be listened to

Comment

Be informed

Advise

DUTY

Be obligated

Do the right thing

Follow

Obey

Have a task

Satisfy others

Prove self

Be devoted

Have a cause

ORDER

Perfection

Symmetry

Consistency

Sequentiality

Checklists

Unvarying

Rightness

Literalness

Regulated

PEACE

Quietness

Calmness

Unity

Reconciliation

Stillness

Balance

Agreement

Respite

Steadiness

RECOGNITION

Be noticed

Be remembered

Be known for

Well regarded

Given credit

Acclaimed

Heeded

Seen

Celebrated

WORK

Career

Performance

Vocation

Determination

Initiative

Tasks

Responsibility

Industriousness

Busyness

POWER

Authority

Capacity

Results

Omnipotence

Strength

Might

Stamina

Prerogative

Influence

SAFETY

Secure

Protected

Stable

Fully informed

Deliberate

Vigilant

Cautious

Alert

Guarded

Now pick a pivotal personal need (PPN) you want to work on—

not necessarily the hardest one, but a significant one. _____

_____

Now pick another personal need—not necessarily the easiest one, but one

that matters. _____

THRIVE ON THE DETAILS

Subtleties, Details, and Nuances
Are More Attractive than the Obvious

He who can take no great interest in what is small will take false
interest in what is great.

—JOHN RUSKIN

Trifles make perfection possible—and perfection is no trifle.

—MICHELANGELO

One way to make sure that the progression of time works in your favor is
to thrive on the too-often unseen links between small details and big
movements. For example . . .

Not very long ago, a perennial New York City problem was growing to
the point where it threatened to undermine a huge sector of the city's
economy. Tourists, conventioneers, and traveling businesspeople had
always rained dollars on New York's hotels, restaurants, clubs, cab drivers,
etc. But visitors faced an increasing daily onslaught of panhandlers,
"squeegee guys," petty thieves, and other small-time criminals.

A client of mine is a culinary professional. A few years ago she was
thrilled about attending her first Fancy Foods Expo—until she had to
climb over several sleeping, malodorous drunks in the stairwells of the
enormous Jacob Javits Convention Center. And subway travel, for years
the most efficient and inexpensive way to get someplace quickly, was
becoming something only the most adventurous would do.

Derelicts and addicts deserve compassion for whatever pain has weak-

---

DISTINCTIONS TO DRAW

THRIVE VS. NOTICE—To thrive is to enjoy immensely the details you notice. Most people notice or consume details yet don't respond to them.

SUBTLETY VS. NUANCE—A subtlety is slightly different in concept and requires discernment. A nuance is a slightly different shade or gradation of the same thing. Subtleties open up new worlds. Nuances simply recolor the existing world.

PRECURSORS VS. PREDICTORS—A precursor is a detail that PROVES what's coming. A predictor is a detail that indicates what's PROBABLY coming.

INKLING VS. INTUITION—An inkling is a hint, an intimation. It's subtler than an intuition. Most people trust their intuitions somewhat but their inklings not at all. To thrive on the details, you need to start trusting your inklings most of the time. They occur before intuition does.

---

ened their power to live. At the same time, everyone deserves livable public spaces free of urine stench, sidewalks not littered with spent crack ampules, and a chance to use those sidewalks without hearing pleas—or vociferous demands—from beaten-down individuals who can't focus on anything but their next bottle, their next fix.

The New York Police Department's resources were hard-pressed fighting major crimes like murder, arson, and extortion, of which there was plenty. But they undertook a small-details-oriented policy shift: more attention on the petty crimes pushing everyday life in the city from unappetizing to untenable, which Mayor Giuliani called "quality-of-life crimes."

We all know what happened. It's now being repeated in several other cities around the country. Paying attention to petty crime made the city more attractive to live in and visit and also dramatically reduced major crime.

The statistics are getting better each year. In 1997 there was an additional 9.1 percent decrease in crime. So now the hotels are frequently booked solid, weeks ahead. The subway is once again a pretty darn good way to get around.

In short, a micro (small details) approach generated macro (whole system) benefits. Which is exactly what Step 14 is all about.

Not having an enjoyable, fulfilled life is a type of quality-of-life crime against yourself. Why not take a tip from the Big Apple and consider a micro approach? Subtleties, details, and nuances can help you unlock the bigger changes.

Novelists and film directors like to say "God is in the details." That's the essence of this principle. The more you start paying attention to the details of a project or of your life, body, environment, ideas, trends, changes, and so on, the sooner you'll be able to do something profound with it.

Of course, it's completely appropriate that this concept involves a host of (that's right!) subtleties, details, and nuances.

How to know you're making progress with this principle

- You start to "popcorn" the details (which means to quickly and significantly expand a vital kernel of information). Instantly, you've got something much bigger and more valuable on your hands.
- You start to ENJOY the details because you can learn from and leverage them. You may delegate less often.
- You start to LOOK for more details underneath the ones you do see. You become more sensitized. It's a great way to live.

TOP 10 WAYS TO THRIVE ON THE DETAILS

1. DETAILS, SYSTEMS, AND BIG PICTURE: WHAT'S THE RATIO?

"Think globally, act locally." This quote is very popular with environmentalists, and supports a great idea: letting the macro view of your project or goal inspire you to work on its micro aspects. Because micro equals doable. And when enough micro is handled, the big picture snaps into focus almost automatically.

If I could create a magic formula, I'd come up with something like 50 percent micro, 48 percent system, and 2 percent big picture. In other words, pay just enough attention to macro so that you understand what details need either improving or tweaking and what systems you need to install to improve those details. The biggest differences emerge from making lots of little differences.

However, that 2 percent macro focus is essential to showing you the right "little" things to address.

2. THRIVE ON THE DETAILS = BE IN THE PRESENT.

One of the Attraction Principles is to focus on and overrespond to the present. Details generally occur in the present, right? You *can* do something about them and you *can* apply other Attraction Principles to improve them.

Goals (another type of macro), however, are in the future, so attraction doesn't work nearly as well with them, unless you trust that taking great care of the present is what attracts a desirable future. Which is a very sane thing to believe. This, then, is the bridge that connects a focused present with a wished-for future.

3. THRIVE ON THE DETAILS = START THE RIPPLE EFFECT.

There are two ways to create a ripple effect: You can either shake an entire lake or stand on the shore and toss a pebble in.

Think of small details as if they were pebbles you can use to start a ripple effect.

You simply can't underestimate the value of "unimportant" details. Many CEOs focus on the "important big-picture stuff" like strategy and numbers and trends. They'd be a lot smarter to spend 98 percent of their time at the front lines, noticing and improving every single detail of their operations. Because a steady flow of tiny improvements ultimately adds up, like steady bank deposits, to become a huge competitive advantage.

Dealing with details 98 percent of the time equals one heck of a ripple effect. As CEO of your own life, why not give it a try?

4. THRIVE ON THE DETAILS = IMPROVE INSTANTLY.

A detail is something you can instantly improve—straightening a picture, helping a customer service agent to deal better with an individual caller, helping a client solve a small problem. These are things you can do fairly easily.

People sometimes feel so desperate to fix a whole problem that they overlook small, doable fixes they can start making right away. One day down the line, that problem might disappear. Or, at least, it could become a lot less vexing.

Many folks may not see the value in the details, but you can. Focus on what you can instantly fix. You'll get instant gratification. You'll get the perspective that there will be something else you can fix tomorrow, and the next day.

Or you can try to fix it all in one stroke, acting on an inspiration that's bound to come just as soon as you've put yourself under enough stress. Sound plausible? Not really, unless you're attracted to self-sabotage.

The bigger goals and problems really can start taking care of themselves. This is the formula: perspective plus commitment, advanced by realistic, rewarding, and doable micro steps.

5. THRIVE ON THE DETAILS = NOTICE NUANCES AND EARLY MESSAGES.

Just because something is inconsequential, even seemingly irrelevant, doesn't mean that it will always be that way. Think of Detroit in the late sixties, ignoring quality and durability issues at the same time Japanese carmakers entered the U.S. market. The U.S. manufacturers then responded by making ever-uglier, ever less reliable machines and tried to win customers back with "Buy American" advertisements. Except for some of the high-horsepower "muscle cars" of the seventies, collectors show practically no interest in American cars made after the mid-sixties. Relatively recently, the quality and value of Detroit cars has caught up to some degree with those of imports. But not before their industry changed forever and the slow-witted companies lost billions.

Think of Xerox, establishing a research lab in Palo Alto and fostering many innovations that would later put Apple, Microsoft, and many other companies into orbit worldwide, yet squelching their own development of these innovations because they weren't in tune with the existing corporate culture. A staid, established East Coast manufacturer of copiers really didn't care about a West Coast technological plaything like a point-and-click GUI (graphical user interface). Why should they?

You can bet that the corporate culture at Xerox has changed radically since then—out of necessity—just as it has at Ford, GM, and Chrysler.

Details, like the first few Toyotas seen on California's roads, are sometimes valuable precursors or early warning signals. They alert you to something positive or negative about the future.

For some time, businesspeople had the luxury of waiting for real evidence of a trend emerging. But now, things are changing fast and lots of savvy folks *are* paying attention to nuances and details, so you cannot afford to wait.

In your personal life as well as your profession, details are GOLD. Treat them that way.

6. THRIVE ON THE DETAILS = OVERRESPOND TO OPPORTUNITIES.

Another Attraction Principle—overresponding—works well with the Details Principle. Details are the perfect things to overrespond to! They are small, understandable, easily responded to. They also generate immediate feedback.

The next time you're surprised by even a *slight* change in something, overrespond and see what happens. Eddies and ripples in a stream can tell you where the fish are biting!

Once you've become an overresponding type of person, you'll start looking at details with a gleam in your eye! They become your playground. You suddenly have plenty of stuff to overrespond to, right?

7. THRIVE ON THE DETAILS = UPDATE YOUR CAPILLARY SYSTEM.

The ripple effect mentioned earlier is somewhat similar to the Capillary System. (The Capillary System is an Attraction Principle of its own, you'll recall. It says you're better off nourishing a network and marketing system than hard-selling to people who aren't already a part of your system.)

Something that fits into your Capillary System needs to be small. The capillaries in your body can't do a lot with a potato, but they can do a lot of good with the potato's nutrients—after they've been separated out by your gastrointestinal tract.

In order to get integrated into your Capillary System, new information needs to be brought to it in little pieces. Well, details *are* little pieces.

In other words, you can integrate a new idea or detail, such as a small action step, into your life more easily than you can swallow a huge opportunity, either which will give you indigestion (stress), or upon which you'll choke (fear), or which you'll avoid because it seems too big to handle.

Opportunity usually comes to you in stages and movements, a few details at a time, not in big bundles. Ingest lots of wonderful little details during your day, rather than frantically trying to gulp down and digest a huge opportunity.

People who thrive on details will profit. Others will lose.

8. THRIVE ON THE DETAILS = MAKE FEWER ERRORS, SUFFER FEWER CONSEQUENCES, ENJOY LOWER COST.

Two points here: First, it is *extremely* expensive these days to make mistakes. Second, customers are *much* less tolerant of any mistakes.

Consumers want the best for their bucks, and the Internet is just one of many ways for them to make comparisons before they buy. Blind loyalty is now an anachronism, as it should be. Savvy people know how to use all their shopping-around resources, at little or no effort.

That's why reliability and trust are key to customers today. Innovation is a great thing, but once people have dealt with products that don't really deliver on what their advertising claims, they learn to prize reliability more. This means paying strict attention to details. Make sure that what you're offering works 100 percent of the time, not 99 percent of the time.

Many entrepreneurs enjoy starting the next project before the current one has been perfected. The market just won't tolerate casual attention to the details. And, as you know, the last 10 percent of a project often takes the same amount of time and effort as the first 90 percent.

Perfection is an investment, it's rarely simple or automatic. But, like God, it is found in the details.

9. THRIVE ON THE DETAILS = CREATE BETTER MATCHES.

Customers are demanding a perfect fit between what they need and what you offer them. It didn't used to be this tough to please customers, but it sure is now. "Good enough" isn't good enough anymore!

Your computer DEMANDS perfect software code or a modem connection in order to work. Even one misplaced digit messes up the system. And in the same way, you want the details of what you offer to fit 100 percent with the exact needs (details) of the person buying. You want, as much as possible, to create a perfect mix, hookup, connection.

If you are online, or have access to an online system, take a look at a site that I developed for CoachV, *http://www.SuperSensitivePerson.com.* It's all about strategies that can turn being sensitive into an advantage, instead of a hindrance.

The SSP is a pretty exact type of person-to-program match. It lets a specific type of person turn a potentially crippling "fault" into a powerful source of personal evolution. So, when the notion and the label were developed, there was instant attraction. It was a perfect match. It soon became (and still remains) one of CoachV's most popular Web sites.

The same is true in coaching. Clients don't just want good, competent coaches. They want a coach with some exactly relating expertise to solve their precise problems in record time. Without this level of detail, this person-to-program match, coaches won't get hired as readily.

10. THRIVE ON THE DETAILS = INTEGRITY IS MADE EASY.

I believe a lot in the INW model. It goes like this: "Put your *Integrity* first, then your *Needs,* then go do whatever you *Want!*"

Very simple, and very definitely true.

Since integrity comes first, whoever fails to pay attention to integrity-related development has little chance of making it to any further steps. Most integrity problems start with details—early warning signals that we simply ignore until they have become a problem.

That leads to another descriptive model, one that I call the opportunity model: Occurrence>Message>Lesson>Problem>Crisis.

Many of us wait for what has come at us (occurrence) to turn into a noticeable message. Not bad, but you've missed the opportunity already!

Even more of us withhold our response until the ignored or unseen message becomes a lesson or problem. Or, in worst cases, a crisis.

The lesson of this model is that if you immediately respond to things (positive and negative; wanted and unwanted) *as* they come to you, almost all of them can immediately become opportunities. And if you don't, they can turn into something really unpleasant.

Respond to all details immediately. You'll begin seeing and enjoying the opportunities *as* things occur, and you'll completely short-circuit the progression of Message>Lesson>Problem>Crisis.

TOLERATE NOTHING

*When You Put Up with Something,
It Costs You; Unnecessary Costs Are Unattractive*

If you wish to drown, do not torture yourself with shallow water.
—BULGARIAN PROVERB

I don't want no drug-store woman.
—JOHN LEE HOOKER

It's a big part of the human condition to be asked to tolerate a lot of things we don't like. "Don't complain," we're told. "Life is difficult . . ." "Don't rock the boat . . ." "To get along, *go* along . . ." "Be grateful for what you have . . ." "Be *understanding*."

None of the above is bad advice. Being flexible, adaptable, having gratitude—these are all virtues. But sometimes we operate at such a virtuous level that the virtues turn into vices. And we all know it. Beyond a certain point you are simply tolerating too much.

Let's define *tolerations* as things that bug us, sap our energy, and could be eliminated! For most people I've coached, as much as 80 percent of their lives involved carrying tolerations around. There's a small payoff to carrying tolerations—you get to feel kind of noble about your burdens and your forbearance. But, believe me, it's a very expensive source of self-esteem.

Tolerations are holes in your personal success cup; they drain away your contentment and your good fortune. They drain YOU. They make you feel less attractive to yourself. They may even reflect deeper problems, involving self-esteem, which are serious but also fixable.

DISTINCTIONS TO DRAW

TOLERATE VS. COPE—When you tolerate, you view the thing you are tolerating as solvable. When you cope, you've basically resigned yourself to the problem's long-term presence.

TRUTH VS. ACCURACY—When something is accurate, it's provable using current measurement systems like calculators or known facts. Something may be true and yet not provable right now. Truth evolves; accuracy is static.

SYSTEM VS. RACKET—When you behave in ways that cause friction or are costly, you are running a racket. Basically, you are getting what you want the hard way. Tolerations are often a racket. When you realize the inefficiency of rackets, you're ready to evolve a sustainable, low-cost (or no-cost) system to get what you want.

COST VS. PAYOFF—Everything you are tolerating has a positive (albeit expensive) payoff. But as soon as you recognize the high cost, you'll end the toleration.

EXPLANATION VS. JUSTIFICATION—To explain means to make something clearer or plainer. To justify is an attempt to prove something, usually to free oneself of blame or consequence. When you find yourself justifying a part of your life, you are tolerating something.

SOFT COST VS. HARD COST—A hard cost is a traditionally measured and recognized expense, such as money, time, or resources. A soft cost is less tangible but even more important, such as space, opportunity cost, attraction level, timing. Many tolerations are justified because the hard cost is low. But once you start seeing how expensive tolerations are, you recognize the power of soft costs.

TOLERATION FREE VS. INTOLERANT—Someone who is intolerant refuses to allow others the enjoyment of their opinions, rights, or worship. To be toleration free simply means that you don't put up with other people's behavior, or with situations, when they are bad for you. You can be tolerant and at the same time toleration free.

HIGH STANDARDS VS. RIGHTEOUSNESS—When you have high standards, you enjoy holding yourself to high-end behavior. When you are self-righteous, you may do the same thing, but you are also rigidly judgmental of others.

BOUNDARIES VS. WEAPONS—When you say no in a phrasing that is helpful and informative to the other person, you are creating boundaries. When you are combative or piercing, your "no" is being used as a weapon.

If you are like the people I've coached—and most of them have been very together, nonneurotic, and well adjusted—you're probably tolerating not just dozens but literally hundreds of things right now. No matter how deeply entrenched your tolerations are, you can start performing laser surgery on them. Great progress is possible, both short-term and long-term.

Tolerations often represent compromises you've talked yourself into. Maybe it's disrespect from a co-worker. Maybe some parts of your role in a relationship are distasteful to you. Maybe something in your physical surroundings dampens your spirits. But when you were a kid, you didn't tolerate much. You announced your displeasure with a scream or a cry. Later, you got socialized. You were directed to stifle your feelings. Because screaming and crying isn't good behavior to carry into adulthood.

On the other hand, neither is self-negation. There are ways to unlearn tolerating, and there are skills that will let you signal your preferences in smooth, effective, nondisruptive ways.

Tolerating is essentially about desensitizing yourself. If you put some beautiful music on your stereo and suddenly a lot of racket fills the air—horns honking, people yakking, whatever—you're going to have to strain to tune out those unwanted noises. Part of your energy is going into hearing, part into not hearing. Since some of the musical notes are going to be of the same frequencies as the unwanted noises, you'll hear much less music. In the same way, tolerations make you block out a lot of life's happiness, just because you're trying not to be affected by what annoys you.

Because gaining the kind of life you really want means becoming *more* sensitive, not less, tolerations have to go! Only then will you have maximum energy on tap for whatever's most important to you.

WHEN YOU TOLERATE: You and your work become mediocre. Your natural creativity is squelched. You are too often tired.

WHEN YOU STOP: You'll be happier, more fun to be around! You won't be busy tending to ego-bruises, so you'll have extra energy to express your values. You'll have the edge: You'll waste no energy stepping over or around things.

If you proceed intelligently, with a plan, you can reduce and eliminate the drag of tolerations. For some people, blowing up at frustrations is a good first step. But go beyond simply being angry. Don't let yourself get looped into the "No More Mr. Nice Guy!" syndrome—venting, spending emotions, then going back into the same patterns.

Here's how to erase Mr. Nice Guy: Deal with your tolerations in four steps. First, recognize the many actual benefits of tolerating. What payoff are you getting? Is it really something substantial? Or is it simply that you get to avoid standing up for yourself and/or your values?

Second, develop a goal or raise a standard that doesn't permit you to tolerate in that area. Maybe it can be expressed in numbers—how many seconds you'll allow someone to be boring before you redirect, or stop, their routine; how many hours or days you'll invest in a thorny project before you tell yourself, "Enough. Too expensive. Move on!"

Third, reduce and/or eliminate whatever consequence you fear or whatever risk you run in ridding yourself of the toleration. Would super-reserves of time, money, space, etc., help? Very probably. But sometimes all it takes is a resolve not to be pushed around by fear.

Fourth, develop a healthy respect for your tolerations. They might signal an area that needs strengthening: Let them be your "Seeing Eye dog." Before you eradicate your tolerations, learn from them.

How to know you're making progress with this principle

- You don't let yourself near situations or people that will cause problems for you. You catch yourself before you get there.
- You take pride in standing up for yourself in situations when you might previously have been a wimp.
- You go a lot further than usual to correct or improve things that have been bugging you.
- You develop the confidence to speak up and change things, because you want to.
- Draining people walk away from you because they see that you don't tolerate them.
- Your communication skills improve.

THE 10 STEPS TO A TOLERATION-FREE LIFE

Check these items off as you complete them.

1. ____ Understand that putting up with things is good for no one.
2. ____ Make a list of ten things you are tolerating at home.
3. ____ Make the requests and/or take the actions to eliminate those items.
4. ____ Make a list of ten things you are tolerating at work.
5. ____ Make the requests and/or take the actions to eliminate those items.
6. ____ Understand that you're getting payoffs by tolerating things!

7. ____   Be willing and committed to being toleration free.
8. ____   Stop complaining; instead, make a strong request.
9. ____   Invest $1,000 to handle the tasks and/or chores that pain you.
10. ____   After doing steps 1–9 above, do them again!

TOP 10 WAYS
TO TOLERATE NOTHING

As an infant and as a child, you didn't tolerate ANYTHING, did you? (Those were the days!) But as you were raised, you were told to not be so selfish, so it's normal to have coped with this terrible news by learning how to tolerate (aka, accept, be patient, wait your turn, be understanding, look on the bright side, compromise, etc.).

Unfortunately, most of us learned these skills so well that we've become All-Star tolerators. Now it's time to unlearn. Now you know that the more you tolerate, the less attractive you'll be to yourself and to the people to whom you matter most.

The tips below will help you reduce your tolerations by 90–100 percent—hopefully without getting divorced, losing your job, or flinging your Rolodex out the window (unless any of those results would be best for you, of course).

1. REALIZE WHAT TOLERATIONS DO
AND WHY YOU HAVE SO MANY.

Tolerations are like brakes slowing your naturally rapid personal development and evolution process. *Rapid personal development* sounds like a wonderful thing (and it is), but it can also be scary. When there's a wished-for change, we enjoy the exhilaration for a while and then suddenly realize how attached we have been to both the good and the bad of the old situation. Like falling in love, for example, and then later starting to wonder if this is the right person or if it would have been better to stay unattached.

In other words, fear leads us to install tolerations—*anything* that slows things down enough to let us feel a bit more safe. Consciously or unconsciously, we hook up with tolerations in order to feel more secure, especially in key relationships, where the thought of a failure is extremely scary. But when we link a toleration to a relationship, it's like tying a small weight around the neck of a bird. In other words, tolerations hold down our potentials and the potentials in our relationships.

Don't get mad at yourself over this. But do resolve to grant yourself more freedom! The less you tolerate, the better you'll be at saying no to anything that would slow you down. You probably think that it's impossible to eliminate tolerations and fulfill all your roles—parent, wage earner, artist, etc.—at the same time. But you can. It just means responding to things differently.

2. MAKE A LIST OF THE FIFTY THINGS YOU ARE TOLERATING IN YOUR LIFE, BIG AND SMALL.

You *do* have at least fifty things, and it should take you less than twenty minutes to write them down. Writing them down is very important. Instead of just having your mind think about them, let your eyes *see* them.

In particular, write down the tolerations that seem impossible to solve. The big, confrontative ones. It's essential that these are included, because most of your smaller tolerations will usually hinge somehow on big ones.

Include tolerations from the following categories or areas in your list: work / job / business / spouse's habits and behavior / *your* habits and behavior / equipment / car / home / office / other people's attitudes or communication styles.

Nancy White runs a weekly coaching group with six women. When she taught them the Tolerate Nothing Principle and had them write lists of all they were tolerating, they began to get overwhelmed. The lists were growing huge! "A" said she could no longer tolerate sleeping on a futon instead of a traditional bed, but she didn't have enough money to buy one. "B" said she couldn't tolerate being bogged down by errands and having chores eat up her time. Nancy suggested the obvious solution, which they both embraced. B hired A to take some chores off her plate on a weekly basis. A went out and bought a deluxe new bed with her earnings. A very quick win/win solution emerged from writing out a couple of lists. It's as simple as that.

3. IDENTIFY THE BENEFITS OF HAVING
AND MAINTAINING YOUR TOLERATIONS.

This may sound a bit odd, because most people don't like their tolerations at all. Nevertheless, they *are* working for you in some way. Otherwise, they wouldn't exist.

They probably work just like whiskey "works" for an alcoholic, eliminating present-moment pain and/or fear while causing unseen, cumulative damage.

It's important to recognize and admit, very specifically, just how your tolerations *are* paying off for you—maybe even in very practical, and perhaps even healthful, ways.

Note at least one benefit for each of the tolerations on your list. Next, try to weigh cost against benefit, using both your mind and your gut feelings. Which are the most expensive tolerations in your life?

The answers will come, along with the power to act on what you've realized.

4. STUDY THE LIST AND IDENTIFY THE HARD
AND SOFT COSTS OF THOSE TOLERATIONS.

Hard costs are those that are known and measurable—they can be either short-term or long-term costs. Soft costs are those costs that are not as clear—an undercurrent of feeling that something about this toleration is really expensive, but you can't quite express it precisely or completely in words or numbers.

Now that you can identify what is "expensive" about your tolerations, go one step further. Identify, as much as possible, the hard and soft costs for each of your listed tolerations.

5. DECIDE WHETHER IT'S WORTH IT FOR YOU
TO EVOLVE INTO A TOLERATION-FREE ZONE.

In doing the exercises in numbers 2, 3, and 4, you've probably gotten to understand yourself a bit better and also to understand the dynamics (both positive and negative) of tolerations. At some point along this process, you can choose to become a toleration-free zone, or TFZ for short.

Basically, it's an internal change or shift: Tolerations become no longer acceptable to you, so you identify and eliminate them (and their sources).

This doesn't mean that you won't tolerate things in the future. And it doesn't mean that you become intolerant. Rather, it signifies that you realize the hard and soft costs of tolerations and are ready to stop paying. From then on, whenever you encounter tolerations, you'll move quickly to take care of them.

Becoming a TFZ is *not* a promise you make to yourself or to anyone else. Rather, it's just a place you've gotten to that consistently says no to tolerations. This attitude helps you eliminate tolerations more easily, as soon as you discover them, before they can become long-standing habits.

6. PICK THE COSTLIEST TOLERATION ON YOUR LIST AND ELIMINATE IT 110 PERCENT.

110 percent? Yes. The extra 10 percent is the source of the toleration. Let's say that someone can't tolerate her husband's squeezing of the toothpaste tube from the middle. (Some might call this person anal retentive, but that's another Top 10 List.) Rather than just asking hubby to change his habits, or telling him that he must, she might simply start buying toothpaste in a pump dispenser or in a tube that squeezes without a "middle."

This example is simple, imperfect, and probably seems silly. But it does illustrate the 10 percent principle. Another way of looking at it: In a psychology class I took years ago, the professor emphasized that, when faced with an argument, most people want to attack the other person and "take the wind out of their sails!" "But," he always added, "it's much more effective and much easier to take *your* sails out of *their* wind."

So, whether you're confronting a big-scale toleration or a minor one, change something behind it. Create a situation in which it will never come up again. Otherwise, you'll be swatting down the same tolerations over and over. That's not progress.

7. TELL THE PEOPLE CLOSEST TO YOU ABOUT THIS NEW TRACK YOU'RE STARTING.

It's only fair to tell people in your family, at work, and in the other environments of your life that you're undertaking change. Say it in terms they can relate to, but basically let them know that you aspire to be a toleration-free zone. Along with fair warning, be gracious about not accepting things that others have seen you accept in the past. You can be firm and definitive without being hell on wheels.

Rather than pouncing on people, just let them know how much you're changing in that particular area. Spend a little time with them, talking about what has recently become "not okay" with you. In other words, don't get righteous. Be kind. It's only fair, because, in effect, you "educated them" previously that you were okay with some of what you're no longer going to accept.

You may even want to invite them to join you as a TFZ. That's usually the easiest way to include people in the process. They might be thrilled, and empowered, by your strength and resolve. And as they discover the benefits of eliminating some of their own tolerations, they'll have even more respect for you and your wishes to change.

8. FIND A FRIEND, COACH, OR THERAPIST TO SUPPORT YOU IN THIS AREA.

Tolerations are the tail; your life is the dog, meaning that your beginning to identify and eliminate tolerations is going to cause some unexpected changes. The existing symbiosis, balance, and harmony of your life will be upset by your evolution. There *will be* fallout. Waves of some sort or another will be made.

If this weren't true, you wouldn't have tolerated so much for so long.

But now you know that the long-term payoff of subtracting tolerations will be worth the risk of short-term upsets. To make sure the changes you initiate build to the good, and are far more constructive than disruptive, have a highly trusted friend, expert coach, or therapist help you respond, react, and step quickly through. That way, you'll see better how the surprises that come into your life are probably gifts.

Yvon LaPlante, a coach who lives in Montreal, hooked up with a client who had no trouble at all seeing the changes in his life as gifts. It was right after Yvon had completed an attraction telecourse. He'd applied Tolerate Nothing to his own life, because he was a little skeptical. Just as he was beginning to feel some terrific benefits in his own life, a new customer showed up. One who had no money. Although he was a great interior decorator with some impressive work in his past, he had gone bust three years earlier and been on welfare ever since.

First, Yvon had him write down the things he was tolerating—everything from his scruffy shoes to the food he was eating, the way he was speaking, and the way he was behaving. They narrowed his biggest complaints down to ten, including: "Why am I tolerating being on welfare? What's there for me? Why do I want to do that? What's stopping me from doing the things I want to do?" And it boiled down to conversations with his dad, who disapproved of his career and always told him he was no good, that he'd never achieve anything.

Three years earlier, when he lost everything because he honored the demands of an ill-advised contract, his father's words came back to haunt him. So he got discouraged. And he was tolerating being discouraged. That was the linchpin of all his tolerations.

What all ten had in common was that they were energy-taking. His "homework" was to take action on his tolerations every day, and call Yvon at a specific time. The first two days he didn't call on time. Yvon said, "I won't tolerate that." Thereafter, he never missed a call. And things started to change.

The client had an agreement with a maker of reproduction fourteenth-century tapestries to act as a sales representative. But in three years he hadn't sold one. With his coach's help, he developed a positive approach to potential customers. Then he was told to list everyone he knew who might want to buy a tapestry. He didn't think he could come up with more than a handful, but the list gathered momentum as his memory clicked, and soon it held 400 names.

In the first month of his comeback he scored $7,000 in sales. The second, $35,000. Even after more months of similar results, he regularly confers with Yvon to track down more tolerations and eliminate them.

9. PROGRESS DOWN YOUR LIST FOR THE NEXT NINETY DAYS.

Put yourself on a thirty- or ninety-day track and focus on handling thirty or ninety tolerations in that time frame—one a day. You'll find that the momentum this creates makes the process occur faster and with less effort. Why? Because you'll experience more than enough immediate gratification and encouragement to offset any fear.

Realize over these days that even if you don't completely eliminate each toleration you've targeted, you have at least gotten a process started. Even partial elimination is progress and a strength-builder.

10. MAKE SOME IMPORTANT INFRASTRUCTURE/GOAL CHANGES TO SUPPORT YOUR PROGRESS.

As you identify and eliminate tolerations, you'll probably find the need to install some new infrastructure in your life—for two reasons.

First, the tolerations *did* provide support and/or focus for you, even if they were expensive.

Second, the people, job, beliefs, and projects that provide support for *anyone* may change, given how much *you* are changing. Some people will gradually (or perhaps abruptly) leave your circle. And you'll attract new folks with better attitudes. Your goals will change, either subtly or radically.

You'll need to recognize that you will be experiencing a sense of loss, even if it is accompanied by wonderful relief. You'll need to install people, projects, routines, habits, and new behaviors that will create a full and reliable system of support. You're only human (which is high praise, by the way).

STEP 16

SHOW OTHERS
HOW TO PLEASE YOU

Don't Make Them Guess

Is you is or is you ain't my baby?
—LOUIS JORDAN

If this is coffee, please bring me tea, but if this is tea, please bring me coffee.

—ABRAHAM LINCOLN

If you've been able to grasp and accept the first Attraction Principle (Become Incredibly Selfish), then this one will be easy!

There are two parts to the act of showing others how to please you. First, let people know what makes you happiest. Don't make them guess. Second, educate people on what you *require* of them to please you.

Both are different; each is highly important.

It's only fair that the people in your life be told whether you're talking about something you really like or about something you really need from them (as an employer might, for example). The more you can embrace being incredibly selfish, the easier it will become for you to accurately voice what you like, what you want, what you truly need from others. Your being selfish, you see, is really beneficial to the relationships of your life—and to all the people they encompass. No more need for withdrawal and brooding. No more "If he/she REALLY cared, they'd understand that . . ."

When people are shown how to please you, they're usually going to be

---

DISTINCTIONS TO DRAW

REQUEST VS. EXPECT—When you request, you ask for things directly and specifically. To expect is to hope, yet say nothing, or to drop hints.

HAVINGNESS LEVEL VS. NEED—One's "havingness" level is that person's ability to accept and maintain the good things they've attracted or earned. (Many people can't handle success, and so they bring themselves back down.) A need is something that you must have to make the most of your talents or resources. Coaches can help you work on both.

SHOW VS. TELL—It's best to directly show people exactly what you want. Take them shopping. Demonstrate just how to touch your face or kiss you. Don't just tell them what you need—that's too much work for both of you.

SPECIFIC VS. GENERAL—Asking for long-stemmed red roses with baby's breath in a crystal vase on Friday is specific. Saying "Get me flowers, honey" is general. Being specific makes it easy for the other person to please you exactly.

---

very happy that all the agonizing guesswork has been removed—just as you would be if they were equally direct. And if, somehow, they realize that they can't do the things that please you, then everyone is free to reformulate their relationships—instead of waiting for toxic levels of disappointment and resentment to build.

As a coach, I've spoken with people who offered up some very deep revelations about their lives and relationships. I've come to the conclusion that most disruptions occur when one or more people in a relationship—whether it's based on business or on love—start feeling their wants and needs aren't respected. Because those people eventually start thinking how unfair that is and, by damn, how much they've got a right to grab whatever or whoever they can in order to get what they've got coming.

In a sense, they're perfectly right. But among people skilled in showing others how to please them, there are much fewer disruptions, more satisfaction, and—when change is called for—more graceful transitions.

If that sounds like what you want for yourself, please try the following ten points on for size.

How to know you're making progress with this principle

- You start to ask people for things way before you actually need them. In other words, you give people plenty of time to adapt to, or provide, what you need. FYI, it's not fair to demand certain things without properly conditioning the request.
- You feel that you CAN get what you want or need in the exact way that you want or need it.
- You start relating with people who are EAGER to please you because they want to, for smart, healthful reasons.
- You're eventually able to accept and enjoy people who cannot give you want you want or need, because you are getting enough from others.
- You learn what really pleases you.
- You're pleased by others most of the time, not by chance.
- You get better service from your suppliers and have fewer delays, conflicts, or errors.
- You save a lot of wasted time and you stop playing games (just as others stop playing games with you).

TOP 10 WAYS TO SHOW OTHERS HOW TO PLEASE YOU

1. SHOW PEOPLE HOW TO TOUCH YOU PHYSICALLY.

Where on your body? How long? How lightly or strongly? Stationary or moving? Tightly or loosely? Hugs? Handshakes? Proximity?

Some people don't like to receive a kiss, even a light one on the cheek, from anyone except the few people to whom they feel exceptionally close. Women are usually unabashed about kissing close friends of either gender. Lots of men simply are not. They're worried about how they'll be perceived, or about losing some sort of competitive advantage by demonstrating seeming connectedness instead of dominance. And yet there are some men, straight or gay, who can greet another man with a kiss on the cheek as naturally and easily as accepting a handshake.

Touch is a language all its own. And we all need to "get in touch" with what it expresses, and what forms of being "addressed" please us the most. Some people like a few pats on the back to accompany a hug. Others feel that they add a note of condescension, like "There, there, little one, everything's going to be fine." Some people feel uncomfortable hugging a person of the opposite sex. Many are uncomfortable hugging someone of the *same* sex. They still have too much fear left over from adolescence, taunts and worries about sexual identity.

A male friend of mine was in the Peace Corps long ago, stationed on a small island in the mid-Pacific. It was normal there for men who were good friends to walk side by side, holding hands. So one day a native man took my friend's hand as they walked down a path. He felt a shiver in his spine. And he realized he was caught in a dilemma. To pull his hand away would be insulting. But to let it remain was unlike anything he'd ever done before—at least with a man.

After a few seconds of the heebie-jeebies, the strangeness subsided. He realized, "This is just about friendship. I'm a foreigner here and it really feels terrific to be liked."

We all have a lot of unconscious conflict regarding touch and closeness, gender and identity, boundaries and the need for warmth and contact, which is why expressing how you like to be touched will make you much more aware of yourself.

2. TRAIN PEOPLE TO LISTEN TO YOU.

Feeling unheard is one of the most frustrating things in life. It's important to your evolution in life to make sure people receive and somehow respond to your words. To your feelings. To the spirit of what you're saying. Even if you feel you're being rude by demanding that level of respect.

Can you allow them to listen with a critical ear, or do you need a generous one? There's nothing wrong with wanting an honest reaction, tempered with kindness. In business especially, you have to accept that your ideas will sometimes get shot down. The search is always on for approaches and concepts that will bring advantage. But the idea you put forth is not you, just a transitory and renewable part of yourself.

All the same, criticism should be constructive instead of vicious. Take the initiative. Show people how to criticize you and your ideas effectively, how to lead you to improvement instead of rancor.

How long should people listen to your thoughts? What will make you feel that you've been wonderfully heard? Let everyone know. It's not rude to clear a path toward mutually rewarding relationships. It's smart and fulfilling.

3. TEACH PEOPLE HOW TO SHOW THEY CARE.

What would you like to receive? What gift? What color? What size? How often? From where? What kindness? Time? Love? Surprises? Trips? Intervention? A book? Concepts? Wisdom? Flowers? Music?

Gifts are yet another form of language. Every Christmas, every birthday, people try—sometimes way too frantically—to speak that language from the heart. Take away the strain. Don't force people to guess. Coyness and bashfulness in this area really aren't virtues. Give everyone lots of options and ideas, representing lots of "price points," so they can make you feel cared for without busting their budget.

People like to say, "It's the thought that counts." More exactly, it's the recognition that counts. And only you know for sure what things, or what gestures, will elicit your best feelings.

4. SHOW PEOPLE HOW TO RESPOND TO YOU.

This is an extension of number 2 above. Take pride in—and responsibility for—showing people what to say and how to say it, what part of your communication to respond to, what tone of voice to use, how rapidly to respond and for how long.

Again, it's not pushiness; it's the opening of a door. Minor flusters are possible, especially while you're new at this skill. But major breakthroughs are going to result soon.

5. TELL PEOPLE WHAT YOU NEED FROM THEM BEFORE IT BECOMES A PROBLEM.

Sometimes it's appropriate to be stoic. Sometimes you're making the best of a bad situation, dealing with someone who's a "problem child" and hoping you'll never have to again. But the very act of bearing up signals to others that you've got talent for dealing with stress. So they'll remember to direct it your way again and again.

Whether you're dealing with a difficult person, or a very nice person, tell them what you need. It might be that you need more time. Maybe even less time. Or more space. More attentiveness. More concern. Sensitivity. Respect. Tolerance. Acceptance. Endorsement. Different performance. Different results. A change of attitude or perspective.

The simple act of stating your needs reveals how important they are to you. Good people will find a way to make accommodations. Others may not, and then you'll know it's time to break a negative pattern and get yourself out of a stressful, untenable situation or relationship—which sounds like a win to me.

Last year, a woman who has since begun a coaching practice in addition to her regular job found herself in a bind at work: There was a bullying, harassing person in her office. Management was clearly not going to do anything about him. And she wanted to move to Colorado, anyway, to be closer to her parents and siblings. But she couldn't afford to quit.

Her coach encouraged her to start telling people—the bully in particular—NO. She stopped tolerating things such as being "volunteered" for extra work and being insulted by mean-spirited "humor." Management soon moved her to a temporary job, where she found people valued, respected, and honored her. Three weeks later, a job application she'd sent in five years earlier somehow worked its way to the top of the pile. So she suddenly had a brand-new job—in Colorado Springs.

This new job drew her into a more human relations–oriented area, which she had really wanted to enter. And she became clearer and closer emotionally with her family than before. "It is as if the rewards go on and on," she told me. "I took care of myself, I told the truth, and everything else fell into place."

6. TRAIN PEOPLE HOW TO SPEAK TO YOU FOR MAXIMUM IMPACT.

This is related to numbers 2 and 4 above, but it turns the tables. When you're in the role of listener, what's the best way to ensure that both you and the speaker get the message and respond constructively? Help people strike the right tone and deliver the most useful content with the most appropriate timing and suitable style.

Jennifer, a teacher in a well-to-do suburb, consulted a coach recently. After fifteen years in the same school, she had just accepted a position in a new one. The principal was known to be very old-fashioned and prone to yelling at people who displeased him. Since Jennifer is naturally assertive and vivacious, she was worried that her new boss would have a hard time with that. She wanted to let the principal know that she was committed to being herself and yet to keeping him happy with her performance as well. If there was a problem, she wanted him to come and tell her. At the same time, she didn't want to tolerate being yelled at. So she was coached to tell the principal that if he ever became angry, rather than yelling and screaming, he would come to her and say, "Dear Jennifer . . ." The endearment would let her know she'd done something wrong but would also soften the anger and let Jennifer be open to hearing the problem.

Such a small adjustment, but one that could make a world of difference.

Fun doesn't automatically happen just because you go on a vacation. Satisfaction doesn't happen just because you eat a meal or make love. Communication doesn't happen just because someone says something to you. A lot depends on style and grace.

In all of the above areas, and in many more, you have a right to have preferences and a duty to make your preferences clear. When you do, you'll be receiving more "messages," with more satisfaction and more potential for stirring your personal growth.

7. Inform people how to reach you in a way that will get you to say, "Yes, I want to buy."

A relationship with a merchant or vendor is, in many ways, like a relationship with a friend, spouse, or lover. The aim is mutual satisfaction, on a sustaining basis. Anything else erodes the situation and forces a change of "partners." And you'll save tremendous amounts of precious time if you're definite about what you want: features, functions, benefits, value, pricing, flexibility, dependability, availability, fittingness, quality.

Again, it's a skill-set. Skill number one is selfishness-based. It involves understanding that you're worthy. In your passage through this world, you deserve to get what you want! It gets stronger with each usage. And it doesn't mean that you're being rotten.

Businesspeople—like lovers, or any other kind of associates—are very happy when they know how to please you. If you're not sure what will do the trick, engage them in dialogue. Ask them to educate you on what's good and valuable about what they offer. If they can't, or won't, it's time to "date" somebody else.

8. SHOW PEOPLE HOW TO DELIVER SERVICE
IN A WAY THAT WILL INSPIRE YOU TO REFER OTHERS.

This builds on number 7 above. Word of mouth is the surest and sweetest form of advertising for any businessperson. Let them do the calculations on how much they're willing to "spend" to get it. You supply them with a clear view of how to get you satisfied enough to make recommendations to others.

It may be as simple as extra time spent ensuring you get the maximum good from their service. Or genuine care and concern that you are well pleased. Obvious and sincere perfectionism. Matching their delivery of service to your exact needs. Professionalism. Follow-up. Listening. What-ever will make the transaction undeniably win/win.

When you give someone word-of-mouth advertising, you're giving them something of huge value: your good word. If a friend takes your recommendation and gets anything less than great service, you'll look like a fool. So don't be afraid to say it flat out—"If you're good, I'm willing to recommend you to friends. What are you willing to do to convince me how good you are?"

Everyone likes to perform at their best, and everyone is responsible for knowing how much they're willing to put out and what they deserve in return. Good people take pride in pleasing an exacting, well-informed customer.

9. TELL PEOPLE WHAT THEY CAN DO
THAT WILL CAUSE YOU TO ADORE THEM.

Give people the opportunity to make it EASY for you to love, respect, and enjoy them fully. Help them make it impossible for you to resist. Instruct and coach them in all areas of what will make you adore them—don't make them guess what to do. Sure it's NICE if they figure everything out by themselves, but don't wait for that to happen. Assuming you want to adore and fully enjoy someone, and they want to be adored and enjoyed, they'll be open to learning how to make the magic happen.

10. TELL PEOPLE THE SHIFT OR FUNDAMENTAL CHANGE IN ATTITUDE YOU WANT OR NEED FROM THEM.

From negative to positive. From closed to open. From unwilling to willing. From rigid to free. From righteous to humble. From acquiring to grateful. From seeking to enjoying. Because attitude conditions results, shifting to a positive direction can be one of the most important events in your relationship with someone. An attitude you dislike makes you feel you need even more result—more money because of what you have to put up with, more service because of surliness or an unpleasant atmosphere, more goods for the money, and so on.

In an environment of mutuality and freely given respect, demands soften and people find mutually agreeable ways to arrive at win/win outcomes.

ENDORSE YOUR WORST WEAKNESSES

When You Can Accept and Honor the Worst Part of Yourself, You're More Accepting of Others

To the dull mind all of nature is leaden. To the illuminated mind the whole world sparkles with light.

—RALPH WALDO EMERSON

A strong and well-constituted man digests his experiences (deeds and misdeeds all included) just as he digests his meats, even when he has some tough morsels to swallow.

—FRIEDRICH NIETZSCHE

If you're like most people, you probably either ignore, hide, deny, or attempt to compensate for or overcome your weaknesses. After all, they *are* weaknesses, right? And weaknesses *aren't* good.

True—until now. Because now you're going to look at those flaws differently. Not through rose-colored glasses but through a filter that blocks out shame and blame, letting you see so-called weaknesses as your gateways to higher potential.

The trick is to find a way to love and honor your worst weaknesses—and to forget trying to improve on them. Sound impossible? Afraid you'll lose your humility? Stop growing? In fact, you may be better off with a little less humility anyway, and you will actually open yourself to tremendous growth, personally and professionally.

DISTINCTIONS TO DRAW

ENDORSE VS. ACCEPT—To endorse is to approve, to sanction. To accept is merely to consent or agree to.

WEAKNESS VS. FAULT—A weakness is a lack of something, a feebleness. A fault is a defect. Weaknesses can be strengthened; flaws must be fixed.

HONOR VS. PROTECT—To honor your weaknesses means to respect and even revere them. To protect means to defend, preserve, cover, or shield your weakness.

FEEL PROUD VS. HAVE PRIDE—To feel proud of your weaknesses means that you admire them as part of yourself. To have pride means that you are arrogant about them and thus resistant to change.

SURRENDER VS. COMPENSATE—When you surrender to a weakness, you accept it and can go on from there to discover what is extraordinary about it. To compensate means to make up for the weakness, which is a limiting approach.

The following Top 10 List will direct you to a new, more affirmative way of seeing the personal aspects you've wanted to change or eliminate for so long.

How to know you're making progress with this principle

- You see the link between your worst weakness and your strength. It's very exciting to grasp the connection.
- You care less about your weaknesses and enjoy your strengths more.
- You really DO feel terrific about your weaknesses.
- You recover a lot of energy you'd been wasting on self-recrimination.
- You quit fearing and running from the truth about yourself and others.
- You stop trying to become someone you are not.
- You're able to look at all the parts of yourself, which releases your potential.
- You're released from shame about your past.
- Life begins to make more sense because you see how your weakness has actually helped you significantly.

TOP 10 WAYS TO ENDORSE
YOUR WORST WEAKNESSES

1. YOUR WORST WEAKNESS MAY BE THE FASTEST WAY
TO ACCESS THE BEST PARTS OF YOURSELF.

What IS your worst weakness? Are you a wimp? A liar? Insensitive? Impatient? Selfish? A dilettante? Or worse?

Just for now, pick one vexing flaw. If you get to the bottom of your worst weakness you WILL find something of incredible value. For example, if you feel you are a wimp, it may just be that you are a supersensitive person (which is a real gift). If you tell lies, you may be someone who is built for a much better life (one that brings truth to the lie)—reason enough to set high goals! If you are insensitive, perhaps you are associating with the wrong people and it's time to freshen up the Rolodex. And so forth.

Instead of trying to fix your worst weakness, look to understand what it points to, what it tells you. When you see behind the curtain (which is much easier to do if you've decided to give shame a rest), you'll know what the next level of your life should include.

Weaknesses, then, can really be great signposts. They can tell you where to go and/or what to focus on next. Use your weaknesses to get rid of role and goal confusion.

2. WHAT IF YOU BEGAN ACCEPTING/FEELING PROUD
OF YOUR WORST WEAKNESS?

Hopefully, the comments in number 1 above will make weakness sound and feel, well, less weak. It's pretty common advice today to accept your weaknesses instead of criticizing yourself for them, or blaming others. However, I am suggesting that you go a lot further than mere acceptance.

Here's a story that will illustrate what I mean. It's from Madeleine Homan, a coach who lives in the Hudson Valley in New York and does particularly great work with creative people.

One of her clients, a writer in his early thirties whom we'll call Lawrence, writes a very respected, successful newsletter in a booming industry. It's a massive publication, always intelligently written, with extremely valuable information flowing through long essays. It's a huge job, and Lawrence has produced terrific results. A recent magazine article called him "the most desired man" in his field.

His company hired Madeleine, though, because he was having trouble meeting deadlines. It was a nightmare. Meanwhile, he was stressed out. No social life. No self-care. She advised him to cut expenses, which backed off some of the stress, and to get to a gym, which made him healthy enough to withstand whatever stress he couldn't get rid of yet.

Tied in with his deadline problem was what Lawrence considered his major flaw: He had a way of "procrastinating" before getting down to work. Once he got started, though, he wouldn't stop for twelve or fourteen hours. He wanted to change or eliminate this procrastination habit.

His coach felt he should just realize, and endorse, the fact that that was just how he worked. As an accomplished artist in her own right, Madeleine believes that in any kind of point-of-creation work, some amount of "wasted" time is necessary to the creative process and therefore is not something that we can dispense with.

What Lawrence saw as a weakness, she asked him to see as strength and as a necessary part of his creative process. Together they created a whole new schedule and time structure that included "wasted" time—sometimes up to half a day. Once he stopped judging himself, he observed that the longer he procrastinated, the longer he worked and the more he got done. Time freed up for him. He was able to work on projects of his own that really interested him. That gave his existence something that had been missing because he'd been so obsessed with his newsletter that there was no room for anything else, which caused some resentment. And some of Lawrence's inability to meet his deadlines was an outgrowth of that resentment.

There were other steps, certainly. But once he saw his natural creative style as a strength, not as procrastination, all resentment and all deadline problems vanished.

Acceptance implies giving up or giving in. Endorsing means being grateful for, and proud of, your weaknesses.

Wouldn't that be an amazing evolutionary step for you—actually feeling great about your worst weakness? What might happen if folks could hear and feel this new excitement on your part? Imagine the ease you would feel inside and the reserves of energy you'd have for focusing on positive directions.

Acceptance heals, and that's good. But to actually embrace your weaknesses is to embrace the TRUTH, and doing that will set you free. Big difference. Get it working for you.

3. YOUR WORST WEAKNESS CAN BECOME A COMMUNITY-NETWORK BUILDER FOR YOU.

What's your worst weakness? How are you dealing with it? What have you learned? What other weaknesses do you have as a result of having this weakness? Who else is in the same boat?

Your weakness may be the admission ticket to a "club" of others dealing with the same thing. And by getting to know others with a similar weakness, you'll find some of the support you need to convert your weakness to a strength. You suddenly have many minds working on a common goal, instead of you slugging it out by yourself.

Lots of people have a tough time asking for help with anything. But it can be one of the wisest choices you'll ever make. And an opportunity for someone else to be proud of what they've done.

Most of the time, helpers get more positives out of the deal than the one who is helped. And they know it. That's why they're so willing to extend themselves.

Of life's many paradoxes, this is one of the sunniest. Why not take advantage of it?

4. ACCEPT AND ENDORSE YOUR WORST WEAKNESS BY BEING GRATEFUL FOR HOW WELL IT'S GOTTEN YOU TO **THIS** PLACE IN YOUR LIFE.

Give credit to your greatest weakness. It's helped you get to where you are today.

Write down a list of ten very specific ways it has helped you (whether these were positive or negative at the time) in events, situations, conditions, or relationships that were either triggered or exacerbated by your weakness. Include in your list all the times you were in some way protected by your weakness.

Take your time. Before long you'll find a pretty impressive list!

One of my clients felt a bit down on himself because he'd always both idolized and quietly resented a very accomplished older brother. But in trying to override that weakness, he'd become an NFL standout, with a couple of Super Bowl rings. And he realized that without that goad, he might never have gone half as far.

Your own story may not have that much high-profile drama, but I'm sure it includes important accomplishments that were somehow spurred by trying to overcome a weakness. This is a theme in almost everyone's life.

But if you let a weakness continue to be a spur, you become like a person trying to satisfy their thirst by drinking seawater. So be thankful, and also be confident that you've grown enough that you no longer need to be driven by shame and/or overcompensation.

5. LINK YOUR WORST WEAKNESS TO YOUR BIGGEST STRENGTH— SEE THE RELATIONSHIP BETWEEN THEM.

My biggest weakness? I am WAYYYYYY too sensitive to other people's energy, criticism, even to their praise. It either upsets, devastates, or seduces me. I feel that I have no control over it. Yet, it's also become my biggest strength.

To honor the weakness, I've had to change my life, my priorities, and how I work. I've become even MORE sensitive in the process. But now it's a skill, and a gift. Instead of trying to overcome it, I now use it to create new businesses. My sensitivity means that I can feel what other people want and need in their lives. And since I've designed my lifestyle and my workstyle to my own psychological dimensions, through Web sites, frequent vacations, lots of mobility, and enough privacy to offset all the communicating I do, I don't get torpedoed anymore by being so sensitive to other people. I don't get overwhelmed. I get inspiration. And I start asking myself, "What would be a great, really valuable product or service to take care of this need I sense?"

What you might call your biggest weakness is really your body or your spirit saying, "There's something really great down here. You'd better make some changes before I'll let you see what it is!"

In other words, a "weakness" represents a secret you're keeping from yourself. So, why not decide to trust yourself with it? Use a coach, or a therapist, or a good and savvy friend to help you get through.

6. FOCUS ON YOUR STRENGTHS, BUT INCLUDE YOUR WEAKNESSES AND THEN DELEGATE THEM.

I've coached a lot of clients who get some sort of satisfaction from improving their weaknesses. For example, if they are really bad at keeping up on filing, they'll take pride in setting up the world's best filing system—only to have it dismantle itself within a month.

All that effort for a short-term sense of "success," which is followed (unless their attitudes change) by a sense of shame or defeat. Not such a good return on investment.

Better to focus on your strengths, until they bring you to a point where you can afford to pay others to handle your weaknesses.

For example, I'm really bad with paperwork, follow-up phone calls, dealing with the public, and paying bills. So what? My virtual assistant does ALL of that for me. Instead of pushing myself uphill, I concentrate on things that come easier and reward me more.

She happens to be good at these things, and to her they're just a piece of business, not an interruption or an unwanted chore.

Sure, I could MAKE myself do all this stuff (after all, I'm a CPA), but it would be at a high cost personally, emotionally, spiritually, and financially in terms of lost time and lost opportunity.

Any service that covers your weaknesses for you, especially if it keeps you from having to try to become someone you're really not, is really a smart investment. The cost is quickly absorbed and a nice profit begins to build, because you're now dealing from strength nearly all day long.

Part of becoming irresistibly attractive is to become superconductive. How can you become superconductive while forcing yourself to overcome a weakness? Forcing yourself to do unwanted stuff is a high-friction enterprise. You may feel like it makes you noble, but it doesn't. It just makes you numb.

I've learned to USE the fact that I'm lousy with paperwork and dealing with the public. I used to be embarrassed and ashamed. Now I let it be an asset, a strength. I deal with lots of people, but they're "prescreened," because they've worked their way up through my Capillary System. They wouldn't be talking to me if they hadn't already figured out, on their own time, that I have something to offer that could give them a lot of benefit. And I know we're likely to have low- or no-friction, mutually rewarding dealings.

Make that leap in your own life. Give yourself permission to let your strengths take care of you. Let someone who's strong in other areas take care of your weaknesses. It's one of the best investments you can make.

7. EDUCATE PEOPLE ON WHAT YOU DON'T DO WELL, UNTIL THEY FULLY UNDERSTAND.

Part of the process of "converting" your weaknesses into strengths is to educate others about exactly what those weaknesses are. In other words, be human. Take the attitude "I'd rather be hated for who I am than adored for who I'm pretending to be."

Of course, it'd be nice to be adored for my weaknesses, but that's a corner of Fantasyland the folks at Disney haven't gotten around to building yet.

Until they do, here are the types of things to say to yourself or others about specific weaknesses: "I'm really bad at responding to this type of E-mail [phone call, etc.] from someone I don't know. I need to pass on this."

"I'm terrible with secrets; I gossip. Please don't tell me anything you don't want broadcast."

"Paperwork is the bane of my existence. That's why I invoice you by telephone."

"I don't have the attention span to take notes of our coaching sessions. You'll need to keep track of your own goals and progress."

Get the point? You don't get arrogant with your weaknesses: You let them help you to be more truthful. As soon as you stop covering them up, they can become strengths. Use them to shape all your relationships to your liking.

8. BY KNOWING WHAT YOU CANNOT DO AND CANNOT CHANGE, YOU ARE FREE TO ENJOY WHAT DOES WORK WELL.

Taking the path of least resistance is an important strategy in the Attraction OS. So is surrendering to what is so.

The point is this: Spend your energy where it flows and pulls you forward. It's far more attractive than getting your self-esteem and success by overcoming your limitations and natural preferences. If you have strong character (see Step 20), the line of least resistance can actually lead you upward—without striving.

9. WHEN YOU CAN ENDORSE YOUR WORST WEAKNESS, YOU CAN ACCEPT THE HUMANNESS OF OTHERS.

This is key. When YOU get to the place where you see, recognize, accept, and endorse your worst weakness as a strength, or at least a potential strength, you'll be able to see other people in a similar light. You'll take things less personally and be less affected by the weaknesses of others. Unpleasant or unfocused behavior becomes more like an interesting movie you're watching, less like a threat or even an annoyance.

Putting up a front is very expensive to your own humanity. Because you not only feel you have to be stronger but also feel that you have to shun people who don't meet the false standard you're trying to reflect. That's why false fronts actually increase the feelings of insecurity they're meant to mask.

Learning to view your weaknesses with some benevolence will open you to being less judgmental about those of other people.

I'm not saying *tolerant*. You still shouldn't tolerate things that bug you. I'm saying nonjudgmental, which means that you give everybody else the same freedom and respect you give yourself, weaknesses included.

And THAT will really make you attractive—to others as well as to yourself.

10. ENDORSING YOUR WORST WEAKNESS IS JUST THE BEGINNING OF THIS ATTRACTION PRINCIPLE.

You probably understand this, but let's make doubly sure: This principle is not about feeling good about saying to someone, "Listen, Jack, this is my weakness; get over it!" You aren't handing yourself a license to be a jerk, or adopting an excuse not to evolve through your weakness.

To truly endorse your weakness you WILL need to become 100 percent responsible for how it affects you, your life, and everyone around you. Don't ever be ashamed of your weakness, but you also shouldn't wear it like a badge of honor.

Endorsing your worst weakness, then, is just a beginning, a way to see new possibilities, a necessary step toward freedom.

SENSITIZE YOURSELF

The More You Feel, the More You'll Notice
and Respond to the Many Opportunities in the Present

> The aim of life is to live, and to live means to be aware, joyously, drunkenly, serenely, divinely aware.
>
> —HENRY MILLER

> Marta keeps telling me I should try to be more aware of things as they're happening. I think it's Marta who says that.
>
> —JACK HANDEY

It's fair to say that, compared to the exhortative, self-sacrificing, claw-your-way-to-the-top approaches that many people use, attraction is a quieter, more subtle approach to living and success: a sophisticated, high-end personal operating system.

To benefit from attraction, you need to become more sensitive to yourself, your environments, and to subtle changes in others. Why become more sensitive? Because the less sensitive, more numb, or more loud you are, the less you will notice what is actually going on around you.

For attraction to work well, you need to sense things earlier than the average person. That will allow you to respond earlier, with more precision and higher effectiveness.

If you don't sensitize yourself, opportunities pass you by before you have a chance to respond to them. Numbness perpetuates ignorance, causes delayed reactions, and is just plain dumb.

It's likely that you don't have to sensitize yourself very much at all.

DISTINCTIONS TO DRAW

SENSITIZED VS. SENSITIVE—To sensitize is to make something more sensitive. To be sensitive means to be able to feel, to be able to receive impressions. Most people haven't been sensitized enough to feel the nuances, subtleties, and opportunities of life.

SUPERSENSITIVE VS. SENSITIVE—Supersensitivity is a trait affecting about 20 percent of the population. Supersensitives feel and experience much more than the average person and are often overwhelmed by situations, events, environments, and other people. Supersensitives who develop additional skills can really thrive.

NUMB VS. UNAWARE—Some people numb themselves with behaviors or substances. They may be quite aware of things, but their numbness keeps them from responding to what they are aware of. End the numbing and the awareness emerges. Other people are simply not clued in to life. They are ignorant of concepts and dynamics. The solution is training, intellectual stimulation, and sensitization.

AWARENESS VS. KNOWLEDGE—Awareness means that you are conscious, tuned in, apprised. Knowledge means a clear perception of the facts. Awareness can include things that aren't yet perceived as facts, yet are still very real. These subtleties can be the richest part of life.

FEELING VS. KNOWING—To feel is to sense, to be impressed, to be touched. To know is to have information. Both are important; high levels of both are extremely powerful. Most folks favor one over the other.

ENVIRONMENTS VS. SITUATIONS—An environment is a surrounding condition, influence, or force. A situation is a relative position amidst circumstances. Most folks are busy trying to improve their situation when they should focus on changing their environments.

MOTIVATION VS. PAVLOVIAN REACTION—To be motivated means to be moved to do something, usually with room to choose how you'll do it. A Pavlovian reaction occurs when you're moved to do something but lack the capacity to think or choose.

CHOICE VS. PRIORITY—When you prioritize, you put in order what you have. When you choose, you can select something from available options or from what occurs to you at the moment.

FEELING VS. EMOTIONAL REACTION—To feel is to sense what is occurring right now. When you have an emotional reaction, you are reacting to more than what has just occurred, usually because an unresolved memory of a similar incident has been triggered.

You're probably already at a high level and likely to realize big gains from simply getting away from people and/or behaviors that now desensitize you.

Of course, *sensitive* has a bad name in some circles. Some folks think anyone described by that word is a hothouse flower—too delicate for the real world. Talented, maybe, but not up to dealing with reality.

Don't believe that nonsense for a second.

It is true, though, that people who are sensitive need to be aware of how they are different from average folks, and how to manage their more feeling, more perceptive nature so it works as an asset. Sensitivity is like sexuality, wealth, or any other powerful force in life: charged with energy that can be richly enjoyed but that must be guided so it doesn't work against you.

The Top 10 List below will help you get in touch with your innate sensitivity and show how it can be used to create success.

How to know you're making progress with this principle

- You notice things earlier or more deeply than you ever did before.
- You take steps to remove those things that have kept you desensitized.
- You put more credence in what you're feeling and sensing than in the facts you know and the opinions you hold.
- You notice and leverage details others miss.
- You understand your body's signals, so decisions are easier to make.
- You can instantly self-correct because when you've taken a wrong turn, you sense it immediately.

TOP 10 WAYS
TO SENSITIZE YOURSELF

1. IDENTIFY AND REDUCE OR ELIMINATE NUMBING SUBSTANCES.

Alcohol, narcotics, and sugar are proven numb-ers. You may be able to use them without causing yourself obvious problems. But you ARE reducing your body's natural ability to consistently feel and be present.

You may feel more while under the influence, but the experience is always temporary and not sustainable. It's a seduction. Yes, alcohol does shut down anxiety. That's why people call it a "social lubricant." But it never advances you beyond those anxieties lastingly, the way counseling, coaching, or modern medicine can. Cocaine will lift you away from your insecurities to a temporary sense of near-limitless power. But it ultimately drops you lower than before, and it costs you plenty along the way, both in money and in mental and physical health.

Most experts see substance abuse as a sign of depression. Actually, that's good news. Depression, though terrible and reaching epidemic proportions in modern society, is also now highly treatable.

Newer medicines, which succeed in some 80 percent of cases, don't hype people up or slow them down. They simply allow brain chemistry functions to flow at normal levels. Sort of like cleaning a clogged fuel line so gas can get from tank to engine. Typically, people who are prescribed these medicines soon hear themselves saying, "I feel like myself now!"

If you're drawn to numbing substances, look at that fact closely. Get trusted and expert medical counsel. It could be the best favor you'll ever do yourself.

2. IDENTIFY AND REDUCE OR ELIMINATE NUMBING BEHAVIORS.

Watching television, overeating, "zoning out" on unpleasant realities, love and/or sex addiction are all examples of numbing behaviors. They involve overloading your senses with too much input or not being able to "feel" unless when engaged in a specific activity.

Of course, nothing is necessarily evil about any of these items, if they aren't happening too frequently. But, as in number 1 above, the "overload" experience is always temporary and not sustainable. And a need to overindulge may signal a deeper, yet very fixable, problem.

3. IDENTIFY AND REDUCE OR ELIMINATE NUMBING ENVIRONMENTS OR SITUATIONS.

If you're reading this book, you're interested in success. Good for you! There's no reason why you shouldn't be. But the pursuit of success, by old-fashioned means, can be extremely stressful. Especially if it involves overwork, traffic jams, rushed or skipped mealtimes, neglected family or social life, intense pressures, and so on.

If you're in a stressful home, work, or lifestyle situation, you probably can't *afford* to feel all that is going on. It may be too much for your body, your heart, or your mind. So, the best thing might be to get out of that environment before opening up your senses.

Does this involve quitting your job, divorcing, moving away? It might. Nobody but you can answer that question. But finish this book before you decide. And get more acquainted with the infinite number of ways you can get positive change rolling. With the right attitude and skill-sets installed, you might be more able to influence others positively than seems possible to you right now.

In itself, the process of becoming sensitized is usually enough to steer a person toward big environmental and situational changes—without having to "decide" to. When your body has been sensitized properly, it won't PERMIT you to remain in situations that are no good for you. Your body knows even if your mind resists. And being tuned in to the body's reactions is a high form of wisdom.

4. IDENTIFY AND CLEAN UP WHAT MOTIVATES YOU.

It's hard to feel what's present around you when you're busy striving. Striving energy calls up adrenaline, overriding your more subtle "feeling" energy. It's like television—a powerful, overstimulating force that can make it hard to keep much awareness of your larger senses.

Much of what motivates us is fairly expensive and future-oriented. Feelings live in the present. However, emotional reactions, often confused with feelings, live in both the past and the future.

Feeling and reacting are two very different things, then, with very different consequences. Feeling unites you with the present. Reacting sees a cue in the present and is triggered to call up unresolved material from the past.

Feeling is constant renewal, characterized by sensing open horizons and fresh potentials. Reacting is entrapment, characterized by unpleasantness and a sense of stale inevitability. It's obvious which of the two any sane person would choose. And it's vital that you see and embrace the distinction. Many people are completely clueless on this one.

For those who understand the differences between feeling and reacting, it's very, very possible to be 100 percent motivated by the present—although this is a major shift for almost everyone. Here's a wonderful example: One of our CoachV graduates has a client who is a minister and a writer. For ten years he had been planning a deeply philosophical book. It took more than a year's worth of his spare time to create a manuscript.

But he was not able to complete the book because he got completely stuck. He was frustrated and discouraged.

He was so attached to the outcome that he couldn't feel joyful in creating. His coach asked about *other* books he might someday write. And it turned out that he'd been, in quiet moments, writing modern-day stories based on the parables of Jesus, and these stories flowed effortlessly for him.

Suddenly his course was clear: Park the "important" project for now and write his parable-based book. He finished *that* book in three months without any strain, motivated by joy instead of fear. Even so, he worried whether it was good enough to be published. He sent excerpts to friends in the coaching community. One of them happened to know an agent, who decided he liked the manuscript enough to try to get it published.

The minister now sees himself as someone who creates for the joy of it, not for perfectionism or praise. Once he cleaned up his motivation, doors began to open.

5. MAKE THE CHOICE, SET THE PRIORITY, IN ORDER TO SENSE AND FEEL ALL OF WHAT IS OCCURRING INSIDE AND OUTSIDE OF YOU.

When it comes to feeling and sensing, it's common to play the "ignorance is bliss" game. Many of us would simply rather not know! And that's completely understandable.

However, once you choose to WANT to feel and sense more, you soon become intrigued and fascinated by all that you are sensing and feeling. And you really WANT to know, because it really is interesting.

To take this step, you have to believe your feelings are so worthwhile that you're going to become an expert in them and, ultimately, going to respond to them just as faithfully as you respond to facts and statistics.

Your feelings are a kind of undiscovered truth, too evanescent to be expressed in numbers but often more valuable than anything that's been properly validated and added up.

The shift toward crediting what you feel and sense is really profitable, but it takes some people a while to see the tangible benefits. That's all right. Proceed at your own pace.

6. IDENTIFY AND REDUCE OR ELIMINATE
THE EMOTIONAL BLOCKS TO YOUR NATURAL ABILITY TO FEEL.

Therapists can be very helpful in the process of emotional healing. Sometimes, emotional scars from childhood or adulthood get between us and our ability to sense and respond to the *full* spectrum of life and its feelings.

If you've got some emotional damage or baggage, you're tethered to the past. And you know it because the same wrong situations keep recurring in your life, like bad dreams you just can't shake.

It isn't weakness to look for help, it's self-enabling and very intelligent. You'd never hesitate to take your car to a mechanic if its valves clattered or its exhaust gases leaked into the passenger compartment. Believe me, the health of your psyche holds more sway over your present and future happiness than the condition of your car! If you even *suspect* a problem, have the courage to get it checked out.

7. REALIZE THAT MORE KNOWLEDGE IS CONTAINED
IN FEELING AND SENSING THAN IS CONVEYED LITERALLY,
INTELLECTUALLY, OR LINEARLY.

If you've been looking for a practical or financially beneficial reason to get on the sensitivity track, you've just found it! As the information age progresses, many more customers will be attuned to what real quality is. Sensitivity will become an ever-greater business asset.

Words and language simply aren't able to keep up with changing events in business or evolving customer preferences. By the time a subtle change is first noticed (usually far later than it should be) and this information is converted into English and passed up to those empowered to make changes, then sold to the buyers, and eventually made available to consumers, the *original* trend that was noticed may have changed again. Or, more likely, some key aspect of the original information got lost in the chain of command. That's why there are so many "me-too" products out there, fighting for whatever market share is left, while more visionary, more sensitive companies keep evolving their products in tune with consumer preferences as much as possible. That's why the Mazda Miata, which evoked the look and feel of classic early sixties British sports cars like the Lotus Elan and thus captured the imaginations of Boomers who were car-hungry youngsters in 1962, was a great success from day one.

While the similarly sized but not so carefully designed and engineered Mercury Capri evoked only an unflattering nickname: The Not-a-Miata.

If a company wanted to be REALLY smart, they'd place a gifted and "sensitized" person on the customer service hotline once a week, just to pick up on the problems and requests that customers have, both subtle and obvious.

There are experts in the music business called "ears," people who are good at sensing whether or not a band has a marketable sound. Coffee and tea tasters can recognize subtle differences in flavors and quality. Their taste buds have been sensitized to the point that they recognize, and can put into words, what 99 percent of the population cannot. And yet, even without such expert input, consumers will know when they are missing something.

8. LEARN TO FEEL VERSUS JUST REACT EMOTIONALLY.

I mentioned this distinction earlier in the list, but it's so important that I want to take it deeper. As Winston Churchill once said about speech-making, "If you have an important point to make, don't try to be subtle or clever. Use a pile driver. Hit the point once. Then come back and hit it again. Then hit it a third time—a resounding whack."

So here goes: Feelings are true for you all by themselves, *right now.* Emotional reactions are really just echoes of something you felt in the past. A lot of us mistake emotional reactions for feelings, which is why feelings often get a bad rap.

If you're often busy emotionally reacting to stuff, you won't be *feeling* a whole lot. And without really feeling, you won't become sensitized.

9. DELIBERATELY RESPOND TO INKLINGS, BARE TRACES, OR SENSATIONS—INSTEAD OF WAITING FOR "ENOUGH EVIDENCE."

In other words, let your new mantra be "Guess and trust."

Feeling is a skill. For many of us, it takes experimentation to practice and develop it. But there's a great payoff waiting. As you find yourself sensing things earlier and deeper—and responding creatively—you'll start moving ahead faster. You won't have to decide to respond; you'll just do it. Your body won't give your slowpoke mind a chance to slow things down.

The trick is to "give in" to feelings and sensations even before you can fully describe them. It takes getting used to, but it's a skill that builds exponentially. Compared to weighing and measuring each decision, trusting your insides is very advanced—sort of like the difference between dog-paddling and bodysurfing.

10. REALIZE THAT BY THE TIME YOU CAN FULLY EXPLAIN, DESCRIBE, OR ARTICULATE SOMETHING, MOST OF THE OPPORTUNITY HAS ALREADY PASSED.

This takes number 9 above a little bit further.

The greatest opportunities occur far sooner than most people are ready to notice them. Now, just because you didn't notice an opportunity immediately, that doesn't mean you can't eventually benefit from it. But some of the fun in life and business is to be at the leading edge—on the curve instead of behind the curve.

The idea is to be flexible and fast on your feet, eager to play in newly dawning arenas. When you relocate your personal zip code to this place, you'll find some really cool people who have been waiting for you to join them.

PERFECT YOUR ENVIRONMENT

*The Attraction OS Is a Sophisticated System
and It Requires a First-Class Environment*

Say, mister, I want a yellow convertible four-door DeVille
With a continental spare and wire-chrome wheels.

—CHUCK BERRY

Be steady and well ordered in your life so that you can be fierce
and original in your work.

—GUSTAVE FLAUBERT

As you move along the Attraction OS track, you'll notice more things, and you'll also notice things *more*. In part, this is because of increased sensory awareness—feeling things more, seeing things more clearly, being affected by others and your surroundings more than ever before. It's a natural part of the process.

One of the key areas to work on actively is to improve the quality, stability, and order of your environment. There are ten areas below to buff up. The attention you pay them will make attraction work at optimum levels.

To buff something up, by the way, means both to make it as fine and excellent as possible and to make sure that it's an expression of YOU—that it carries your personal stamp and is appropriate to your sense of self.

If the idea of perfecting your environment makes you feel materialistic, shallow, or phony, you've got a rich source of discussion to share with a coach or counselor. Because it's possible to shape your environments with

DISTINCTIONS TO DRAW

PERFECT VS. PREFERRED—Something that is perfect is pure, whole, right for you, sound. Something that is preferred is "better than" or favored. Set your sights on perfection, and in the meantime enjoy having that which is preferred.

BUFF VS. EXCELLENT—Something that is excellent is of the highest quality. Excellence + Personal Style = Buff. In other words, when something is buff, it has your personal stamp on it, it reflects your personal style. It IS you.

STANDARDS VS. RULES—A rule is a prescription, a regulation, a guide for conduct or action. A standard is a choice you make about how you will behave or what you will have in your environment.

STANDARDS VS. BOUNDARIES—Standards are the set of rules that you choose to live by. Boundaries are imaginary lines across which people, events, or situations may not cross. A boundary is "No, you can't yell at me, even if you think it is warranted." A standard is "I do not yell at people."

ENERGY VS. FEELING—Energy is a feeling of power that drives you. A feeling is a sensation that enriches you.

an attitude of self-nurturing and yet to keep all of the negatives from the previous sentence totally out of the picture.

I've said before that gradualism is a key concept in attraction. In other words, don't bust your piggy bank over this buffing-up process. But don't deny yourself improvements you could afford, either. Only you—perhaps with the guidance of an accountant or a financial planner—can determine how fast to pursue this step in your evolution. I can only guarantee that being very self-rewarding will open up new vistas for you and will help other people to understand and respond to your inner self.

Although we're talking largely about material things here, we're really talking about what one of my students called "honoring yourself with more vigor."

For additional clues on how to accomplish that, after studying the following Top 10 List, start CoachV's CleanSweep Program (p. 231).

How to know you're making progress with this principle

- You notice how much more energy you have, and that things seem to happen better, faster, and easier than before. And if you take a moment, you CAN trace this back to what you did to improve your environment.
- You find that as you improve or perfect one aspect of your environment, the improvement of other aspects becomes easier. Call it momentum.
- You're more creative in your perfect, self-designed environment because you have more available bandwidth.
- You have less stress as you streamline the details of your life and get rid of the less-than-perfect aspects.

TOP 10 WAYS TO PERFECT YOUR ENVIRONMENT

1. PERFECT YOUR CAR.

How do you feel driving your car? How does it affect you? How would you *like* to feel? What would you have to change to get that feeling?

There are two important yardsticks: feelings and affordability. Keeping them balanced, get yourself the best possible wheels—new or used. Questions of size, year, model, condition, type, brand, styling, convenience, reliability, cost, ride, handling, features, options, color, are easy to answer once you prioritize your feelings.

By the way, the Internet offers lots of helpful tools for car buying. If you live someplace too small to have lots of competitive dealers nearby, you can still learn about the best prices to be had. And small-town dealers are very anxious to keep local folks buying locally.

2. PERFECT YOUR CLOTHES.

This applies the same standards to a new question: How do you feel when wearing your clothes?

People who earn their livings selecting costumes for movies and television shows will often, once they find something that feels perfect for them, buy two or three exactly the same or in different colors. Being highly attuned to clothes, they know what the right choices can communicate.

Like so many other things, clothes are a kind of language—one that changes constantly for some people, and very little for others across a lifetime. Having a personal style in clothing is like having a personal style in speaking, writing, drawing, photography, or anything else that's expressive. You need a few distinctive fundamental elements, a willingness to be playful with them, plus an ability to have fun with maverick choices.

Without that playfulness, there's a danger that the style will have you, instead of you having the style. Big difference. So take chances, guided by your feelings, and confidently reflect your inner self through what you wear.

3. PERFECT YOUR HOME.

Same process here. How do you feel while in your home now? How would you prefer to feel?

Some changes are costly, others only slightly expensive. The important thing is to know that you do have options, at several price points, and can begin perfecting your home environment right away, at least to some degree. Look for ways to adjust upward in terms of location, size, design, furnishings, light, placement, quality, color, materials, condition, livability, suitability, air flow, appliances, storage, kitchen, bathrooms, living room, bedrooms, electronics, security, homeyness, neighborhood/neighbors, comfort, artwork, decoration, bedding, style, layout, whatever else spells ease and supportiveness for you.

Sharon Eakes, a wonderful coach who lives in western Pennsylvania, recently wrote to me about the late poet Carl Sandburg, someone she (and millions more) holds in tremendous regard.

For the last twenty-two of his eighty-nine years, Carl Sandburg lived in an 1860-vintage farmhouse in the Blue Ridge Mountains of western North Carolina. He lived simply, lovingly, and selfishly with his wife, three daughters (two of whom were handicapped), two grandchildren, and 14,000 books. His environment supported him perfectly. He had several comfortable writing places inside the house and one outside on the porch. He liked to work in the stillness of the night, slipping into bed just as the rest of the family woke to do the work of running the farm, on which they tended a herd of 200 goats.

He slept in a room that was quiet, rose for a midday meal with his family, then spent his afternoons walking with his children or grandchildren on the many paths through the woods that were adjacent to his farm. The evening meal was usually very sociable, followed by reading aloud or singing. After everyone else retired, he began writing again.

Among other things, Carl Sandburg showed that perfecting your home doesn't have to mean overspending, going for the glitz, or creating some kind of Yuppie paradise. It simply means creating, as much as possible, an environment that's perfectly supportive of you and your aims, providing lots of what you need to be at your best.

Self-indulgent? Yes, in the best possible sense. And tremendously attractive.

4. PERFECT YOUR OFFICE/WORK ENVIRONMENT.

How do you feel while doing your job? Whether you're self-employed or work for someone else, there are several variables. They include the job itself, the company, your office or workspace, desk, chair comfort, filing systems, support services, computer, printer, fax, artwork, lighting, air, co-workers, stress level, suitability, compensation, role, respect, requirements, travel, perks, security, pension, raises, etc.

Which, among the above, can you change for the better? Should you "divorce" your current employer, for example? Is physical discomfort distracting you? Could you perform better if you could always instantly put your hands on the information you need?

Employer/employee relationships are in many ways similar to romantic relationships. If it's too often a struggle, yet you cling to the notion that someday there'll be a change in attitude—more recognition of your value, an opening up—chances are that you're waiting in vain. Somehow, the longer it takes people to realize this, the more angry and bitter the eventual parting will be. So don't wait for your mind to construct an ultimate proof as to whether you should stay or go. Listen to your body and your feelings. Is there a culture of complaint where you work? Are you often tempted to join in? Or is there a win/win dynamic between employers and employed?

And, of course, look for big and little physical changes you can make that will support you in making your best work performance. Pat Riley, the future Hall of Fame NBA coach, has written that the most important aspect of his job is "to create an atmosphere where the players' talent can flourish." He makes sure his teams are booked into top-flight hotels, with tall stacks of soft, plush towels waiting in their rooms. The theory is that first-class amenities will elicit first-class effort. With the right people, it works!

Why not apply that theory to yourself?

5. PERFECT YOUR BODY.

How do you feel about inhabiting your body? How much time per week do you budget for maintaining your shape, your weight, hair, eyes, teeth, chin, cheeks, chest, stomach, butt, legs, feet, hands, skin, vitality and energy levels, breath, breathing, fitness level, skin tone, muscle tone, nails, arms, ears, forehead, shoulders, back?

Just like building financial health, it's best to accumulate steady investments, even if they are fairly small, and be patient while they grow into something impressive and self-sustaining. Your body is the most important machine you'll ever own. (It's much more than just a machine, of course.) It deserves—and repays—a smart investment of time and effort. Personal trainers, well-cushioned athletic shoes, gym memberships, bicycles, free or machine-mounted weights, massages, yoga instruction, pickup basketball games, aerobics classes: Whatever you can do to build and maintain healthy tone while also generating fun and/or fulfillment is something you should consider a well-deserved gift you're giving yourself.

6. PERFECT YOUR FOOD AND LIQUIDS.

How does your body feel about what you ingest? Are you on a first-name basis at the local LumpyBurger franchise? Are you nodding like a circus horse before the kid even finishes saying, "D'you want fries with that?"

Diet is a very personal thing. It's also cultural. Strands of your identity reach into your food choices. Some suggestions that are perfectly good for others may be too far-out for you. And vice versa.

This much I'm certain of: You can move in healthier directions without experiencing hard-core deprivation. Eating should be pleasurable, not penitent. Fear of food can be just as much a malady as being overweight. But eating should also be an investment of sorts—one that balances pleasures of the moment with health dividends of the future. Like any kind of lifestyle upgrade, you have lots of elements to play with here: snacking habits, juicing, vitamin or mineral supplements, adding fruits and vegetables, deciding how much dairy to ingest, minerals, frequency of eating, size of portions, including more grains, health food, total or partial vegetarianism, purified water, among others. There are diet books, health-oriented cookbooks, and specialized training programs beyond counting out there.

Realize that you may need time, and that any positive change may set the stage (or the table) for many more to develop.

7. PERFECT THE ENERGY AROUND YOU.

As you become more aware, you'll be like a top-quality radio receiver that pulls in all signals with clarity. A key idea is to "preset" your dials to the best broadcasts, which means opting for the most soul- and self-nourishing choices in love, stress levels, friends, coaches, family relationships, work, spouse, finances, intellectual stimulation, music, contact with nature, neighborhood, lifestyle.

You CAN upgrade, either gradually or rapidly, in any of the above areas. You can shift your choices or be a catalyst for improvement in relationship to existing choices.

Here's another key: Improvement in one area will make it easier to upgrade another. Any big and/or little things you do to reduce your stress level will reduce the amount of adrenaline pumping through your system. Adrenaline is a good thing in genuine fight-or-flight situations, but daily jolts of it lead to unwanted consequences—from making rash choices to experiencing sleep deprivation and worse.

8. PERFECT YOUR LIGHTING, SOUNDS, AIR, VISUALS.

These are some more environmental variables that could be a lot more influential over your happiness than you realize. For example, there's a health problem called, appropriately, SAD (seasonal affective disorder). For people vulnerable to SAD, low levels of sunlight can trigger mild or severe depressions.

SAD is most likely to strike in climates where winter is exceptionally sunless, although it can also be caused simply by staying indoors too much. One study found a high percentage of people living in San Diego (which has one of the most agreeable climates in the United States) weren't getting enough sun to stave off SAD. There was plenty of sunshine. They just stayed indoors so much that they failed to absorb enough of it.

If you have mysterious fatigue, weight gain, or weight loss during winter, make the most of every bit of winter sun.

And everyone could benefit from more natural lighting, mood-setting sounds, fresh air, resonant artwork, inspiring views, and other spirit-lifting forms of visual and auditory stimulation. They are all inputs. Choose the ones that make you feel best.

9. PERFECT YOUR INTEGRITY.

Not to say that you're a scoundrel or a backslider right now, but everyone, myself included, should be open to micro or macro improvements in how "together" they are. It could be as simple as installing a system that keeps you as up to date as possible in paperwork and organization, so the right responses are always generated quickly.

The same applies to being on the curve, instead of behind it, when it comes to handling taxes, having adequate insurance, being current on registrations and debt repayment, being available in the present moment for key relationships and agreements, and staying rooted in truthfulness and forthrightness.

Integrity is more than just honesty. It's about being INTEGRATED, so that all the parts of your life and yourself are cooperating smoothly to honor your best interests. Since we ultimately can't possess anything more important than our good name, any upgrade to your integrity will eventually be an addition to your well-being.

10. PERFECT/UPGRADE YOUR TOOLS, COMPUTER, EQUIPMENT.

Within reason and within budget, acquire the best of everything you use to be effective in the world. Like having the right car, the right home, etc., the right equipment is not only pleasing, it puts you in a position to do your best. Apply that belief to perfecting or upgrading your computer, printer, scanner, modem, phones, voice mail, washing machine, dryer, kitchen appliances, shop tools, storage, everything that extends or supports your capabilities.

THE CLEANSWEEP PROGRAM

This is a tool to help you sweep away some of life's debris. When you do, you're going to become more rock-steady as a person, and that will allow your successes to grow taller and broader.

The CleanSweep Program consists of 100 items that you'll review, firmly but fairly, rating yourself on twenty-five points in each of four key areas. Doing it will give you a sense of where you are, a baseline from which you can gauge progress.

These 100 items will also raise lots of important issues in your life. But, remember, you don't have to tackle every one of them now. Just bringing them to a level of consciousness is great progress. Then you can start thinking about how to respond to the challenges.

For today, address whichever one you feel is the most important unresolved issue or relationship in your life. Success with that single issue will help you feel more complete, and it will relieve you of significant pressure. Soon you'll realize that you're enjoying added strength and vitality, which will be fun to apply to the next item.

Let yourself take on the others when the timing feels right to you. Your feelings of personal strength and your appetite for growth will tell you when. What may at first have seemed difficult, or at least daunting, will become play.

When you do complete the CleanSweep Program—whether it takes you a month, a year, or even more—you'll be standing tall!

There are four steps to completing the CleanSweep Program:

Step 1. Answer each question. If true, check the box marked True. Be rigorous; be a hard grader. If the statement is sometimes or usually true, please DO NOT check the True box until the statement is virtually *always* true for you. If the statement does not apply to you, or will never be true for you, check the True box. (You get credit for it because it does not apply or will never happen.) And you may change the wording of any statement to make it better fit your situation.

Step 2. Summarize each section. Add up the number of True boxes for each of the four sections and write those amounts where indicated. Then add up all four sections and write the current total in the adjacent box.

Step 3. Color in the Progress Chart. If you have nine Trues in the Well-Being section, color in the bottom nine boxes, and so on. Always start from the bottom up. The goal is to have the entire chart filled in. In the meantime, you will have a current picture of how you are doing in each of the four areas.

Step 4. Keep playing until all the boxes are filled in. You can do it! Don't push yourself, but do be determined. Take a month or take a year—whatever's the right amount of time for you to achieve a CleanSweep. Feel free to use a coach or a friend to assist you, though. Because the sooner you complete the program, the sooner your life takes on the qualities you're after!

On the lines below, jot down specific benefits, results, and breakthroughs that happen in your life because you handled an item in the CleanSweep Program. _____

_____

_____

_____

_____

_____

_____

_____

_____

_____

_____

_____

PROGRESS CHART

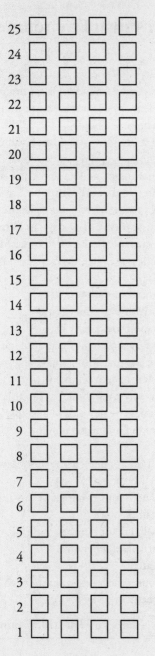

Physical Environment

TRUE STATEMENT

____ My personal files, papers, and receipts are neatly filed away.

____ My car is in excellent condition; doesn't need mechanical work, repairs, cleaning, or replacing.

____ My home is neat and clean—vacuumed, closets organized, desks and tables clear, furniture in good repair, windows clean.

____ My appliances, machinery, and equipment (refrigerator, toaster, snowblower, water heater, toys) work well.

____ My clothes are all pressed, clean, and make me look great (no wrinkles, baskets of laundry, or torn, out-of-date, or ill-fitting clothes).

____ My plants and animals are healthy (fed, watered, getting light and love).

____ My bed/bedroom lets me have the best sleep possible (firm bed, light, air).

____ I live in a home/apartment I love.

____ I surround myself with beautiful things.

____ I live in the geographic area of my choice.

____ There is ample and healthy lighting around me.

____ I consistently have adequate time, space, and freedom in my life.

____ I am not damaged by my environment.

____ I am not tolerating anything about my home or work environment.

____ My work environment is productive and inspiring (synergistic, ample tools and resources; no undue pressure).

____ I recycle.

____ I use products that do not deplete the ozone layer.

____ My hair is the way I want it.

____ I surround myself with music that makes my life more enjoyable.

____ My bed is made daily.

____ I don't injure myself, fall, or bump into things.

____ People feel comfortable in my home.

____ I drink purified water.

____ I have nothing around the house or in storage that I do not need.

____ I am consistently early or easily on time.

____ **Number of True (Maximum 25)**

Well-Being

TRUE STATEMENT

____ I rarely use caffeine (chocolate, coffee, colas, tea, fewer than three times per week, total).

____ I rarely (less than three times per week) eat sugar.

____ I rarely (less than five hours per week) watch television.

____ I rarely (fewer than two drinks per week) drink alcohol.

____ My teeth and gums are healthy (have seen a dentist in the past six months).

____ My cholesterol count is healthful.

____ My blood pressure is healthful.

____ I have had a complete physical exam in the past three years.

____ I do not smoke tobacco or other substances.

____ I do not use illegal drugs or misuse prescribed medications.

____ I have had a complete eye exam within the past two years (glaucoma check, vision test).

____ My weight is within my ideal range.

____ My nails are healthy and look good.

____ I don't rush or use adrenaline to get the job done.

____ I have a rewarding life beyond my work or profession.

____ I have something to look forward to every day.

____ I have no habits I find unacceptable.

____ I am aware of the physical or emotional problems I have, and I am now fully taking care of them.

____ I consistently take evenings, weekends, and holidays off and take at least two weeks of vacation each year.

____ I have been tested for the AIDS antibody.

____ I use well-made sunglasses.

____ I do not suffer, either mentally or physically.

____ I floss daily.

____ I walk or exercise at least three times per week.

____ I hear well.

____ **Number of True (Maximum 25)**

STEP 19

Money

TRUE STATEMENT

____ I currently save at least 10 percent of my income.

____ I pay my bills on time, virtually always.

____ My income source/revenue base is stable and predictable.

____ I know how much I must have to be minimally financially independent, and I have a plan to get there.

____ I have returned or made good on any money I borrowed.

____ I have written agreements and am current with payments to individuals or companies to whom I owe money.

____ I have six months' living expenses in a money market–type account.

____ I live on a weekly budget that allows me to save and not suffer.

____ All my tax returns have been filed and all my taxes have been paid.

____ I currently live well within my means.

____ I have excellent medical insurance.

____ My assets (car, home, possessions, treasures) are well insured.

____ I have a financial plan for the next year.

____ I have no legal clouds hanging over me.

____ My will is up to date and accurate.

____ My investments do not keep me awake at night.

____ I know how much I am worth.

____ I am on a career/professional/business track that is, or will soon be, financially and personally rewarding.

____ My earnings are commensurate with the effort I put into my job.

____ My services are so exceptional, people gladly pay me premium rates.

____ I have no loose ends at work.

____ I have relationships with people who can assist in my career/professional development.

____ I rarely miss work due to illness.

____ I am putting aside enough money each month to reach financial independence.

____ My earnings outpace inflation, consistently.

____ **Number of True (Maximum 25)**

Relationships

TRUE STATEMENT

____ I have told my parents, in the past three months, that I love them.

____ I get along well with my sibling(s).

____ I get along well with my co-workers/clients.

____ I get along well with my managers/staff.

____ There is no one whom I would dread or feel uncomfortable running across (in the street, at an airport or a party).

____ I put people first and results second.

____ I have let go of the relationships that drag me down or damage me. ("Let go" means to end, walk away from, declare complete, no longer be attached to.)

____ I have communicated or attempted to communicate with everyone I have damaged, injured, or seriously upset, even if it wasn't fully my fault.

____ I do not gossip or talk about others.

____ I have a bank of friends/family who love and appreciate me for who I am, not just for what I do for them.

____ I tell people how they can satisfy me.

____ I am fully caught up with letters and calls.

____ I always tell the truth, no matter what.

____ I receive enough love from people around me to feel good.

____ I have fully forgiven those people who have hurt/damaged me, intentionally or not.

____ I am a person of my word; people can count on me.

____ I quickly correct miscommunications and misunderstandings when they do occur.

____ I live life on my terms, not by the rules or preferences of others.

____ I am at peace with past loves or spouses.

____ I am in tune with my wants and needs and get them taken care of.

____ I do not judge or criticize others.

____ I do not take personally the things that people say to me.

____ I have a best friend or soul mate.

____ I make requests rather than complain.

____ I spend time with people who don't try to change me.

____ Number of True (Maximum 25)

DEVELOP MORE CHARACTER THAN YOU NEED

Integrity Is Not Enough to Become Irresistibly Attractive

Character is not made in a crisis—it is only exhibited.
—ROBERT FREEMAN

I am a writer who came from a sheltered life. A sheltered life can be a daring life as well. For all serious daring starts from within.
—EUDORA WELTY

Being known as a person of character, a class act, is the highest compliment you can ever get. But just what is character? What does it take to become a class act?

People often define character in terms of integrity or honesty. That's a good start, but character is also a whole lot more.

I believe that ten distinct areas compose character. I've used them to formulate the following Top 10 List, which is designed to help you understand where you are along this path right now, and show you which areas it would be worthwhile to develop further.

Each of the following ten components of character goes with a ten-point checklist. Taken all together, they're a 100-point analysis tool that's called "Class Act 100." It's a detailed look at character traits, life skills, special qualities, and personal practices that will help you to both become and feel like a class act, naturally.

DISTINCTIONS TO DRAW

CHARACTER VS. PERSONALITY—Your character is the sum of your qualities; that which distinguishes you from others; your strength of mind and emotion. Personality is how you come across, how you relate to others.

HONOR VS. COMMITMENT—To honor is to respect. To commit is to promise and follow through.

HONOR VS. INTEGRITY—Honor is how you relate to yourself and to others. Integrity is the quality of wholeness that you maintain for yourself and your environment.

How to know you're making progress with this principle

- You realize that you enjoy the process of building your character, even if you were a little scared at first.
- You feel better about yourself and less affected by disappointments because your CHARACTER now matters more than results do. The more you strengthen your character, the more it carries you.
- You're not held back by self-doubt because you are sure of what matters most to you.
- You naturally impress others without having to promote yourself.

Special thanks are due to Coach Winston Connor, who did so much development work on Class Act 100. To evaluate yourself, respond to how true each statement is for you by circling N (for Never, as in "I don't do this right now in my life"); S (for Sometimes, as in "I sometimes do this" or "I try to when I can"); O (for Often, as in "I often do this, at least when I can"); AA (for Almost Always, as in "This is the kind of person I am and I almost always do this well"); or A (for Always, as in "This IS who I am at this point in my life. I consistently do this and it's very, very natural").

At the end of the Top 10 List, you will have answered all 100. You'll find instructions there for tabulating your score. Note: A score of 100 probably means that you're just visiting this planet from Valhalla, Mount Olympus, or some other home of the gods. It's not unusual for regular human beings to score closer to 30. So don't be discouraged by this first assessment. It's amazing how quickly you can upgrade and become a class act, once you've reviewed this checklist.

TOP 10 WAYS TO DEVELOP
MORE CHARACTER THAN YOU NEED

1. HONOR

In a poignant short story by F. Scott Fitzgerald, a man much like the author himself had lived a sybaritic, irresponsible, alcohol-laced life in Paris. He revisits the city with his growing daughter, trying to make sense of his new, sober life and trying to feel worthy of being father to a smart, sweetly innocent girl he'd neglected so much.

Significantly, the daughter's name is Honor. The story's core emotion is deep sadness for how much he had neglected Honor and the realization of how vital it now was to bring all he could of her into his life.

Let's shift from literature to accountancy: Honor is something that pays dividends. The same is true of the other aspects of character reviewed in this step. They bring in many ultimate payoffs. One of the most obvious is this: When you're completely clear about the rightness (as opposed to self-righteousness) of how you operate in life, you won't have any questions in the corners of your mind about whether you deserve the best. You'll know that you deserve a great life, and you won't experience self-sabotage or feelings of emptiness as you reach out and grab it. So anything that distracts you from being a class act is glitter, not gold.

I think of honor as the integration of fairness, conviction, courage, truthfulness, morality, loyalty, accountability, responsibility, commitment, and diligence. Take note of what you think while responding to the following ten statements. Circle your answers by the guidelines given above.

REGARDING HONOR

N S O AA A   1. Fairness. I do only what's right and just.
N S O AA A   2. Conviction. I stand for at least ten things, and I am steadfast.
N S O AA A   3. Courage. I respond to danger without fear.

N S O AA A   4. Truthfulness. I have not lied in at least a year or been deceptive in any of my dealings.

N S O AA A   5. Morality. I have a moral code, and I live my life by it.

N S O AA A   6. Loyalty. I stand by my family, friends, and others I am committed to.

N S O AA A   7. Accountability. I keep my word 99 percent of the time.

N S O AA A   8. Responsibility. I can always be counted on to meet agreed-upon expectations.

N S O AA A   9. Commitment. My actions demonstrate my commitment. I "walk my talk."

N S O AA A   10. Diligence. I do not waver until whatever I am involved with gets signed, sealed, and delivered.

Section Total _____

2. INTEGRITY

I define integrity as the extent to which someone embodies honesty, wellness/wholeness, prudence, thrift, orderliness, attention to details, an absence of unmet needs, punctuality, and, of course, balance in his or her life.

REGARDING INTEGRITY

N S O AA A   1. Honesty. I always deal fairly; I am not sneaky.

N S O AA A   2. Wellness. I am in optimal emotional, spiritual, and physical condition.

N S O AA A   3. Prudence. I have and use excellent judgment in all of my actions.

N S O AA A   4. Thrift. I save 10 to 30 percent of what I make.

N S O AA A   5. Simplicity. I live an honest, simple, easy life.

N S O AA A   6. Orderliness. I am neat, tidy, and orderly.

N S O AA A   7. Detail-Oriented. I make sure details are handled.

N S O AA A   8. Needs Met. I add to a room; I don't drain it or exhaust others as I add.

N S O AA A   9. Punctuality. I am on time 98 percent of the time.

N S O AA A   10. Balance. I am juggling nothing; I fully understand that it's not worth it.

Section Total _____

3. PERSONAL STYLE

Personal style is much more than owning a closet full of Milan's finest tailoring. Personal style is all about how you carry yourself in the world. It includes excellence, trustingness, polish, cleanliness, being well dressed, gracious, appropriate in your actions, passionate, consistent, and resilient.

REGARDING PERSONAL STYLE

N S O AA A 1. Excellence. I buy and deliver quality only.

N S O AA A 2. Trusting. In my dealings with others, I assume that people are trustworthy.

N S O AA A 3. Polished. I come across as polished.

N S O AA A 4. Clean. I maintain the highest standard of personal hygiene.

N S O AA A 5. Well Dressed. I always look exceptionally good, even when very casual.

N S O AA A 6. Gracious. I am always charming and warm and offer appropriate courtesies.

N S O AA A 7. Appropriate. I act according to the saying "There is a time and a place for everything." And I consistently pick the right times and the right places.

N S O AA A 8. Passionate. It's clear to all what I feel strongly about and what I most enjoy or believe in.

N S O AA A 9. Consistent. People know what to expect from me. I am predictable when it matters.

N S O AA A 10. Resilient. I bounce back from adversity quickly (two to forty-eight hours) and/or willingly. I recover.

Section Total _____

4. CARING

Caring is based on knowing that we're not really as separate from one another as surface realities may lead us to believe. The most nurturing and lasting relationships derive from an "everybody wins" mentality. That's what caring is about: wanting everybody to come out okay. It includes respect, availability, concern, tenderness, tolerance, sharing, kindness, patience, generosity, and hospitality.

REGARDING CARING

N S O AA A 1. Respect. I don't violate any aspect of another person.

N S O AA A 2. Availability. I am very willing to help.

N S O AA A 3. Concern. I take an interest in others.

N S O AA A 4. Tenderness. I am lovingly considerate and highly respectful.

N S O AA A 5. Tolerance. I welcome diversity because it expands me emotionally and spiritually.

N S O AA A 6. Sharing. I do not hoard, nor am I stingy. I give.

N S O AA A 7. Kindness. I don't hurt people or even squash bugs.

N S O AA A 8. Patience. When waiting is appropriate, I can do it easily.

N S O AA A 9. Generosity. I give freely; I enjoy it.

N S O AA A 10. Hospitality. I make people feel comfortable in my home or in my space.

Section Total _____

5. EFFECTIVENESS

Character counts the most when it's applied to real life. And that means it's vitally important to be effective. Which means you assimilate easily; have a vision, mastery, productivity; are accomplished, causal, enrolling, an investor, practical; follow through on your intentions; and have adequate bandwidth.

REGARDING EFFECTIVENESS

N S O AA A 1. Bandwidth, Absorption. I easily handle/assimilate lots of input from any source.

N S O AA A 2. Vision. I see clearly what is possible for people and am willing to help them attain it.

N S O AA A 3. Mastery. I am at the top of my game at work.

N S O AA A 4. Productive. I get more done in a day than most people get done in a week.

N S O AA A 5. Accomplished. I have a track record of doing well and contributing to life.

N S O AA A 6. Causal/Initiating. I create my own path and do not wait for others to direct me.

N S O AA A 7. Enrolling. I can enroll anyone into something that's good for them.

N S O AA A 8. Investing. I consciously invest time and money in people, concepts, equipment, and opportunities.

N S O AA A 9. Practical. I do what makes sense.

N S O AA A 10. Follow Through. What I begin work on gets done.

Section Total _____

6. SENSE OF SELF

A sense of self is both an aspect of character and a by-product, too. Your sense of self allows you to be confident, secure, content, integrated, self-caring, self-motivated, capable, compassionate, mature, and self-respecting.

REGARDING SENSE OF SELF

N S O AA A 1. Confident. I feel confident, from deep inside myself.

N S O AA A 2. Secure. I am safe. I fear almost nothing.

N S O AA A 3. Content. I am very satisfied with myself and my life.

N S O AA A 4. Integrated. I don't lead separate lives; all of my goals work to support all of me.

N S O AA A 5. Self-Caring. I am aware of my needs and get them satisfied continuously.

N S O AA A 6. Self-Motivated. I don't rely on others or on potential consequences to motivate me.

N S O AA A 7. Capable. I can handle all that life brings.

N S O AA A 8. Compassionate. I naturally forgive and am always understanding of others' mistakes.

N S O AA A 9. Mature. I never behave childishly.

N S O AA A 10. Self-Respecting. I am well educated, well trained, and well read. I know my strengths and use them.

Section Total _____

7. OPENNESS

Openness is the virtue that lets things happen and allows them to come into your consciousness and your life. It's the great difference between being self-directed and being controlling and rigid. A person who is open is accepting, intuitive, aware, willing, adventurous, spiritual, visual, present-oriented, creative, and flexible.

REGARDING OPENNESS

N S O AA A   1. Accepting. I don't resist what is so. I let people be who they are. I embrace reality.

N S O AA A   2. Intuitive. I listen to my hunches and that little voice inside me. Evidence is optional.

N S O AA A   3. Aware. I understand what awareness is, and I am on the path of becoming more aware.

N S O AA A   4. Willing. I am always willing to try and to help.

N S O AA A   5. Adventurous. I actively seek new people, ideas, activities, and projects.

N S O AA A   6. Spiritual. I value the notion of a higher plane or being. I understand that we're all connected.

N S O AA A   7. Visual. I see all of what's around me, and I respond to it.

N S O AA A   8. Present-Oriented. Life is occurring right now. I live here, not in yesterday or tomorrow.

N S O AA A   9. Creative. Great ideas, opportunities, and things just come to me; I don't have to work at creating them.

N S O AA A 10. Flexible. I adjust quickly and readily.

Section Total _____

8. DELIVERY

A person with character "delivers the goods." That means they orient around win/win and results; are proactive; add value; underpromise; are interdevelopmental, adaptive, innovative, direct, and resourceful.

REGARDING DELIVERY

N S O AA A   1. Win/Win. Everyone I work with wins as much as I do.

N S O AA A   2. Results. I deliver results when needed.

N S O AA A   3. Proactive. I anticipate needs and act early.

N S O AA A   4. Add Value. I leave people better off, always.

N S O AA A   5. Underpromising. I deliver more than promised.

N S O AA A   6. Interdevelopmental. I learn as much from others as they learn from me. We all grow.

N S O AA A   7. Adaptive. I quickly adapt to new situations, ideas, technology.

N S O AA A   8. Innovative. I continually experiment and make things, processes, and relationships better.

N S O AA A   9. Direct. I am up-front and candid, always.

N S O AA A 10. Resourceful. I can find solutions instantly.

Section Total _____

9. LIFE SKILLS

An old R&B song title poses the question, "What Is Hip?" Well, "hip" actually derives from a West African word that means, approximately, "having your eyes open." And a person with strong life skills is truly hip, as well as loving, clever, light, humorous, diplomatic, savvy, generous, wise; and has perspective.

REGARDING LIFE SKILLS

N S O AA A   1. Loving. I rejoice in my love of others and in the love I receive from them.

N S O AA A   2. Clever. I take advantage of opportunities to accomplish my objectives.

N S O AA A   3. Light. Things matter to me, but they don't take on excessive meaning, significance, or heaviness.

N S O AA A   4. Humorous. I can see the humor in almost anything.

N S O AA A   5. Diplomatic. I seek to build relationships, even if it takes an investment of time.

N S O AA A 6. Savvy. I have street smarts and understand what
motivates people.

N S O AA A 7. Generous. I share what I have.

N S O AA A 8. Wisdom. I am very, very wise.

N S O AA A 9. Perspective. I understand history, and I see where we
are in relationship to the past and to the future.

N S O AA A 10. Hip. I GET IT! And it shows.

Section Total _____

10. COMMUNICATION

This is, to me, among the greatest of all life skills. As a youngster, I felt
barely able to express myself in words. I focused on it relentlessly, especially on making fine but crucial distinctions between things that seem
similar but really are different. This turned out to be one of the most
important skills I ever acquired.

I recommend that everyone latch on to the idea that he or she can
become a great communicator. What's involved is awareness of tone and
"dance" (going easily back and forth from speaker to listener) and being
articulate, clear, appreciative, congratulatory, constructive, encouraging,
friendly, and expressive.

REGARDING COMMUNICATION

N S O AA A 1. Tone. I speak in warm, clear tones.

N S O AA A 2. Dance. I can speak and hear simultaneously

N S O AA A 3. Articulate. The words I need flow naturally out of my
mouth.

N S O AA A 4. Clear. I speak simply. I am easily understood.

N S O AA A 5. Appreciative. I thank people, and I mean it.

N S O AA A 6. Congratulatory. I am excited for the success of others.

N S O AA A 7. Constructive. I reinforce the positive side of a person;
I don't criticize.

N S O AA A 8. Encouraging. People need encouragement, and I am
unstinting in my support.

N S O AA A 9. Friendly. I like people and let them know it.

N S O AA A 10. Expressive. My spirit, love, emotions, and excitement come across when I communicate.

Section Total _____

SCORING

An "N" scores zero points. An "S" is worth 1/4 point, an "O" is 1/2 point, an "AA" is 3/4 point, an "A" is one full point. Tally up your score for each section, then total up your overall score below. If you understand now how useful it will be to develop even more character than you need, hire a coach or counselor to help you get to a perfect 100.

Grand Total Score _____

SEE HOW PERFECT THE PRESENT REALLY IS

Especially When It Is Clearly Not

The "what should be" never did exist, but people keep trying to live up to it. There is no "what should be," there is only what is.

—LENNY BRUCE

This time, like all times, is a very good one, if we but know what to do with it.

—RALPH WALDO EMERSON

This is perhaps the most challenging of all of the principles—until you understand it. Then it becomes completely obvious. It's a challenge to actually live this belief, but the more you address the challenge, the more positive momentum your life will acquire.

This is the essence: When you recognize and accept that things are the way they are, and that the present is all we truly have, then it's not too much of a leap to believe that the present is perfect.

Maybe it's not optimum, but it is perfect to *learn* from and perfect to *grow* from.

In other words, accepting and embracing the present—warts and all—doesn't mean you give up hope for a finer future. It doesn't mean your dreams are unattainable. It's actually just the opposite: Being in sync (and in love) with your present is just about the best way to optimize your future.

It's a bit of a conundrum, but stick with it and you can work through it.

DISTINCTIONS TO DRAW

PERFECT VS. PREFERRED—See "Distinctions to Draw," Step 19 (page 224).

REQUEST VS. COMPLAINT—To request is to ask for something you need or for someone else to make a change. To complain is to blame, find fault, kvetch, and so on. Most people complain about other people or about life but don't make a clear request.

Once you do, you may forget it again when you need it most. But it'll come right back in seconds and pull you back on track just as fast.

How to know you're making progress with this principle

- You are less likely to lose your composure when you get bad news.
- You become a very curious person and enjoy discovering the perfection in the present, even the bad parts.
- You relax and enjoy the present, even if it's not what you wanted.
- You set fewer goals and instead seek and find the opportunities in the present.
- You make the most of reality because you're not wishing it were different.
- You save energy because you don't battle the universe daily.
- You notice and benefit from the gifts that lie buried under every apparent problem.
- You are free to do more with what you already have.

TOP 10 WAYS TO KNOW THAT
THE PRESENT IS PERFECT

1. THE PRESENT IS PERFECT
BECAUSE THE UNIVERSE IS IN BALANCE.

The forces of nature have had millions of years to work out the balance of all things. Remember, balance doesn't mean that you like or agree with how things are balanced, but that there is something called "balance" and it's always working.

I sometimes call it "cause and effect." The past is the cause. The present is the effect. Only by relaxing into full acceptance of the present can you start seeing clearly. To avoid it is like using drugs to avoid scary-feeling emotions. The dose wears off, and you find yourself in the same bad movie again—or worse. Meanwhile, all the clues for attracting a better future are really staring at you. The trick is to keep your eyes open and remain bright, calm, and nonjudgmental.

By nonjudgmental I mean not beating up on yourself, or anyone else, because of frustrations you may feel or blame you may want to place as you rush to decisions about who and what must change. Instead, let the decisions dawn on you, in their own time. Maybe they'll come in a dramatic moment, but more likely they'll just start showing up as the mists of confusion and stress start to lift. And you'll recognize them as elements of how your life stays in its present balance, elements that you're free to play with in order to start causing a more agreeable effect.

2. THE PRESENT IS PERFECT
BECAUSE THE PRESENT IS ALL THERE IS.

You can create a case for thoughtfully planning your future and acknowledge that we are all very much affected by the past. But you can also begin living as if the present were all there is to work with right now, at this exact moment.

You can't change the future—although things you do now will steer it. You can't change the past—although things you do now will unlock its grip on you.

The past and the future are too important to ignore. But the present is much bigger (and more interesting and powerful) than either one. It *is* what is. The less emphasis you give the other two, the more control you can take over your reality.

3. THE PRESENT IS PERFECT
EVEN THOUGH IT MAY NOT BE WHAT YOU WANT.

Perfect doesn't mean desirable, fair, just, or preferred. Perfect refers to the idea that, in the bigger scheme of things, there's a perfect explanation for why things are the way they are—even if that explanation eludes you at the moment.

George, an entrepreneur in his mid-forties who was very frustrated and angry, recently came to coach Bobbi Gemma. He talked in a flippant, sometimes almost paranoiac way about his lifelong series of start-up businesses. Taken all together, they had made enough money to support his family—but never enough to sustain and become rewarding.

His goals were concrete: to get help in staying focused on a business and to decide what he most wanted to do. He was looking at his life and thinking, "I'm always just hanging on by my fingernails. I need to make some profound changes here."

George, whose projects usually involved sales, is like a lot of us who are very entrepreneurial: driven, restless, project-oriented more than career-oriented, and prone to judging himself by outside criteria.

Bobbi started out by validating him, letting him know he was okay just as he was. That alone helped George a lot. He'd always felt like an outsider, as though there were something wrong with him. When he would say, "Maybe I just need to get a nine-to-five job," she would answer, "But you won't be happy doing that. You'll stay a few months, it'll get on your nerves, you'll move on."

Next came focusing exclusively on his current projects, deciding what to work on, and narrowing him down to get some things off his plate.

Soon George agreed that working on just three things at one time would be better for him. Reaching this decision, he also decided it was smart to deal with his internal workings, as well as the external, concrete goals. And the first internal thing was to ease up on his self-generated pressures. Anger had made him very harsh on people. He was in the habit of strong-arming them, pushing them from point A to point B. Now he can laugh about the fact that he tends to be an "in-your-face" person. And he can soften up his style and still be okay. As he lightens up on himself, he lightens up on other people. His interactions go better—so much so that he's started exploring the Web for Principles of Attraction material. It made sense to him, and he now insists on spending half of each session with Bobbi on attraction, the other half on his career concerns. The story is ongoing, the career developments will take time to manifest, but notice that George's progress started out with accepting who he is, right now. Then it moved to a sort of unclenching, which meant he'd stopped fighting the present. Now, he's better able to see the clues about where to really focus.

4. The Present is Perfect
because you CAN do something about it.

As mentioned in number 2 above, what's great about the present is that you CAN change it, and a lot more than you think. Changing the present is really taking the easy way out. The tough way, the one that lots of folks keep trying, is trying to change the future because of being rooted in the past. That's the very definition of inner conflict. So whenever anything in your life seems to be a fight, ease back, keep your eye up ahead, on your ultimate intentions, and look for the present-time path of least resistance.

5. The Present is Perfect
if you're evolving with reality.

The present may not appear to be "enough," given how rich the past is and how much potential the future has. If this is true for you, think about this: You as a person are evolving (instead of just changing). The changes aren't your focus: They're just little marking points in the bigger, overall process of your evolution. From that point of view, the present becomes really exciting. If you're evolving, there's no limit to how rich the future can turn out to be.

It's also important to realize that the rest of the world (other people, genes, memes, technology, philosophy, and so on) is also evolving. We're all part of a global process. That makes the present even more interesting and gives us even more reason to relax, find the flow, and go with it, instead of being (to adapt F. Scott Fitzgerald's last line from *The Great Gatsby*) "boats against the current, borne back ceaselessly into the past."

6. The Present is Perfect
because there is a gift in everything.

I often quote the old saying "Why do you think they call the present a gift?" It means that there is always a positive in every present moment, if you're willing and able to see it. (Usually, we're either too upset, frustrated, or self-righteous to even want to look.)

There's an important caveat: Don't arbitrarily latch on to something and call it "a gift" just because you need a justification for bad things that are happening. Just be open to the idea that you'll learn a lot more from the present if you believe there's a gift to discover, even when you encounter something bad.

7. THE PRESENT IS PERFECT BECAUSE YOU CAN LEARN QUICKLY FROM IT.

You can learn from the past, but you can generally learn more, and faster, from present-time events. And when I say *learn,* I mean to grow and change, not just add skills and acquire information. Information acquisition is a substitute for actual learning, because learning occurs during the process of *living,* not during the process of studying. And, as any good coach will tell you, there's no better way to refine skills than through hands-on involvement. That means getting into the game, as opposed to withdrawing, and focusing on the present, as opposed to obsessing over the past or future.

8. THE PRESENT IS PERFECT BECAUSE IT'S LEVERAGEABLE.

The present is so rich because so much is happening in it. Most people can't see, feel, or experience it, so they can't benefit from it. If, on the other hand, you actually can see, feel, or experience it, that skill is leverageable.

By this I mean that you can do more with the present than you can with the past or the future. The present is like yeast, or like a pulley or a fulcrum—anyone who is aware of, and sensitized to, all that is occurring in the present will find that they can do a lot with it.

9. THE PRESENT IS PERFECT BECAUSE IT'S THE CULMINATION AND SYNTHESIS OF THE PAST.

Studying history is a good way to understand why things are occurring as they are in the present.

Although we can learn about the present from the past, I say we can learn a lot more about the past by understanding the present perfectly. That combined understanding will help us enormously in conceiving the future.

There's always a two-way dialogue in progress: past to present and present to past. Make any sense? Well, the first cars were just primitive engines attached to state-of-the-art buggy technology (minus the horse, of course). Engines, transmissions, wheels, brakes, frames, axles, and every other conceivable part of automotive technology has evolved, tremendously. But the "ghost" of buggy technology is still visible if you use some intuition while looking at the essentials: a frame, a carriage (or body), two axles, four wheels, and suspension springs. To conceive what cars will become, consider that durable "ghost." In some form or another, as modified by whatever advances in technology affect its elemental parts, it will probably persist.

The present is always a window on the past, clarifying the lessons it provides, making the future a little bit less mysterious.

10. THE PRESENT IS PERFECT BECAUSE YOU SAY SO.

I know this is cheating, but some things are easier just to declare so because *you say so.* If it's your definite opinion that the present is perfect—and you choose to live by that belief—that should be good enough for anyone. In other words, your determination that the present is perfect is going to eventually gather enough force to actually make the present perfect—and optimum at the same time!

Try saying it out loud: "The present is perfect!"

What do you hear in your mind next?

Whatever your response is, it's a perfect one. Because you're not stuck. You're evolving. The present, which you fully embrace, is only a reference point along the way.

BECOME AN UNCONDITIONALLY CONSTRUCTIVE PERSON

High Levels of Respect Are Very Attractive

How far you go in life depends on your being tender with the young, compassionate with the aged, sympathetic with the striving, and tolerant of the weak and strong. Because someday in your life you will have been all of these.

—GEORGE WASHINGTON CARVER

If you must be candid, be candid beautifully.

—KAHLIL GIBRAN

There are three parts to the statement at the top of this page:

1. *Unconditionally.* This means always, regardless of circumstances, with no conditions or exceptions.

2. *Constructive.* This means that what you say and do will always build the other person up, never destroy or belittle that person.

3. *Become an Unconditionally Constructive Person.* This means not only to be unconditionally constructive (as a technique or practice) but to evolve into the type of person who is "naturally" this way, without stopping to think about it.

DISTINCTIONS TO DRAW

CONSTRUCTIVE VS. COMPARATIVE—If you compare someone's actions or results to another person's, or if you point out how someone has improved, you're not being unconditionally constructive. Don't point out progress. Simply state what the person is doing well.

CONSTRUCTIVE VS. POSITIVE—When you're positive, you build the other person up. When you're constructive, you help the other person to build something bigger.

RESPECTFUL VS. HONEST—To be honest means to tell the truth as you see it. To be respectful means that you care more about the person than you do about the truth in the situation. This is a tricky, but valuable, distinction.

ACKNOWLEDGE VS. COMPLIMENT—To compliment someone is to share what you like about them, their actions, or their possessions. To acknowledge a person is to compliment who they ARE.

WHO VS. WHAT—This is a fundamental distinction. The *who* of a person is their essence. The *what* is their role, their attainments, their possessions, and so on. Focus on the who, and the what will follow.

EMPOWERING VS. EMPOWER—To empower a person is usually a deliberate act. To be empowering means that you empower people without having to try. Big difference. People who are unconditionally constructive are usually empowering.

POSITIVE VS. PUFF—Puffery is seduction by hyping or exaggerating something good about a person. To be positive means to focus on the good qualities or progress, and to be optimistic without exaggerating.

OPTIMAL VS. POTENTIAL—Both are fine words. But *potential* is a perception that may mislead. If you focus on a person's potential, you are, in effect, limiting them. If you focus on what would be optimal, you create a gap the person may be inspired to step into.

How to know you're making progress with this principle

- You stop criticizing people and find you become much more respectful of other people.
- You don't feel the need to point out unpleasant things to others.
- You listen and respond to what is special and positive about the other person instead of what's wrong or weak about them.
- You surprise yourself by being direct and constructive simultaneously! You discover better ways to phrase things.
- You say truly helpful and affirming things, rather than empty compliments.
- You fully enjoy others just as they are. You come to enjoy yourself fully, too.
- People tell you the things that are most important to them because they trust you to respect them.

TOP 10 WAYS TO BECOME
UNCONDITIONALLY CONSTRUCTIVE

1. TELL THE TRUTH, THE WHOLE TRUTH.

There's one particularly damaging way that this unconditionally constructive principle is often misunderstood: People who take it seriously tend to put being UC *ahead* of telling the truth. Whenever you're in doubt, and in danger of tripping over yourself in the struggle to say what you have to and still be UC, then by all means TELL THE TRUTH—even if it isn't UC. Don't beat around the bush or make up some "nice" comment. Don't sugarcoat or in any other way hold back what NEEDS to be said.

Eventually, you'll learn phrasing and awareness skills that will permit you to simultaneously tell the truth *and* be unconditionally constructive. But it takes practice.

In the meantime, err on the side of truthfulness.

Marlene Elliott is a coach who lives in Sarasota, Florida. This is a very funny—and truthful—story she told me from her own life.

Very recently, Marlene went to a large post office near her home. It was jammed. The line continued out the door. She needed assistance, and asked for it. A man wearing a shirt and tie came over, talking very loud and with a superior attitude, telling her what he *thought* she needed to hear but not answering the question she'd asked. In the middle of his high-decibel discourse, Marlene said, "Excuse me. You don't have to yell. I can really hear you."

"I ALWAYS TALK THIS WAY. IF I TALKED ANY DIFFERENTLY, I WOULDN'T BE MYSELF."

"Would you mind JUST lowering your voice?"

"IF I LOWERED MY VOICE, I WOULD BE TALKING DOWN TO YOU."

"Right now you're being condescending. If you don't stop, I'm going to ask for the postmaster."

"I DON'T CARE IF YOU ASK FOR THE POSTMASTER!"

"Do you know how to whisper?"

"I'M NOT GONNA WHISPER!"

"Very good. Get me the postmaster."

"YOU CAN'T SEE THE POSTMASTER!"

This man didn't know it, but his life was going to be forever altered by dealing with a bona fide graduate of CoachV.

A supervisor came over. "I want to file a complaint against the gentleman I spoke with," Marlene said. A woman nearby added, "He was rude to you and he was condescending." Marlene, of course, wrote down her name.

After the supervisor gave her the postmaster's number, Marlene went home and called. Calmly, she said there was a complaint, she had a witness, and her intention was to take it as far as she needed to go with it. "I want this man to be reprimanded," she said. "But not in the way you normally do it. I'm really interested in you providing some kind of training or coaching so that he can actually understand customer service better than he ever has before. I'd like to give input, and I'd like you to have the steps of his training be put into writing."

The postmaster was intrigued. He invited her to come to his office and meet with him and his second-in-command. "In all the years I've been in the post office," said the postmaster, a man nearing retirement, "I've never had such constructive criticism to use to support my people."

The upshot? They asked Marlene to be the man's coach for three or four months. (She declined.) And they offered her a position on their Customer Service Council. (She's thinking it over.)

The point is, she told the truth—relentlessly—both with determination and with a positive outlook about making a difference. But she did so without any kind of sugarcoating. In coaching jargon, this is called "getting off it." That means taking the focus away from making the other person a villain and working instead to change things for the better.

"The guy was being arrogant, rude, unaware of customer service, and was banking on the idea that he's got a job where no one can fire him," Marlene concluded. "But if all I did was prove that his attitude was all wrong, I certainly wouldn't have gotten these results."

By the way, one day later she returned and found that the post office was running like a clock. Plenty of customers. No lines. No yelling.

2. DEAL WITH WEAKNESSES OF OTHERS BY POINTING TO THE OPTIMUM POSSIBILITY.

Old way: "You seem to be awkward when you shake someone's hand." Or: "Let me know if you want some tips on how to shake someone's hand better." Or: "You sure have a weak handshake."

UC approach: "People really enjoy a firm handshake." Or: "Tell me what you experience the moment you realize you'll be shaking someone's hand." Or: "I like a firm handshake, don't you?"

In other words, point out the end result you want the most "for them" and focus on that. They'll see the gap between where they are and where they can get to. In most cases, that alone will pull them toward the optimum.

3. NEVER MENTION PROGRESS, TIME, FUTURE, PAST, OR RATE OF DEVELOPMENT.

Old way: "You look so much happier than the last time I saw you!!!" Or: "You've lost so much weight!!!" Or: "It's been so long; we shouldn't let it go this long next time."

UC approach: "You look terrific, John." Or: "It is such a delight to spend time with you."

When you compare the person with how they used to act or how much "better" they are now, all you do is immediately bring them back to where they were before. Believe me, the person DOES know how "far" they have come. Acknowledge their progress by identifying them with what and how they are in the present moment. If you bring up a comparison instead, that's like saying, "Today you're somewhat different from the *real* you that we all know. Must be some kinda fluke, right?"

4. TELL THE TRUTH IN A WAY THAT EMPOWERS A PERSON.

Old way: "I think it's really important that you know blah blah blah about yourself." Or: "You need to work on that stutter; I know the perfect speech therapist." Or: "I know you didn't ask, but . . ."

UC approach: "I know exactly what you mean, Bob, it's a big change to make. But you're so disciplined and centered, I know you'll do great with it." Or: "That must have been a surprise for you; was it serendipitous?"

5. NOTICE IMMEDIATELY AND COMPLETELY ALL YOUR REACTIONS TO THE PERSON.

If you're having ANY negative reaction to the person, it's just about impossible to be UC and authentic, too. First, get to the source of the reaction. Then decide whether you should start spending time with people who don't bring up that sort of reaction in you.

6. BE THRILLED ABOUT WHERE THE PERSON IS ON THEIR PATH OF DEVELOPMENT.

This is important. I say "thrilled" rather than just accepting, because anything halfhearted can quickly translate into condescension, which is supremely unattractive.

Some well-meaning folks find it irresistibly tempting to "share" what they know or have learned with others—without being asked. It's usually not welcome.

If you have a knee-jerk reaction to share a solution or "next step" for a friend, client, or loved one, you're expressing your own need to make a difference, be right, be accurate, or be helpful. Those are all good things. But don't put the fulfillment of your own needs ahead of the respect you should have for the other person's boundaries. It takes a big person to be happy for where others are along the path of life. And an even bigger person to be happy for where they, themselves, are.

In other words, check yourself out for a second: Are you opening a door or attempting to push someone through?

If you're supplying an unwanted push, people are going to sense some patronization, pity, or judgment. Be sure you're not deliberately hanging around people (friends, clients, colleagues) who aren't "there" yet (at least up to your level) and getting some pleasure out of being the teacher or parent or "smart" one. It's an insidious way to get your needs met!

7. POINT OUT THE CHARACTER QUALITIES A PERSON NATURALLY HAS.

There's a big difference between accomplishments and qualities.

Accomplishments are what you have been able to do successfully. Qualities are the specialness a person has, distinct from skills, talents, or gifts.

A sure way to be unconditionally constructive is to focus on and remind the person about their special qualities. Why? Because it tells them they're already essentially wonderful. When you focus instead on accomplishments, talents, skills, or gifts, you obligate the person to perform and continue performing. You may mean it as a compliment, but it's often heard as "I like you for what you've done for me." The next logical sentence, whether spoken out loud or not, is "What are you going to do for me now?"

Old way: "You're such a good listener; you ought to have become a coach!" Or: "You are very prolific." Or: "You have the gift of patience; children must really adore you." Notice that these three examples ARE fairly positive, yet they still are performance-based, which implies obligation. Saddling people with obligations is very unattractive, and not to be confused with bringing out their best.

UC approach: "You have been very patient with me, and I appreciate it." Or: "The style you naturally have about you is very, very special." Or: "You seem to enjoy being forthright in your dealings."

See the difference? It's subtle, but the UC approach can bring about results that are radically more positive.

8. SPEAK TO THE PERSON AS IF THEY ARE WHOLE AND CAN DO ANYTHING.

Don't patronize or play God. Don't be afraid to ask or expect things from somebody just because you—or they—may doubt whether they can pull it off.

Assume that they can. More often than not, you'll be pleasantly surprised by how well they respond to the challenge! Of course, don't absolutely bank on the person either, if they are untested in an area. Give them room to fail and to bounce back from it a smarter person. Mistakes are great teachers, but people stand to learn more in a nonjudgmental setting.

9. As you develop and master this skill, YOU will evolve.

Being unconditionally constructive IS a skill-set, but as you learn and master it, you'll find yourself changing *and* evolving significantly—for several reasons.

First, it takes some effort, and a strong will, to speak so thoughtfully. This way of communicating is a real stretch, even if you feel you're already constructive.

Second, you'll find yourself seeing the positive sides of other people a lot more. As a result, you'll develop more compassion and respect for everyone, *including yourself.*

With these things working for you, you can't help becoming more conscious and aware. As I never get tired of pointing out, those skills are hugely visible in your career as well as your personal life.

10. Recognize your parents in the words and approaches you use.

One evening at a comedy club some years ago, I heard a singer/pianist named Dale Gonyea do a really clever song he'd written called "Help! I'm Turning into My Parents!"

If you haven't felt that little piece of existential irony yet, don't worry: It's on its way. We all eventually start to recognize our parents, and their relationship styles, in some of our own patterns. It might be a characteristic hand gesture, a certain way of expressing grumpiness, disdain, or even joy. It could be a way of stringing words together, a facial expression, a folding of the arms. And those parental patterns are more likely to emerge when stress or some other factor starts to distract you from the present moment.

I'm not criticizing parents in any way. But now that you've been made aware of the distinction of speaking in an unconditionally constructive way, contrary patterns you picked up from them may stick out a lot more.

Many of the terms and approaches we grew up with, even if meant to be encouraging or supportive, were simply not unconditionally constructive.

After all, parents have a challenging job, and they learned how to do it from watching *their* parents (who learned it from people who grew up in a previous century and probably on another continent).

You, on the other hand, have more evolved communication styles to choose from. Slipping back into preset patterns is just as much of a choice as aiming to be unconditionally constructive. You may miss the mark sometimes but can easily get back to the optimum communication style *if* you stay awake.

ORIENT YOURSELF AROUND YOUR VALUES

When You Spend Your Days Doing What Fulfills You, You Are Attractive

Let the firstlings of my heart be the firstlings of my hand.
—WILLIAM SHAKESPEARE

The privilege of a lifetime is being who you are.
—JOSEPH CAMPBELL

You can orient your life around a lot of things: wants, needs, shoulds, coulds, etc. But if you are clear on your values, and you orient your life around them, your chances of experiencing fulfillment are enhanced to the extreme. What I mean by *values* will get defined a bit more as you read through this step. For now, think of them as those wonderful, intangible things that attract *you*. Think of them also as forces that can make pep talks and motivational speeches totally unnecessary in your life. (And isn't that a relief!)

There are no absolute guarantees in life, but when this principle is intelligently applied, you're as close as possible to having a sure bet. Why? Because when all is said and done, you ARE your values. Orienting around your values, then, offers a perfect pathway to unity, wholeness, centeredness.

Notice that I said this principle must be intelligently applied. That means being awake, taking in messages from mind and body—not just ego. And always keeping some key distinctions clear.

DISTINCTIONS TO DRAW

VALUES VS. NEEDS—Values are activities, preferences, or behaviors that you are naturally drawn to. Needs are resources, people, feelings, situations, or environments you must have in order to be your best. When you get your needs met, you'll have more time for your values!

VALUES VS. WANTS—Values are you; wants are what you enjoy having. Values fulfill you; wants provide gratification.

VALUES VS. PRIORITIES—A value is you; a priority is something you decide to do sooner rather than later.

VALUES VS. GOALS—Values are you. Goals are objectives to achieve. Value-based goals are the most fulfilling type of goals to set.

FULFILLMENT VS. SATISFACTION—When you are fulfilled, your soul is full. When you are satisfied, your body, mind, or heart is satiated.

How to know you're making progress with this principle

- You don't find yourself torn between things. Your values will choose for you.
- You feel less conflicted, more at peace, because your goals are in sync with what is most important to you.
- You enjoy your work, and the different areas of your life flow together—no compartmentalization or juggling.
- You drop draining goals and projects that don't express your values.
- You have no regrets, whatever happens, because you have been true to your values.

TOP 10 WAYS TO ORIENT YOURSELF AROUND YOUR VALUES

1. VALUES ARE THE INTERESTS OR QUALITIES THAT ATTRACT YOU.

A value is something you naturally feel is important to you—whether it's beauty, creativity, family, honesty, friendships, or anything else of worth.

You'll realize its importance by the strength and depth of the feelings it awakens inside you.

As you review the following list, circle the twenty values that most appeal to you.

Adventure	Turn on	Be imaginative
Risk	Unstick others	Be original
The unknown	Coach	Conceive
Thrill	Spark	Plan
Danger	Encourage	Build
Speculation	Influence	Perfect
Dare	Stimulate	Assemble
Gamble	Energize	Inspire
Endeavor	Alter	Discover
Quest	Contribute	Learn
Experiment	Serve	Detect
Be exhilarated	Improve	Perceive
Venture	Augment	Locate
Create beauty	Endow	Realize
Embody grace	Strengthen	Uncover
Express refinement	Facilitate	Discern
Embody elegance	Minister to	Distinguish
Exude radiance	Grant	Observe
Experience magnificence	Provide	Feel
Experience gloriousness	Foster	Experience
Have taste	Assist	Emote
Catalyze	Create	Sense
Have impact	Design	Glow
Move forward	Invent	Feel good
Touch	Synthesize	Experience energy flow

Lead	Experience sensuality	Be awake
Guide	Experience bliss	Relate with God
Inspire	Be amused	Be devoted
Influence	Be entertained	Be holy
Cause	Play games	Be honoring
Arouse	Enjoy sports	Be passionate
Enroll	Relate	Be religious
Reign	Be connected	Teach
Govern	Be part of community	Educate
Rule	Be part of family	Instruct
Persuade	Unite	Enlighten
Model	Nurture	Inform
Embody mastery	Be linked	Prepare
Be expert	Be bonded	Edify
Dominate field	Be integrated	Prime
Be adept	Be with	Uplift
Be superior	Be sensitive	Explain
Hold primacy	Express tenderness	Win
Hold preeminence	Perceive	Prevail
Be the greatest	Be present	Accomplish
Be the best	Empathize	Attain
Outdo	Support	Score
Set standards	Show compassion	Acquire
Embody excellence	Respond	Win over
Give pleasure	See	Triumph
Have fun	Be spiritual	Predominate
Experience hedonism	Be aware	Attract
Experience sex	Be accepting	

2. THERE IS A BIG DIFFERENCE BETWEEN NEEDS, WANTS, AND VALUES.

A need is something you *must* have in order to be your best, such as time, space, money, love, information, food, exercise, or tools. Usually, getting a need met causes you to feel *satisfaction*.

A want is something that you relate to by trying to acquire or experience it, such as a vacation, a promotion, a gourmet meal, sex, a good book, a new car. Usually, getting something you want makes you feel *gratification*.

A value is something that you naturally gravitate toward, prompted from within and not by needs or wants.

The same thing can be a need, a want, or a value for different people, or for the same person at different times. It just depends on you or the situation. Here are some guidelines that will help you draw distinctions:

If there is urgency, it is probably a need.

If there is craving or desire, it's probably a want.

If there is a natural and uncomplicated pull, it's probably a value.

Being able to distinguish among all three takes a little practice, but one of the many benefits is that you'll understand yourself better and make better decisions, because decisions based on your values will have more chance of being right and staying right for a long time. Decisions based on wants or needs are not as likely to be beneficial on a continuous basis.

Look back at the exercise above. Can you now prune away any wants and needs from your twenty selections? After checking out that possibility, add or subtract enough items to bring your list to a total of five. Now you're looking at your core values and at an incredibly valuable reference point for all the choices you'll ever make.

3. IT'S HARD TO DISCOVER AND ORIENT AROUND YOUR VALUES IF YOUR NEEDS ARE NOT MET.

This principle is a bigger challenge for anyone who has not gotten their needs met. Unmet needs usually cloud your ability to identify your values. Until those needs are satisfied, it's pretty tough to distinguish between needs, wants, and values.

FYI, one of the greatest side benefits of getting needs met is that the number and intensity of your wants will decrease measurably. Which puts fewer obstructions between you and your values. It's an amazing thing but true.

4. IT IS POSSIBLE TO ORIENT YOUR LIFE FULLY AROUND YOUR VALUES, VIA WEAVING AND EXPRESSING.

A value is like a theme, not just a focus or an orientation. A theme, say beauty or adventure or discovery, is something you can weave into all aspects of your life. So, technically, you don't have to orient your life entirely around your values—although you can.

A good first step is to get involved in activities that let you express those values. If adventure is a core value, for example, either get a job that has an adventurous aspect, or create adventure in whatever else you do.

5. VALUES HELP YOU SET BETTER GOALS.

A lot of folks spin their wheels for days, weeks, months, and years because they can't decide whether or not a certain course of action would be worthwhile. Whenever you're considering a certain goal, run it by your list of five values. Does it fit in with or express any one or two of them? If so, it's likely to be worthwhile. And you've just saved yourself a lot of stewing.

6. VALUES ARE VERY IMPORTANT BECAUSE, WHEN HONORED, THEY LEAD TO OPPORTUNITIES.

Recently, a growing high-tech company on the Eastern Seaboard hired a coach to help a high-level manager navigate problems caused by a rivalry between her department and another one. Fortunately, those problems resolved quickly. But, since the company had already budgeted four months' worth of coaching expenses, she was allowed to use the service personally.

"So," the coach reports, "we started talking about the fact that she was bored. Her staff was coming to her with really creative ideas, and she was jealous of the fun they were having. Her own job, even if higher up the totem pole, lacked sufficient challenge. It seemed to her that it was time to look for something new."

In the meantime, another high-tech outfit had approached her about starting up a whole new business within their existing company. All she had to do was evolve a plan they liked: Financing and support would follow. But she hadn't written anything up yet because she wasn't sure what they wanted to hear.

The coach suggested doing two things. First, seek more responsibility in the job she had. Make it fun for herself again. In other words, orient around her values by seeking new challenges.

The next thing was to stop worrying about what these people presenting the entrepreneurial opportunity wanted and to get clear for herself what kind of company *she* wanted to create.

She began by writing down what would make her present job more attractive to her. That job done, she memoed her boss—politely but definitively—with her concerns and the solutions she'd like to see. Then she put together a proposal for the potential employers, describing the proposed new business exactly as she most wanted it to be, reflecting not only the strategies she thought could succeed but also creating an environment where she felt her best qualities would always be engaged. In short, a business that would make her feel joyful and challenged, too.

While her boss was mulling her suggestions, she met with the other people, who absolutely loved the business concept she'd designed. They want her to get started right away. However, on the evening she'd presented her proposal, her boss called her at home from his car phone (something he'd never done before) and told her that he was going to expand her role, just as she'd requested, and grant her a big raise.

Which opportunity should she choose? This is the kind of career quandary we should all have. The funny thing is, most people are afraid that being clear about their values will hurt their careers. In fact, what it will do is steer you toward what is right for you—in your work life *and* in your personal life.

7. VALUES ARE VERY IMPORTANT BECAUSE THEY HELP YOU SCREEN AND FILTER NATURALLY.

In number 5 above, I mentioned that by knowing your values, you can set better goals—ones that are more naturally "you." In addition to goal setting, you can also better filter or screen the events, surprises, and people who come your way (aka the content of your life).

Not sure how to respond (or overrespond) to a person, problem, or opportunity? Run it by your core values. See if it fits or qualifies. If not, pass. If so, embrace.

Again, decision making made easy! And it sure beats making a list of pros and cons.

8. VALUES GIVE YOU SOMETHING TO HONOR.

If your self-esteem is weak or is just developing, or if you're in a period of rapid transition, you may not know which way is up or who the heck you are—which is disorienting to say the least. But when you know your values (which generally stay the same all through your life), you can lean on them and honor them. This comes in handy as a backup support system.

If you're upset or confused and can't completely honor yourself in some moment, simply honor your values.

9. PLAY THE "GOALS EQUALS VALUES" GAME.

This is fun. Look at your list of five core values. Then, make a separate list of your five most important goals. Now try to match up each goal to one of your values.

If there's a goal that can't find a "home" (matching value), think of how you might change it so it will line up more closely with your values. It's a great exercise for becoming more true to yourself.

Note: Some goals are integrity- or need-based and deserve to be honored as well, so you don't have to throw any of them out just because you can't find a matching value.

10. USE VALUES AS A CATALYST AND MOTIVATOR
TO GET YOUR NEEDS MET.

Earlier, I coached you to first get your needs met and then work on identifying and expressing your values. That's usually the easiest approach. However, you can start with values first if you want to. This works well for some people, because once they are strongly in touch with their values, they'll find added incentive to take care of whatever gets in the way of expressing their values 100 percent of the time.

This is one of my favorite aspects of the Principles of Attraction: Since they loop back into each other at several points, no matter where you start in the system you'll eventually discover everything that's specifically important to you.

SIMPLIFY EVERYTHING

*Abandoning Nonessentials Leaves
More Room for Attraction*

You can't have everything. Where would you put it?
—STEVEN WRIGHT

We are here and it is now. Further than that, all human knowledge is moonshine.

—H. L. MENCKEN

Starting today, simplify your life. By abandoning at least one project, goal, role, problem, or dream that hasn't been moving forward easily you will—believe it or not—move more rapidly toward your truest, closest-to-the-heart dreams.

The idea here is much like the one you learned about tolerations. It's another facet of being superconductive—getting the greatest possible return on any energy you spend.

Here, though, the lesson relates to a tactic that sports coaches call "picking your spots," which means focusing your sharpest skills and strongest efforts at the right times and in the right places. Any game has turning points. So does a life. When you've simplified your life, you can sense a pivotal moment coming and bring your full concentration into it. And that will put you in a position to win!

Winning has certain psychological contours, certain feelings, and you want to develop those into a personal groove, because your goal is not just to win but to sustain the habit of winning.

DISTINCTIONS TO DRAW

SIMPLIFY VS. ERADICATE—To simplify is to make less complex. To eradicate is to cut things out. Reducing and integrating can lead to simplification; you don't have to lop chunks of your life off unless you want to.

SPACE VS. TIME—When you have room and freedom to think and live, you can better manage your time because you will be anticipating better. When you don't have enough space, time becomes a limited resource. There is PLENTY of time, but only if you first create enough space.

OUTSOURCE VS. DELEGATE—*Outsource* means to hire a professional to take responsibility to handle a matter, function, or problem. To delegate means that you still "own" the problem but are working with someone who will do their best to solve it. Better to outsource than to delegate.

If dream projects, social opportunities, clients, or any other potential breakthroughs have been eluding you, give them up. Stop your pursuit.

This doesn't mean that you're accepting defeat. It means that you're going to proceed, with confidence, into areas where there's more likelihood of a positive return on the energy you'll invest.

Dreams are not foolish in and of themselves. In fact they're wonderful, and they're also one of the most important aspects of who you are. But sometimes they represent themselves, and sometimes they represent other wishes in disguise.

One of my friends is a performing guitarist. He also happens to be a very approachable person. Fairly regularly, people come up to him after a show and say how much they want to play guitar, too. They ask about taking lessons. Some of them even go out, purchase a guitar, and take a lesson or two. But very, very few ever keep playing.

Why? Not because they're lazy, or bad people, but because it wasn't really the right dream for them. It would probably take them hundreds of hours of practice to get the desired return: the ability to express their feelings through an artistic skill. Or maybe just to feel lighter in spirit. So their musicianship dreams really represented something else, which they could achieve in several other ways.

As you become more sensitized, you'll begin to have a more solid sense of what propels your dreams. This is key, because the spirit of a dream is far more important, and lasting, than its exact form.

That's why you have to hold your dreams lightly and not squeeze the soul out of them. Just stay open to the possibility that you might ultimately fulfill them in some great way that you haven't even dared to think of yet.

So . . . Do you really need to get close to that certain, specific person? Do you really have to land that certain blue-chip client? Do you really have to beat down a certain thorny problem, once and for all, in order to feel all right about yourself?

Give up. Wisely. Don't court frustration and anger. As we've noted before, striving is unattractive. Believe in the process of attraction and that a time will come when the answers and the people and the rewards will come to you without being called, simply because they like to be where you are.

One of the most interesting benefits of becoming irresistibly attractive is that you'll attract a LOT of stuff, mostly good. If you start now to simplify your life considerably, you'll be creating the space to respond well to all the new stuff. Without a lot of space, you might find yourself feeling overwhelmed.

How to know you're making progress with this principle

- You feel bored. But that's good news! It's just a way station. Real fulfillment is approaching.
- Before you jump on an opportunity, you screen it first to see if it would needlessly complicate your life, no matter how great it is.
- The feeling of excitement you've previously gotten from complication and stress becomes distasteful, and you easily avoid stirring them up again.
- You spend less money.
- You have much less to manage and a lot more free time.
- You have a lot more emotional, physical, and intellectual space.
- Successes come more quickly because there is room for them!

TOP 10 WAYS
TO SIMPLIFY EVERYTHING

1. STOP DOING ERRANDS.

I don't know if anyone's ever collected the statistics, but my guess is that an inordinate percentage of our free time is spent shopping, schlepping stuff and people around town, getting things fixed, and the like. How much time do you spend doing errands in an average week? Since time is a commodity, and you want to use it in ways that reward you, doesn't your errand-running time feel a little too expensive compared to your bigger goals?

While nothing is really wrong with doing errands, it's likely you'll be less willing to spend so much time on them once you've begun to find more things to do that bring you fulfillment.

How do you get around the need for doing errands? Maybe you can pay a friend who loves to shop, hire a personal shopper, get a delivery service. Or do the shopping in person but pay for delivery—saving yourself the most tiring part of the chore. Reasonably priced solutions can be found, and they're worth it.

2. GET A VIRTUAL ASSISTANT.

I use a virtual assistant for several reasons. First, I tend to put off tasks, and they get to be weighty before long. Second, I am a procrastinator by nature and I know that it can be an extremely high-cost trait if allowed to go on. Third, I am not very good with tasks like dealing with vendors, scheduling appointments, and making requests of people I don't know. Fortunately, my VA is terrific at all of these things.

Finally, my VA acts as my personal "garbage disposal." I E-mail her with the problems, potential problems, stuff I just don't want to deal with, and she "consumes" them by the end of the day. No stopped-up drains on my end! What is a big problem to me is, to her, just a little task. (By the way, her E-mail address is *jkhewett@thebranchoffice.com*.)

3. AUTOMATE ALL ADMINISTRATIVE AND FINANCIAL TASKS.

Whether you're an employee, own a business, or want to streamline your personal chores, there are lots of administrative tasks that you can automate. These include preparing taxes (get a CPA), bill paying (Quicken or CheckFree software), bookkeeping (get a bookkeeper), using a debit card (vs. credit card), having your phone and other bills paid via autodeductions.

Again, you'll open up space in your life that more than justifies the costs. Space isn't a luxury add-on to your process of evolution—it's a necessity.

4. USE A REMINDER SERVICE.

AOL and many other Net providers have free E-mail reminder services that can remind you automatically about birthdays, anniversaries, and other important dates.

True, you *can* keep track of these manually, but delegating this function to a "system" means you have one less document or book to keep around—and perhaps forget to check.

5. ELIMINATE ENOUGH PROMISES, PROJECTS, AND PLANS UNTIL YOU FEEL PLENTY OF SPACE.

Life has become incredibly complicated and busy for most folks today, due perhaps to the fact that we have many more choices regarding work, sideline businesses, self-development, advanced education, travel, hobbies, and entertainment.

You may feel a need to get into some new area of interest, take some extension courses, etc., but most of the time those thoughts are an expression of some other, more underlying desire. Probably a wish for fulfillment. But the activities and interests you've already chosen likely offer more potential than something you'd have to start from scratch.

Catch yourself early enough so that you can say—and feel—that having (and maintaining) plenty of space is more important than getting into yet another hobby, project, or commitment. In other words, make space as important as a new interest could possibly be.

6. Empty your closets of any clothes you don't really like.

This may not seem like a huge thing to some people, but clothes have a lot of symbolic importance. You'll be amazed at how much it will lighten you up, and it usually sets off a chain reaction that will simplify other areas of your life. When it comes to closets, basements, attics, and storage units, adopt the mind-set of a master gardener. Prune mercilessly and confidently, knowing that you're making space for new life.

7. Wean away consuming people.

A coach recently reported to me that one of her former clients had just gotten in touch again. And it turned out that this client had coauthored a book that had been on the best-seller list for several weeks. Now, going back to the drawing board for her next project, she was ready to resume being coached.

Two things got her to the point where she could write the first book. Both involved simplifying. The most fundamental of all was realizing that a lot of her time was taken up with "yakkety-yak" relationships. Because she happens to have a great sense of humor, people just wanted to spend time with her. But she needed to get that sense of humor down on paper! And she recognized that all she got out of those relationships was being able to avoid the thing that she needed to do most, which was to write.

Next came simplifying her finances, so there would be time to experiment as she wrote and get her voice onto the page exactly as she wanted it. The powerful combination, created by jettisoning distractions, has given her the space to create a wonderful career.

Simplify *your* personal relationships. For me, it's worked well to identify the ten most important people in my life and focus on them—instead of trying to juggle my once-large Rolodex.

In my case, the first to go were people who, though nice and helpful, needed me a lot more than I *wanted* to be needed. Sometimes it's tricky to identify these people in your life, because they're often very, very special in many ways. But if you feel drained after spending time with them, and you can't fix the problem, it's probably time to wean them away.

There ARE terrific people you'll be meeting as you become more attractive, and they won't drain you. Happily, they'll be just as rewarded and fulfilled by your company as you are by theirs. You need to reserve space in your life for them, right away. It's that important.

8. Order supplies, equipment, goods, via 800 numbers and the Internet.

Almost anything can be ordered over the phone or on the Web today, and quickly delivered, including new cars, groceries, office and other supplies, tools, computers, electronics, and professional services.

Once you make this leap, you can stop getting trapped at the mall. No more multiacre parking lots. No more trying to recall if your car is in area 3, level C (lilac), or in 12, level E (mustard yellow). No more Muzak. No more wandering in a stupefying maze of advertising overkill. No more elbow-to-elbow crowd movement. Presto. Paying perhaps a little more for delivery (but often saving much more via highly competitive pricing), you'll be rewarded by the removal of great quantities of stress.

Like banging your head against a wall, mall shopping feels so good when you stop it.

9. Delegate most household chores.

Hire a housekeeper, maintenance people, a handyperson, and "special task" people. Will this cost you something financially? Yes, most likely. However, you'll probably find yourself making more money in your job or business if you have this extra time (and the space to be creative that it provides), just knowing that your household is taken care of.

Sure you CAN clean your own home. Some people find certain household tasks are kind of meditative. But if they're costing you ANY creative time, farm them out.

10. Simplify your lifestyle so that you'll have less— and less to have to do—in numbers 1–9 above.

If your life is really complicated, or your lifestyle very busy, you may not be able to reach this place of "space" that simplification brings, even if you apply all of the above nine suggestions. So, before you rush to apply them all, first decide if it's your life (or lifestyle) itself that needs to be simplified significantly. The litmus test, of course, is that your lifestyle should enhance your life, rather than spending your life enhancing your lifestyle. A key realization is that having depth in your interests and activities is usually less expensive and more fulfilling than having a wide but shallow range. Searching for more excitement in your life is like trying too hard to "have a blast" on New Year's Eve or any other special occasion. It's better to become attractive. Excitement will come to you, and you'll be able to select however much of it you may want.

It can be as easy as saying, "Wow, I'm ready for a very, very simple life at this point. What major change would I need to make to get on that track?"

MASTER YOUR CRAFT

The Easiest Way to Become Successful?
Become the Best at What You Do

I am always doing that thing which I can not do, in order that I may learn how to do it.

—PABLO PICASSO

If you practice an art, be proud of it and make it proud of you . . . it will make you a person in your own right.

—MAXWELL ANDERSON

Competency is no longer some great, lofty thing to aspire to; it has become the floor, or even subfloor, of professional success. It's the starting point, not the goal.

That's why good enough isn't good enough anymore, especially if you're adopting the Attraction Operating System. You need to set your sights higher—all the way up to mastery—in terms of what you do for a living and how you do it.

How to know you're making progress with this principle

- You learn more quickly.
- You include others in your learning process.
- You find yourself learning from everything.
- You find yourself drifting away from colleagues and others who aren't learning as fast as you or who aren't on a mastery path.

DISTINCTIONS TO DRAW

MASTERY VS. COMPETENCE—When you are competent, you can do your work at high standards. When you are a master, you invent the next level of your work, craft, or business, which is a lot more attractive, especially to better clients and customers.

SUCCEED VS. WIN—To succeed means to accomplish, to ascend. To win, there must be a loser. Winning implies cost.

INNOVATION VS. IMPROVEMENT—To innovate means to revolutionize, or at least introduce something new and important into the recipe. To improve is to make what you have better, incrementally. To innovate is to evolve, which is far more attractive.

INVENTION VS. INNOVATION—Invention, discovering or creating something for the first time, is even more radically evolutionary than innovation.

EFFECTIVENESS VS. EFFICIENCY—To be efficient means that you get a job done in a smart, resourceful, timely way. To be effective means that you get the RIGHT job done well, whether efficiently or not. Efficiency combined with effectiveness is quite powerful, but effectiveness is *always* more important. Even the most efficient buggy-whip manufacturer won't prosper at this stage in history.

ASSIMILATION VS. INTEGRATION—To assimilate means to absorb and to be nourished and developed by what you are learning, eating, or experiencing. It is incorporated into YOU. To integrate means to link or bond with something else and, as a result, create a new synthesis. Both assimilation and integration are evolutionary.

- You find surprisingly different and better ways to deliver what you offer professionally, even if you are already very good at what you do.
- You enjoy innovating and doing things unconventionally.

TOP 10 WAYS
TO MASTER YOUR CRAFT

1. INVENT SOMETHING NEW IN YOUR FIELD.

It may sound like an extravagant goal, but it's really NOT that difficult. You don't have to be an Einstein or an Edison, but you do have to give yourself permission to tap into your natural intuition, creativity, and, yes, *genius*.

To make it all easier, get closer to your customers. The more you do that, the more ideas you'll have. They'll inspire you whenever they say what they like, what they love, what they hate, and what they wish was part of the available products and/or services in your field. Customers are your research and development department.

Question: What's something that your current customers need but haven't specifically or directly asked for yet?

2. INVENT A BETTER WAY FOR CUSTOMERS TO USE YOUR PRODUCT OR SERVICE.

It's one thing to be a great attorney, coach, or RV salesperson. It's quite another to actually care how WELL your clients use your service or product. Most providers, manufacturers, and salespeople SAY they care about this, but they really don't. At least, as long as this year's sales aren't horrendously worse than last year's figures.

If you really care about how much good people get out of your service or product, you'll start finding ways for them to get even more value. Which will lead to one or both of two terrific things: They'll become more loyal and/or they'll find benefit in buying even more.

Question: If you DID care this much, how would you prove it?

3. GET SMARTER BY TEACHING OTHERS.

One of my favorite moments in novelist John Barth's *The Sot-Weed Factor* is when one character tells another the real challenge is teaching something you haven't learned yet, because "any fool can teach what he already knows!"

Don't try to force yourself to master your craft all by yourself. That's a lot of extra work. A fast way to master your craft is to offer to teach the newer people in your field what you know. They, in turn, will ask YOU questions, which will drive you further in your own learning and progressing. Surround yourself with very smart students, and you'll become a real master of your craft.

Question: What can I learn from new people coming into my field?

4. BRING A PIECE OF WHAT YOU DO AND SHARE IT WITH THE PUBLIC, FOR FREE.

This prompts you to think in terms of serving a much larger market than you may be serving now. What IF you could give away a piece of what you do, know, or have to tens of thousands of people? How would you go about it? Who are the people who could benefit?

Earlier, we discussed the benefits of having a Capillary System versus hard-sell marketing. One of the keys is realizing that, no matter how much you've been conditioned to guard your work and your knowledge jealously, there's probably a lot that you could distribute for free without harming your position. In fact, you're likely to enhance it a little bit now and a lot in the future.

This has always been a central precept behind CoachV, and in a recent two-week span we fielded more potential-student inquiries than we had in our first two *years*. When you give knowledge away for free, you also give people an easier way to come near you, see what you're all about, and possibly become a client. And a well-informed client at that, which is the best kind to have.

5. RAISE AT LEAST ONE STANDARD IN YOUR FIELD OR INDUSTRY.

This is one great way to improve yourself, your industry, and your own professional reputation. Of all the separate components in your product or service, which could you improve slightly and thereby cause a big overall improvement?

Every time one person in an industry or field does this, the bar gets raised. People with a lesser degree of mastery either get caught up or shaken out.

Public appreciation notches higher, and everyone with mastery benefits. Make sure you're part of their numbers and not among those shaken out (unless a change of occupation is what you really want, anyway).

Question: What is the one professional standard you could raise that would make you stand out among your peers?

6. REDUCE THE EMOTIONAL AND TIME COST OF DELIVERY OF YOUR PRODUCT OR SERVICE.

In order to have the time and space to master your craft, you'll probably need to find a way to simplify, streamline, or automate part of what you do to get your product or service delivered. Of course, this alone makes you more attractive right now. The mastery, as it develops, will make you even more attractive in the future.

Question: Is there some aspect of what you do professionally that is unnecessary, time-expensive, or emotionally expensive to your customers?

7. INCREASE THE DEMAND FOR YOUR PRODUCT OR SERVICE.

I believe that whenever you focus on increasing the demand for what you provide (meaning to give more people more and better reasons to buy what you offer), you are in effect getting better at what you do. This focus puts you more in the shoes of your current as well as potential customers, and it helps you imagine features and benefits they will respond to. As a side effect, you'll be evolving the product or service you provide.

Question: What's one thing that almost *everyone* really wants in life; how can I link my product or service to it?

8. INTEGRATE YOUR PRODUCT OR SERVICE WITH OTHER POPULAR PRODUCTS OR SERVICES.

Nowadays, people rarely buy something to use all by itself. Usually it interlocks somehow with other products or services or enhances them as a tool to get more out of life.

No product or service is an island—it's part of a network. For example, there are cars, motorcycles, musical instruments, stereos, and cameras, and there are aftermarket products to help people get more value from those purchases. Sometimes the value is in expanded usefulness, sometimes just in image-related appeal. And, of course, there is the mutually beneficial relationship of hardware and software. When Hollywood makes better movies, attendance goes up and more theaters are built, employing more people, etc. When software makers devise irresistible new computer applications, requiring a little more "horsepower," computer makers can create quicker, brainier machines. And vice versa.

Question: What product or service do people use a lot that I can link my product or service to?

9. TAP INTO THE MINDS OF THE SMARTEST, MOST VISIONARY PEOPLE IN YOUR INDUSTRY.

There are visionaries in every field. One of the fastest ways to master, or simply improve, your skill-sets is to be in touch with these smart people in some way.

I read *Wired* and subscribe to several E-mail broadcasts from supersmart people in the training, development, and Internet industries. Working outward from those resources, I've developed relationships with several brilliant people. I can turn to them with questions. Their responses prompt my thinking in ways that would never occur if I was just working on my own.

This is more than just plain networking. It's highly targeted. And the support you give these people, via subscriptions, trade-outs of services, etc., not only brings you specific help from people whose intelligence runs at exciting levels—it also frees those visionaries to focus even more on unexplored possibilities for your field.

Question: Who is the smartest, most visionary person you know of in your field? How can they be accessed? Do they have an electronic mailing list?

10. INVENT A NEW CRAFT.

This, of course, is cheating. But what a way to win!

There are new professions and crafts popping up all the time, in response to a generation of more educated, demanding, and specialized consumers. Don't be afraid to invent an entirely new service or product, and give it a new name. Everything is based on, or somehow feeds upon, what came before. Movies are an elaboration of the concept of stage plays, and they still use hit plays as content material. Television is an elaboration of the concept of movies, and it uses movies as content.

Your invention will likely take some existing ideas or products, recombine some of their elements creatively, and open up a previously untapped market with a product or service that somehow connects to it better than any predecessors' products or services did.

That's exactly how business and personal coaching got started as a profession. And it has thrived.

RECOGNIZE AND TELL
THE TRUTH

The Truth Is the Most Attractive Thing of All,
but It Requires Skills and Awareness

> Anything more than the truth would be too much.
> —ROBERT FROST

Telling the truth is a skill that may take several years to master. That's because telling the truth is something that doesn't always come naturally. Mark Twain wrote a great line about congressmen being people who would never lie "unless it was absolutely convenient." Well, we all have those same truthful-when-convenient tendencies. Partly because there's a lot about truth—like its power, its changeability, and the skills needed to handle it right.

Recognizing the subtleties and completeness of truth requires plenty of awareness and sensitivity, plus a strong vocabulary (to exactly pinpoint what you see or feel), and enough of a reserve to feel that you can "afford" the truth.

What gets in the way of people telling the truth (besides ignorance) is fear of potential consequences. In other words, their survival needs. So, telling the truth is more than just being honest. It's also creating an environment where you aren't so scared, so close to the edge that it feels like you need a lie to save your bacon.

DISTINCTIONS TO DRAW

TRUTH VS. ACCURACY—Accuracy assumes accepted measures being used to prove a truth. However, the truth may sometimes not be provable by standard measures.

TRUTH VS. FACTS—Truth is what is so for you. A fact is provable by others. Truth is fairly personal and may not be provable in a traditional sense.

TRUTH VS. DOGMA—Truth changes and evolves. Dogma was true at one time but has since been boxed in and now may be untrue or irrelevant.

EVOLVE VS. GROW—To evolve means to change by mutation. To grow means to get stronger or better, more definitively who you already are. Both are terrific.

INTEGRITY VS. HONESTY—Integrity is doing what is best for you that makes you whole. Honesty is about telling the truth. Honesty contributes to your integrity, but there are more aspects to integrity than just telling the truth.

DISTINCTION VS. DEFINITION—A distinction is a subtle difference that becomes clear when you contrast like-seeming words. A definition states with clarity what something is.

DISTINCTION VS. VOCABULARY—Distinctions are a subset of vocabulary. They require that a person be sensitive and aware enough to appreciate the subtleties. Having a rich vocabulary is a great start to realizing distinctions. Distinctions don't just educate you; they evolve you. That's why you should experience distinctions, not just memorize them.

How to know you're making progress with this principle

- You enjoy telling the truth, even if there are significant consequences. In other words, you don't put goals, objectives, or needs ahead of the truth.
- You're able to recognize falseness—yours and other people's—much earlier than before.
- You think more creatively because you don't need to hold on to old ideas or truisms.

- You solve problems faster; truth gives you an incentive to reduce possible negative consequences for you because the cost is very clear.
- You grasp new and subtle distinctions in every situation because you are seeking more than just the facts.

TOP 10 WAYS TO RECOGNIZE AND TELL THE TRUTH

1. REDUCE OR ELIMINATE ANYTHING THAT CLOUDS OR NUMBS YOUR ABILITY TO RECOGNIZE TRUTH AS IT EMERGES.

You can't tell the truth if you can't recognize it. If you're high on adrenaline, stressed at work, if you smoke, drink, or take drugs, then your body is at a disadvantage to recognize what is true and what is BECOMING true at any given moment. By the time you recognize it, it's past. So, in effect, you're always operating *behind* the truth curve.

What's tricky is that people who do adrenalizing things or use mind-altering substances often do so because it makes them feel "more alive." The sad part is they're trading a few moments of acuity for a long stretch in the fog. In other words, they experience something exhilarating, a brief sense of being balanced on the razor's edge, for being part brain-dead the rest of the time. And they do it because real life, as they've been living it, doesn't have enough punch.

It might make you "feel alive" to be tossed by a huge wave, but there's a lot better experience to be had by catching the wave and surfing it beautifully, riding it out to its full potential and yours. Of course, you'll need a well-made board, awareness of how waves tend to break in that spot, sensitive timing of the wave as it crests, plus great balance. And you'll know more fun and fulfillment than any smoker, drinker, overworker, or junkie who ever lived. It's exactly the same feeling when you can afford the truth, and have the skills to tell it well. Anything that subtracts from presence of mind is going to hold you back from fulfillment.

2. YOU CAN'T RECOGNIZE OR TELL THE TRUTH UNLESS YOU HAVE A WELL-TUNED VOCABULARY.

The truth is quite often paradoxical and almost always filled with important nuances. Most people need to expand their vocabulary in order to describe fully what they feel, see, hear, or otherwise sense. What also helps is knowing key distinctions, like the ones shown at the beginning of each of the 28 steps. For even more, visit *http://www.distinctionary.com*. The juxtapositioning of similar-yet-dissimilar words can really make your perception of the truth come alive.

3. BECOME A PERSON OF INTEGRITY, NOT JUST AN HONEST PERSON.

Honesty is just the beginning arc of the truth curve. Next comes forthrightness, then fairness, then integrity.

To be a person of integrity you must understand and honor your own integrity and also that of others, of a situation, of life itself. You have to recognize and live by the truth that your actions or words affect far more than just yourself or the other person—they affect life itself. In a previous step, we talked about profoundly affecting others. To take that further, we affect others profoundly all the time. So why not be someone who does it with grace and style, and always in a positive way?

4. UNDERSTAND THAT TRUTH (OR AT LEAST OUR PERCEPTION OF IT) EVOLVES.

Truth is not dogma. Just as the human species evolves, so does truth. What was truth for someone 100 years ago may not be regarded as truth today. This is an uncomfortable notion for some people. But, for just one example, it took some people centuries to admit they were wrong about the truths Galileo discovered, just because those truths seemed to undercut their ideas of how the universe worked.

Religions aren't the only institutions that sometimes show disrespect for the evolving nature of truth. Governments generate fresh examples on an almost daily basis, as do corporations, schools, and scientists. Actually, what we think of as "truth" is in some ways akin to Napoleon's definition of history: "The lies agreed upon by the winners." In other words, truth is—to some degree, at least—a socially constructed phenomenon. Since people are still a long way from being gods, it follows that "truths" can go in and out of fashion.

But the answer to that conundrum is not to become more cynical. Rather, it's to expand your awareness of what the truth is for *you*—and of how you should always be capable of perceiving its changes.

5. TRUTH UNFOLDS, AND BECOMES CLEAR, CONTINUOUSLY.

This is similar to the evolving nature of truth, as described in number 4 above. But here I emphasize that as one sees and feels more clearly, one can see the truth "better" or more clearly—just as when a fog gradually dissipates, the details on the valley floor are easier to see. Don't glom onto the first bit of truth you recognize. Rather, notice it and stay open to the next thing you'll see on the "valley floor."

The late Father Anthony DeMello, a Jesuit priest of Indian/Portuguese background, wrote a story about when the Devil and an acquaintance were walking together, a discreet distance behind a man who didn't sense their presence. The man suddenly stopped, picked something up that pleased him, and carried it away.

"What's that?" the Devil's friend asked.

"He found a Truth," the Devil answered.

"Doesn't that worry you?"

"No," said the Devil. "Very soon he'll turn it into a Belief."

The moral: Hold the truth the same way you hold your dreams— lightly enough that you don't squeeze the life out of it. Dreams evolve as awareness grows, and so does the truth. Beliefs, on the other hand, tend to turn into dogma.

6. YOU WON'T TELL THE TRUTH IF YOU CAN'T AFFORD IT.

Survival—in its many forms—is more immediately compelling than truth. The fact is, truth can "kill" you, meaning that if you recognize and reorient around something that you recently discovered to be true, you DO take a risk. Because you never know what's going to result when you start telling the truth.

So, as terrific as the truth is, not everyone can fully afford the consequences of telling the truth and orienting around it. Of course, telling the truth really IS worthwhile, for its own sake, but you have to be prepared for the potential fallout—which is just one more important reason to respect the power that having superreserves can bring.

7. NOT MANY PEOPLE ARE ESPECIALLY INTERESTED IN THE TRUTH.

I think it's fairly true that most people aren't that interested in recognizing the truth and orienting 100 percent around it. To do so could be fairly disruptive to the status quo and even to how the person is getting their needs met.

The truth may set you free, but there is often a cost associated with this freedom. As I once heard someone say, "The truth will set you free, but first it will piss you off!" That perceived cost keeps most people fairly content where they are.

The "truth" here, then, is that they don't want to pay the price of the truth, and that's just about as honest as you can get! So don't expect them to embrace the truthfulness you put in front of them. Know your audience! Harsh as it may sound, remember the biblical injunction about casting pearls before swine.

8. PERCEIVING THE TRUTH IS SOMETIMES ALL THAT YOU NEED TO DO.

Here's where "The truth shall set you free" makes real sense. You don't necessarily have to do anything once you recognize and tell the truth! What I've found is that when people do recognize and tell the truth as it emerges, their bodies are naturally guided to reorient around the truth. It doesn't take commitment or willpower.

One might say that the body and the soul seek truth once it's found. They are naturally attracted toward it. You needn't force yourself to change. You don't have to consciously rebuild your belief system. The truth will evolve you. That's how strong it is! So why not trust in that strength and have patience with yourself in the meantime?

9. The truth is what will make you most irresistibly attractive.

Of all the 28 steps along the attraction path, telling the truth is the one that will make the biggest difference for you. Because even though we get scared and put up our internal barriers to truth, it's like oxygen to our minds and our souls. On a spiritual level, becoming more truthful is like experiencing a miraculous recovery from emphysema.

The stronger your skills and reserves are, the easier it will be for you to breathe deeply.

10. Stop searching for the truth.

The truth is not "out there." It's all around you and inside of you. And it's relative, not static.

Use the Attraction OS as a support tool. It can help you recognize what is true FOR YOU—which is the most important truth of all. What's true for you is far more "truthful" than what is broadly agreed to be "true."

Believe what you feel, hear, and see; don't believe in "the truth." There isn't any.

HAVE A VISION

When You Can See What's Coming,
You Don't Need to Create a Future

Where there is love and inspiration, I don't think you can go
wrong.

—ELLA FITZGERALD

That is happiness: to be dissolved into something complete and
great.

—WILLA CATHER

"Have a vision" sounds like such a big or impressive thing, doesn't it? But
don't get intimidated. A vision is a very practical thing. Having a vision is
just a natural extension of being who you are.

This Top 10 List is designed to explain what a vision is, how it works, how
easy it is to find one, and what to do with it once you do see it. For example, Microsoft's vision is a very clear one: "a computer on every desk and in
every home, all running Microsoft software." (I'm paraphrasing a bit.)

If you can't articulate a vision right now, or even after trying to assimilate this step, don't worry about it for a second. Your vision will emerge
before long, once you believe that it can and you recognize the importance
of letting it come through. And it might evolve over time, too. Be just as
accepting of that.

DISTINCTIONS TO DRAW

VISION VS. PURPOSE—A vision is what is clearly visible to you and probably to others. It's not you, nor is it a reason for living. It's simply something you see that's clear to you. You can choose to move toward it or just enjoy it from a distance. It has a tug but not a charge. A purpose, however, is personal. It orients, defines, and identifies you. It is likely to be connected with the past, and thus can sometimes be a burden or a drag.

VISION VS. GOAL—A vision is what you see as likely to occur, whether you actively work on it or not. A goal is what you identify as something to achieve.

How to know you're making progress with this principle

- You notice current trends and easily see how the future will look.
- You stop reading books on discovering your life purpose.
- You start seeing how perfect your life has been, because it's prepared you to do something very special to further your vision. This perspective helps you be very accepting of what has happened in your life thus far.
- Fears about the future are quieted because you can see what's coming.
- You quit chasing goals, objectives, and pipe dreams.
- You don't feel the need to create meaning in your life; it's already in place.

TOP 10 WAYS
TO HAVE A VISION

1. BE CLUED IN TO THE TRENDS AFFECTING SOCIETY, BUSINESS, AND YOU.

A vision is, in one way, about the future. Yet a vision is even more about the present; it's about what is happening TODAY. In fact, I'd even say that the clearest and best visions are NOW-based.

That means that you simply need to identify or recognize a current condition, trend, or event and then EXTRAPOLATE from there. If you notice society making progress in one area, and you sense that the forces behind the progress will likely continue, then you can pretty easily "see" the vision of the progress continuing until it is universal or has reached the point of completion. (Look at Microsoft's vision above and you'll see what I mean. They ARE extrapolating, but they can back it up with data, too.)

2. KNOW SEVERAL VISIONARY TYPES PERSONALLY.

It's one thing to have a vision; it's another to be a visionary. A visionary can see the dynamics ruling change in a number of things, not just one. I'm not talking about crystal-ball gazers here, I'm talking about people who avidly and quickly absorb all the new information they can find, and who have some special talents for mining that information heap to discover the potential and probable futures within.

As you spend time with folks like this, their skills and abstract thinking improve your own and sharpen your vision as well.

Unfortunately, you can't just dial 1-800-VISION. But you can explore thought-provoking magazines, the library, and the Internet. And you can simply ask people you admire whom *they* admire.

3. IDENTIFY A CURRENT TREND AND EXTRAPOLATE IT INTO A VISION.

What is a current trend you see in your field of work or in life itself? Computers are a trend. So is the Internet. In education, there's a dawning awareness that the arts are more than just window dressing but rather a system as old as culture itself, invented for transmitting thought, feeling, and vision.

How about retailing? What's the underlying trend there? What is it in automotive engineering?

Once you've picked an area and identified a trend, ask yourself, "If this trend continues for the next fifty years, what will be TRUE for this industry, situation, product, market, population?"

For example, if current Internet trends continue, between 80 and 95 percent of American homes WILL eventually be connected in some manner (PCs, network computers, Web TV), just as 90 percent of American homes have phones now (compared to a much lower number earlier this century).

Given this 80 to 95 percent Internet penetration factor, what's one of the more obvious visions regarding the Internet and people? The end of ignorance? An explosion of creativity? The end of education as we know it?

The fun thing about this process is that your vision doesn't have to be accurate—a vision is not a prediction or a promise. It's just what you see, given what you see. Its benefit is that it inspires you—and gives you "permission"—to dig deeper into everything you already find fascinating.

4. GIVE UP CHASING A VISION.

Having a vision has become a sexy thing, meaning that people think it's important to have one. And it is. But a vision is usually best as something that you discover as you live your life or engage in your work, instead of something you strain your eyes to see.

You can't *acquire* a vision. However, you can notice what's already occurring around you, feel the feelings that awaken in you, and extrapolate the combination into a vision. So a vision is not the result of a quest so much as it is the by-product of an uncovering process.

5. DROP THE WHOLE NOTION OF LIFE PURPOSE, PRIMARY MEANING, COMMITMENT, AND MISSION.

One can create a case for the value of having a clearly articulated life purpose, meaning, commitment, or mission, and I'll quickly admit that each of these has a value. However, they are not necessary. They can even get in the way. Because they are all future-based, future-outcome-type things.

They are what I call "manufactured" realities or futures—interpretations and other mental creations of people needing to feel more secure in who they are. That's why they can become traps instead of guiding lights.

Someone I respect once said: "Thomas, your life purpose is just to be great. Give up the other stuff and just be yourself. That's plenty." I strongly suspect that the exact same thing is true of you.

6. USE GOALS AS A WAY OF KEEPING YOUR VISION CLEAR AND AVAILABLE.

A vision that I have is that everyone will eventually have the language (definition: vocabulary plus awareness) to get what they want. I clearly see the world already progressing in this direction. It WILL happen universally at some point, even if we're only 1 percent of the way there currently.

I don't even have to have faith in this vision; to me it's just an obvious extrapolation. However, it is fun to identify projects that will accelerate the vision, just as people in the computer industry have fun coming up with new operating systems and applications, creating even more reasons for people to have a computer at work and at home.

7. ADJUST YOUR LIFE SO THAT YOU'RE INSPIRED BY YOUR VISION, NOT EMPOWERED BY IT.

This point is a little tricky. Empowerment, generally a good thing, is not a good thing in this area of vision. Because it would mean that, for you, empowerment is dependent on your vision's development.

Reduce the stress on your vision. Be content about it, and feel inspired by it from time to time. Get empowerment from people, not projects. There's a big difference in levels of humanness to be experienced.

8. LET YOUR VISION EVOLVE BY YOUR DEVELOPMENT AND AWARENESS.

I focus on my vision only every couple of months. I kind of "check in" with it and with what I'm working on. I don't have to check in any more often than this, because the vision is so clear for me that it already guides my actions and orients my projects.

Any projects or ideas that come to me have already been "filtered" by the clarity of the vision. I very seldom have ideas that aren't directly related to the vision being realized. So, I am free to chill out, be myself, grow, enjoy, learn, and develop myself, without having to check in constantly and consciously measure myself against the vision.

Which brings us to point number 9 . . .

9. DON'T CONFUSE YOUR VISION WITH YOUR SELF-IDENTITY.

There is ME and then there is my VISION. There is YOU and then there is your VISION.

You'll know the two have crashed into each other if your vision becomes a CAUSE, and you start basing your life, self-esteem, success, or identity on the progression or success of your vision.

It's not pretty when that happens. You become very unattractive— except to similarly messed-up people, who are so deficient in self-esteem, vision, and identity that they need to latch on to something and make it more valuable than life itself.

Vision is extremely dangerous if you let it become a need. That's why I keep emphasizing that you don't actually *need* a vision, and you should never push to locate one. Remember—it's a healthy by-product of living fully, not a tool for living fully or a reason for living.

10. LET YOUR VISION EVOLVE NATURALLY.

In other words, don't get fixated about your (single) vision. Let it evolve and grow. It needs to, given that you're changing as well.

Think of your vision as one of your friends. Sometimes it will feel very present, and you'll enjoy that presence while it lasts. But don't seek a dependency relationship with your vision. Let it have some freedom. Otherwise, it becomes stunted.

BE REAL, BE HUMAN

When You Are Human,
You Are Attractive

Life is an unanswered question, but let's still believe in the dignity and importance of the question.

—TENNESSEE WILLIAMS

The problem with people who have no vices is that generally you can be sure they're going to have some very annoying virtues.

—ELIZABETH TAYLOR

Even if your life is a real mess, or you're clearly not the person you know you can be, you can still become very, very attractive if you'll be honest (and enjoy being honest, versus enjoying the attention you might get by admitting your all-too-human frailties) about where you happen to be *right now* in your life.

Below are ten ways to become REALLY human and real. If you are for real, good people will want to be around you. Because even though we all want to seek and ultimately claim an optimized reality, the present-moment truth remains very, very attractive.

How to know you're making progress with this principle

- You begin to recognize the tremendous amount of pretense and positioning that other humans do, and, given that others are simply mirrors of ourselves, you see where you are full of it.

DISTINCTIONS TO DRAW

HUMANNESS VS. EGO—Ego is the needy side of yourself. It is a good thing simply because it's true and real. The trick about being human is cutting yourself a LOT of slack by accepting and including your ego. It's something you developed during the growing-up process, a kind of coating over your inner self. You can't simply discard it, not without getting overwhelmed by fears. Why not have a healthful relationship with it?

AUTHENTIC VS. GENUINE—A person who is genuine is being honest but may not be totally in touch with all aspects of themselves, so they can be honest only about the parts they know. Someone who is authentic knows most all of themselves and is thus more available and complete. People trust an authentic person more than they do a genuine person.

NATURALNESS VS. PRETENSE—Someone who is behaving naturally is just being themselves; someone with pretense is trying to be someone they are not, in order to make an impression. Pretense carries a cost; naturalness does not.

SUCCEED VS. STRIVE—To succeed means to have arrived, even if you didn't have to strive to get there. To strive means you're seeking to get somewhere that you aren't at already.

YOU VS. ROLES—We adopt roles, such as mother, father, boss, owner, executive, that may take over our lives, meaning that we are defined more by our roles in life than by who we are. Roles are supportive but may limit one's thinking.

FEEL VS. SEARCH—Some people are continually looking for themselves, meaning they seek answers or purpose in life. Better to feel what is around you, and respond to that, than to get on the searching treadmill—which is very costly and rarely fulfilling. You do not need to search in order to evolve.

- You develop an excellent sense of human. (If you haven't chuckled yet, you're way too human and you are trying not to be.)
- You start to enjoy the faults of others, rather than react to them.
- You enjoy being really human, and you can accept that in others as well.
- Life becomes easier because you are not pretending to be somebody you are not.
- You have more fun and are more fun to be with because you are more genuine.

TOP 10 WAYS
TO BE HUMAN

1. DROP PRETENSE.

Are you trying to appear or sound like someone you're really not yet—or will never be? Pretense, while it might temporarily boost a weak self-esteem, usually is exhausting to the spirit. It generates lies or partial truths and fools only those who are pretending more than you are. A favorite old saying puts it crudely but accurately: "Nobody is easier to bullshit than a bullshitter."

What's the solution? If you're a loser, say so. If you're a fool, say so. If you make lots of mistakes, say so. If you have no money, say so. If you don't like who you are, say so. If you can't EASILY afford the Mercedes, sell it. Good people, those who have enough personal clarity to see the realness of a person, flaws notwithstanding, will still find you attractive. Flaws like those mentioned above are much easier to overcome than the subtle poisons that phoniness, in any form, puts into your cup of success.

2. STOP TRYING TO BECOME SOMEBODY.

It's normal for us to want to become somebody we can be proud of, but often the tendency is to pick a hero or a figure whom we either admire or wish we were like.

Nothing's wrong with being inspired, but the cost of striving to be *like* someone else is extremely high. Striving costs you the opportunities in the present you cannot see because you are too busy focusing on the future. It postpones the process of becoming yourself. And adulation stunts your growth, as well as the humanity of the person who accepts so much of it that he or she begins to *need* it.

Solution: If you are a nobody but think you are—or should be—a somebody, take pride in being a nobody (becoming somebody is pretty stressful!). Admire people of style and accomplishment but don't aspire to grab their coattails in any way. Have confidence that there is a very special and valuable somebody inside you, and that no one else could ever duplicate that person. Just as you could never duplicate whoever it is that you highly admire. "I wanna be like Mike" may be an effective ad slogan, but it's a blindly ignorant, really unworthy goal to pursue.

3. GIVE UP SPIRITUAL AMBITIONS.

This one is tricky. I see a lot of people aspiring to become more spiritual, but it often seems to turn into a quest or a marathon or a track measured by "less ego."

Personally, I feel that ego is very spiritual and that trying to squash your ego is very unspiritual. To me, spirituality is two things—relatedness and lightness.

Relatedness means how well and how easily you relate to yourself, your environment, reality, truth, and other people.

Lightness is about how much you can laugh, how much you can take things nonseriously. Remember what G. K. Chesterton said about angels: The reason they can fly is that they take themselves so lightly.

The problem with so many folks on a spiritual track is that they are so incredibly serious, dogmatic, and heavily concerned about their spirituality. Their weightiness makes them less spiritual than ever.

Solution: Life is spiritual enough by itself. So are you. Stop trying to pour water into a cup that's already full. Start seeing and sensing the fullness you already have.

4. STOP PUTTING POSITIVE SPINS ON WHAT'S TRUE.

Euphemisms and "positive interpretations" are the bane of many people's existence. Rather than call something a problem, they call it a challenge. Rather than call something a screw-up, they call it a breakdown. Rather than call somebody clueless, they call them well intentioned. This one is a little tricky because one of the 28 Attraction Principles is to be unconditionally constructive. And some of the terms I've used here are a far cry from that. But if you're building from a sugarcoated, half-truthful foundation, you can't really be constructive. An unpleasantly expressed truth is more attractive than a half-truth prettified with pastel ribbons and bows.

You'll need to work out for yourself where "a positive attitude" ends and "rose-colored myopia" begins. This is one of those areas where your body will tell you—and has been telling you all along, but you've likely blocked out the messages because they weren't "nice." Being nice is a very harmful pursuit and should never be confused with being unconditionally constructive.

Solution: If something is bad, say so. Don't make it sound less bad than it really is. That would be lying.

5. DROP THE JARGON.

If you buy the idea that truth is the most attractive thing, then anything that isn't true is going to make a person less attractive. Most personal-development-related jargon isn't very attractive because it involves manufactured words and/or meanings. Most people who use that sort of jargon cannot translate it into simple English.

Anyone who cannot translate their terms within ten seconds into incredibly simple English that ANYBODY can understand instantly is using jargon. And *they* likely don't really understand what they're saying. Their payoff is in how good it feels to be part of a movement, which is something that would appeal only to an insecure person and is of limited and short-term value anyway.

Solution: Use very simple terms that anyone can instantly understand.

Note: In this book, the word *attraction* is jargon, so don't use it unless you're teaching it to someone. The simple English equivalent of attraction is "an easier approach to life." Or, more lengthily, "a set of principles and practices that people can use to enjoy their life more." If someone asks you what *attraction* is, use simple English—either the above phrases or, better yet, your own words.

6. ENJOY BEING REAL.

I'd rather be an outstanding failure than constantly struggle to be a success. Make sense? Being real really is a delightful way to live—far more important than success itself. Plus, it's more likely to evolve one day into lasting, sustaining success than any phony style of being.

Solution: Ask yourself, "What's more important—being real and being myself, or becoming successful?" And ask the question knowing that you never actually have to choose between being real and being successful. You simply have to choose between being real and *striving* to be successful. Get the difference?

7. AVOID THOSE WHO AREN'T AUTHENTIC OR GENUINE.

As you adopt more of the Attraction OS, your personal antennae will be able to better (and earlier) detect who's real and who isn't. After all, you're sensitizing yourself more.

Pretty soon, you'll come to recognize and feel the extremely high costs of spending time with those who are still trying to impress, compensate, or strive. And you'll just naturally steer clear of them.

In the meantime, however, don't be surprised if your Rolodex gets smaller. Your world isn't shrinking, it's just jettisoning some deadwood.

Solution: Make a list of the people in your life who are not genuine or authentic. Then identify the reasons (which may well be important and valid) why they are in your life. Start thinking about whether those reasons justify the inevitable drains on your time.

8. BE YOURSELF WITHOUT BEING DEFINED BY, OR DELIVERING, A ROLE.

This one is also tricky: Most of us are very much defined by the roles we adopt or have assigned to us—child, mother, father, provider, sibling, boss, employee, client, vendor, professional, educator, expert.

And yet, those roles are not actually who you are, are they? You may get lots of satisfaction from playing your roles well. There's nothing wrong with that at all. But you can't let that satisfaction turn into your reason for living. Your roles are bound to change—sometimes gradually, sometimes abruptly. And, no matter how good you are, your roles are dependent on things beyond your control. Like other people.

For example, Herman Melville wrote *Moby Dick,* which today is ranked as either the most important American novel or one of the two most important, alongside *Huckleberry Finn.* But it was a commercial and critical failure in its day, and Melville's role quickly changed from esteemed literary voice to customshouse clerk. His genius and his real worth didn't change, just the ability of his contemporaries to notice them.

It's no sin to aspire to elevated roles. But don't let your roles be the only place in which your self-esteem can survive and thrive.

Solution: Who would you be if you had no roles in life? Would you still be yourself? That's the question to work through. Take your time, let the answers come at their own speed. But, to borrow from the Tennessee Williams quote above, believe in the dignity and importance of the question.

9. LAUGH AT YOURSELF, AND AT LIFE, AS YOUR DEFAULT REACTION.

There is a place to get to in life where you can laugh at virtually every aspect of yourself (strengths, weaknesses, habits, failures, IQ, lifestyle, behaviors, blind spots, successes) and also at life itself. This is an amazing place to inhabit: You're in tune with how absurd it all is anyway.

Arriving at this place means you are very much in sync with yourself and life. When you have arranged your life so that you always have plenty of choices, you don't need to take things too seriously.

This is not so much a goal you should strive for as a possibility you should be open to, as well as a by-product of everything you do that helps you evolve.

Solution: Adopt this slogan, which my computer programmer has attached as part of his E-mail signature: "Not one shred of evidence supports the notion that life is serious."

10. BE RESPONSIBLE FOR THE FACT THAT YOU **ARE** HUMAN.

Okay, the nine points above were all about accepting and enjoying the positive and negative sides of being human and life itself. Now that you're giggling hysterically at all of your problems, you CAN become responsible for your weaknesses or tendencies.

In other words, just because you're human doesn't get you off the hook if your fallibility is causing problems for others. People often think of "being human" as meaning prone to messing up. That's a failure-oriented definition. Being human, to me, means being fallible yet at the same time always capable of growing into greatness. It also means accepting others as having the same capacities, no matter how much doubt or disappointment they stir up for you.

Solution: Discover how your humanness affects others and make any necessary changes. Allow others the possibility of changing, too.

BUFF IT UP!

BUFF = PERFECTION + PERSONAL STYLE

Speaking of changes: The Buff It Up! Program is a self-paced personal development program for the individual who wants—and is ready—to have it all and have it right now.

The Buff It Up! Program targets ten areas of your life. Play with it only after you've completed all the other self-tests in this book.

It's designed to be used with the guidance of a coach specially trained in this program. If you go it alone, please realize that this is a VERY rigorous program. Take it one piece at a time. Your first score may be less than 10. Do not worry. You'll get to 70, 80, or 90+ sooner than you may think. Once you start the process, it creates its own momentum.

There are four steps to completing the Buff It Up! Program.

1. Answer each question. If the statement is true, fill in the indicated line. If not, leave it blank until you've done what it takes for a full YES. Be rigorous; be a hard grader. If the item does not apply or will never be true for you, fill it in anyway. (You may do this with up to five items.) Feel free to reword up to five of the items in this program to better suit you, your needs, and your life.
2. Summarize each section. Add up the number of filled-in lines for each of the ten sections and write those amounts where indicated. Then add up all ten sections and write in your current total.

3. Color in the Progress Chart below. If you have five filled-in lines in the My Body section, for example, color in the bottom five boxes, and so on. Always start from the bottom up. The goal is to have the entire chart filled in. In the meantime, you have a current picture of how you are doing in each of the ten areas.

4. Keep playing until all the boxes are filled in. This process may take six months, or it may take five years, but you can do it! Use your coach or adviser to assist you. Every three months, check yourself for progress.

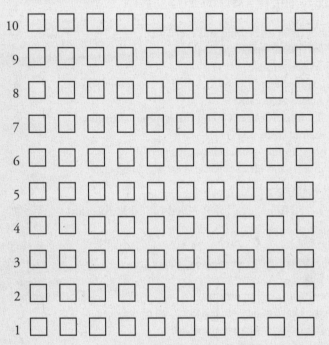

1. MY BODY—THE 10 ASPECTS TO PERFECT

___ My hair is the color, shape, style, and cut that I most love.
___ My skin is toned, clear, and glowing.
___ My eyes shine and are the color I most want.
___ I eat only the foods that my body works best with.
___ I eat only fresh, healthy, and nourishing foods.
___ My fingernails and toenails look perfect and healthy.
___ My posture is great: I stand tall and walk gracefully.

___ My stance is firm and secure, but not rigid.

___ I look ten years younger than I am. I age slowly.

___ I have all the sex I want, and it's great and healthy for both me and my partner.

_____ **Number of Lines Filled In (10 Maximum)**

2. MY SPIRIT — THE 10 ASPECTS TO PERFECT

___ I see the beauty in everything and everyone.

___ I listen more than I speak.

___ I simply do not get sick.

___ I am well connected to my spirit, which is my energy source.

___ Nothing breaks around me.

___ I believe it's possible to get 100 on this without struggling.

___ I never raise my voice.

___ I walk around feeling overwhelmingly grateful.

___ I grasp concepts and ideas quickly; there are no blocks.

___ I feel very connected to others.

_____ **Number of Lines Filled In (10 Maximum)**

3. MY HEART—THE 10 ASPECTS TO PERFECT

___ I have only happy, loving dreams.

___ Every friend I have makes me feel great, all of the time.

___ I simply do not have negative thoughts.

___ All of my emotional needs are taken care of, always.

___ I have virtually no concerns, problems, or worries.

___ I am lighthearted and delightful to be with.

___ I have plenty of love for everyone.

___ I protect myself from people who are needy or insensitive.

___ I always ask for exactly what I need, before I need it.

___ I am fully developed and mature: I no longer react, period.

_____ **Number of Lines Filled In (10 Maximum)**

4. MY SELF-CARE—THE 10 ASPECTS TO PERFECT

____ I have a facial weekly.

____ I have a massage weekly.

____ I have my hair trimmed or styled at least monthly.

____ I treat myself better than anyone I know.

____ I know which colors are best for me, and my clothes make me feel great.

____ I wear only natural fibers.

____ My phone has a pleasant ring.

____ I wear only shined, attractive, and well-heeled shoes.

____ I drink only clean water.

____ I have my car cleaned professionally biweekly.

____ Number of Lines Filled In (10 Maximum)

5. MY HOME — THE 10 ASPECTS TO PERFECT

____ I sleep on 300-thread-count sheets or Egyptian cotton.

____ I love the view from my home.

____ I have the right amount of natural lighting in my home.

____ I am thrilled with the geographic area in which I live.

____ There are no environmental toxins in my home.

____ My furniture is exactly the way I want it.

____ I always have fresh flowers in my home.

____ I feel safe, loved, and inspired in my home.

____ My home is professionally cleaned weekly.

____ I have beautiful art on my walls.

_____ Number of Lines Filled In (10 Maximum)

6. MY WORK—THE 10 ASPECTS TO PERFECT

____ My work, quite simply, is play. I have no hassles at work.

____ My work is a full expression of my four most important values.

____ My files are perfectly neat and orderly.

____ I am working on a fulfilling, creative project right now.

____ The people I work with respect me and support my work.

____ I love my office or work area.

____ I have every piece of equipment I need to do a great job.

____ I am well trained and amazingly productive.

____ I am well regarded in my field.

____ I do my job better than anyone I know in my locale.

____ **Number of Lines Filled In (10 Maximum)**

7. MY QUALITY OF LIFE—THE 10 ASPECTS TO PERFECT

____ I don't do errands.

____ I work out daily and love it.

____ I have more than enough time to do what I want.

____ If I wear jewelry, it's only the finest quality.

____ Adversity and suffering are foreign to my life.

____ Every day feels fresh and new; nothing is carried over.

____ I am adrenaline free.

____ I score 95+ on the Reserve Index.

____ I am proud of the life I lead.

____ I want for nothing.

____ **Number of Lines Filled In (10 Maximum)**

8. MY FINANCES—THE 10 ASPECTS TO PERFECT

____ I have at least $100,000 in savings or liquid investments.

____ I earn at least $100 per hour for my time.

____ I have insurance to protect me from harm.

____ My taxes are professionally prepared by someone I trust.

____ I understand investments fully and am well invested.

____ Money is just a detail in my life.

____ I give 10 percent of what I make in time or cash to those I love.

____ I am saving at least 20 percent of what I make each month.

____ My net income is increasing at least 10 percent per year.

____ I have no money blocks; I live the idea of abundance.

____ **Number of Lines Filled In (10 Maximum)**

9. MY FAMILY AND FRIENDS—THE 10 ASPECTS TO PERFECT

___ I am admired and respected by my family.
___ I know all the people I need to know.
___ Everyone around me is fulfilled.
___ I don't spend time with anyone who upsets me.
___ I love my parents and appreciate what they've done for me.
___ My friends and family go out of their way to show their love.
___ I treat my children and/or siblings very well.
___ I protect myself from family or friends who aren't nice to me.
___ I've stopped looking for new friends. I have plenty!
___ I remember and celebrate birthdays of my friends and family members.

_____ **Number of Lines Filled In (10 Maximum)**

10. MY MAGIC—THE 10 ASPECTS TO PERFECT

___ I seem to be getting points on this program without trying.
___ I am a perfectionist but not compulsive about it.
___ People who come into my life seem to be ready for me.
___ Everything I need consistently comes to me.
___ My plants never die.
___ People are always great to me.
___ When I want something, I always get it, easily.
___ Animals and children are drawn to me.
___ Life is easy for me.
___ I love this Personal Perfection Program!

_____ **Number of Lines Filled In (10 Maximum)**

___ **Total Score   (Maximum 100)**

EPILOGUE

COACHING, FROM PAST TO PRESENT

The past: Coaching, of course, has been around as long as humans have been around—even if it went by other names, like parenting, teaching, mentoring, or consulting. And athletic coaching has been around at least since ancient Greece, where Olympic champions were paid with amphorae full of olive oil. Coaches, I presume, did not go home empty-handed.

The present: Since the late 1980s, coaching has officially been available with both a personal focus and a business orientation. You can now use a coach to get your personal life together, set and reach goals, start and expand a business, get ahead faster in a corporation, improve your job performance, and communicate better with everyone. There are literally hundreds of things you can use a coach to help you solve, master, achieve, or develop.

There are now thousands of full-time coaches practicing in over thirty countries. Most have come from complementary professions such as counseling, teaching, business ownership, training, psychology, management, and the ministry. Over 100,000 clients have used their services thus far, and that number will probably double.

What's new and different about these coaches, compared to their counterparts from the past?

Coaching has now evolved into an integrated success technology. It's more than a couple of principles or techniques. It's a well-woven fabric of hundreds of specialized skills, principles, concepts, practices, and nuggets of wisdom.

Coaching has evolved from a corporate experiment to a standard program being installed in nearly every Fortune 1,000 company in the United States and worldwide as well. A successful manager today must make people *want* to give their best, not just force them to perform incrementally better. Enlightened companies are vitally interested in helping their people maximize their potentials for both happiness and productivity. The best employees are going to come to expect coaching, not management, from their superiors.

Coaching has evolved from a professional service to a synergistic relationship between client and coach. A coach doesn't just recommend; a coach is actively engaged in a client's progress. Both parties are vocal, both committed to making things happen.

Coaching has evolved from a specialty skill to a full-time practice. Thousands of coaches (the number has been doubling every year since 1992) earn from $25,000 to $400,000 per year, with the average around $75,000. My best guess is that the field will level out at between 100,000 and 200,000 practitioners in the United States. As a point of reference, there are now more than 500,000 stockbrokers in the United States.

Coaching has evolved into the mainstream—fast. This is because there is a demand from the public. Clients are usually people who have noticed real-world improvements in their friends and colleagues who have a coach, and have asked them how to get one. The 150 or so newspaper, magazine, and television features covering CoachVille in the past two years have made massive numbers of people aware that there is such a thing as coaching, that it works, and that they can probably afford to hire their own coach.

All of this coverage emerged without a single advertisement being placed. If you work in any media-related business, you know that's a remarkable tribute!

The future: More and more people want ownership of how they earn their living. Working for a paycheck is becoming outdated, especially among the educated. Given that the fastest-growing segment in the economy is information services (versus manufacturing or professional services), anyone with information skills and a powerfully practical idea can make money. The doors of opportunity have never been open wider than they are right now. The only problem is that few people ever had a class called Entrepreneurialism 101. They are eager to play, even though they don't yet know the rules and strategies of the small-business game, and so they lose a lot. A coach can help them learn those rules and strategies very, very quickly. And corporations, eager to hold on to the kind of talented people whose performance can create competitive advantages in the marketplace, are going to be just as eager to provide coaching to improve the workplace and keep people happy, productive, and innovative.

I feel that humans have tapped into only about 1 percent of their talents, skills, or special qualities. That means there's a huge untapped reservoir of potential. Accessing even a tiny bit of it will bring huge increases in personal success and happiness. I think that a lot of people are just now realizing how untapped their potentials have been. Thanks to the Internet, the availability of creative tools and inexpensive (sometimes even free) education on a just-in-time delivery basis, we might get to 2 percent pretty quickly. Coaches are right there, encouraging the process, providing just-in-time help, offering a safety net as well as supportive words.

THE ATTRACTION OPERATING SYSTEM

If you own a computer, you probably know that there's a difference between operating systems and application software. An OS essentially tells a computer how to make use of the facts and capabilities it possesses. Application software lets your computer help you do certain specific tasks, such as play solitaire, lay out a spreadsheet, or write a memo.

When I call attraction an "OS," I'm saying that there is a strong analogy to be made between computers and human beings. The comparison doesn't take anything away from people, it just recognizes that computers are something we've made "in our own image." That is, computers have a brain (the central processing unit, or CPU), sets of skills (application software), data (accumulated information), and an overarching method for using the brain to work with the data and to apply the skills (an operating system).

As we can do for our computers, we humans can upgrade our CPUs, our application software, our data, and our operating systems. Formal education is the best-known, most-used way. But our world is evolving so quickly now that, for some people, coaching is more relevant, and more targeted, than formal education systems, which are wonderful repositories of information yet notoriously slow-changing, late-adapting, highly politicized entities. Experience is another acknowledged teacher. As Ben Franklin put it, "Experience keeps a dear school, but fools will learn at no other." And yet experience has its limits—unless you are clever enough to understand exactly the lessons it teaches you.

The Attraction OS doesn't take the place of formal learning or of experience, just as it doesn't take the place of therapy. Attraction is highly now-oriented, seeking to augment or update whatever things may need attention, in order to help people make the best use of their capabilities. It doesn't make sick people well, it helps healthy people become extraordinary.

THE ZEN OF ATTRACTION

"Zen in its essence," wrote the Japanese sage D. T. Suzuki, "is the art of seeing into the nature of one's being, and it points the way from bondage to freedom."

Zen, like attraction, is often taught by unorthodox methods. Zen is often expressed in puzzling statements such as, "Act without doing; work without effort," which comes from the Tao Te Ching. Attraction may seem puzzling and paradoxical at first, but it also involves seeing into the nature of one's being, and it also leads to effortless effort.

Attraction, in its essence, can be expressed by fourteen brief pairs of sentences. Please note, though, that these words describe an ideal state. You and I may never completely get there. But our lives can become easier, more remarkable, and more fulfilling with every step we take.

1. Promise nothing. (Just do what you most enjoy doing.)
2. Sign nothing. (Just do what doesn't require a signature of any kind.)
3. Offer nothing. (Just share what you have with those who express an interest.)
4. Expect nothing. (Just enjoy what you already have; it's plenty.)
5. Need nothing. (Just build up your reserves and your needs will disappear.)
6. Create nothing. (Just respond well to what comes to you.)
7. Seduce no one. (Just enjoy them.)
8. Adrenalize nothing. (Just add value and get excited about that.)
9. Hype nothing. (Just let quality sell by itself.)
10. Fix nothing. (Just heal yourself.)
11. Plan nothing. (Just take the path of least resistance.)
12. Learn nothing. (Just let your body absorb it all on your behalf.)
13. Become no one. (Just be more of who you already are.)
14. Change nothing. (Just tell the truth and things will change by themselves.)

INDEX

About the Author

Thomas J. Leonard (1955–2003) has been called the coach's coach. He mentored and coached hundreds of business, corporate, and personal coaches worldwide. He founded CoachVille in 1992 and Teleclass.com in 1998. Although based in Seattle, Thomas spent much of his time touring the United States in his motor home. His Web site is located at *www.thomasleonard.com*.